Nobel Laureate Prof. Albert Szentgyörgyi de Nagykapolt, Chairman of the Hungarian Word 80th Anniversary Committee.

Hugo Gellért, outstanding Hungarian-American artist/muralist, Co-chairman of the 80th Anniversary Committee.

THIS NOBLE FLAME

PORTRAIT OF A HUNGARIAN NEWSPAPER IN THE USA

1902–1982

AN ANTHOLOGY

EDITED BY ZOLTÁN DEÁK

HERITAGE PRESS
1982

5

Table of Contents

In Hungarian ⸻ 9
Editor's Note ⸻ 11

Oh, How High the Sky Is! 15
About Hungarians ⸻ 16
Oh, How High the Sky Is! ⸻ 18
Brutes ⸻ 24
Vision in Union Square ⸻ 37
Rebellion Rides the Ocean ⸻ 39
The Family Hearth ⸻ 40
Adventure in Uniform ⸻ 46
The Importance of Learning Foreign Languages ⸻ 56
The Circus ⸻ 59
Whitman's Trumpet Hangs on a Dusty Wall ⸻ 64

The Torch Bearers 67
The Eternal Task ⸻ 68
Hugo Gellert Reminiscences ⸻ 69
Bartók the Man ⸻ 92
An Evening with Béla Bartók ⸻ 96
Béla Bartók on New York's Kossuth Radio ⸻ 99
On the Causes of Wars ⸻ 100
András Ösze ⸻ 104
Autumn's Branches ⸻ 106
The Art of Julius Zilzer ⸻ 107
You Are History ⸻ 111
Three Hungarian Giants of Science ⸻ 117
Leo Szilard ⸻ 120
Hungarians in the Labor Movement ⸻ 122
My First Strike ⸻ 124
Organizing the Copper Workers ⸻ 125
Louis Weinstock ⸻ 126
James Lustig and the Great Phelps Dodge Strike of 1946 ⸻ 128
Paul Dömény ⸻ 131
Julius Emspak: A Giant of American Labor ⸻ 133

The Diamond Rollers 135
The Miners of Hazelton ⸻ 136
Hungarians in the Mines ⸻ 138
How and Why the Verhovay Association was Founded ⸻ 143
The Founders ⸻ 144
The "Subversive" ⸻ 145

The Tower Warden Looks Back 147
The Tower Warden Looks Back ⸻ 148
Excerpts from the Writings of Rev. L.A. Gross ⸻ 150
On All Soul's Day, 1915 ⸻ 154
Christmas in the Camp ⸻ 156

John Reed's Farewell _____159
They Deported My Mother_____163
The Dead Are Warning _____165
Two Soldiers_____166
Storm Clouds of the Revolution_____168
For Peace_____169
In Defense of the Workers' Sick-Benefit Society _____170
The Crime of Sacco and Vanzetti_____171
Support the Striking G.M. Workers _____172
For the Spanish People _____173
Israel and the New Golden Calf_____174
Ordeal of the Bier_____175
Watergate _____178
Prometheus of the Moneybags_____180
Condemning the World's Children _____182
Letters to the Editor _____183
    A Greeting from Porcupine Plains _____185
    Elegy _____186

Hungary, Oh Beloved Land!   187
A Message to Our American Brethren _____189
Hungary is Songs _____190
Once I Rang the Church Bells _____192
"Farewell, Aelia Sabina!" _____194
Elegy _____197
I Don't Know _____199
For a Happy, Free Hungary _____201
Hungarian Good Friday _____203
Hungary, A Special Country_____205
An Address by Paul Robeson _____207
The Destruction of the Hungarian Jews_____209
Questions on Hungarian Society _____212
Transylvanian Feast _____217
Transylvanian Sunday Soup _____219
The Secret of Strudel Making _____220
My Mother's Starter Dough _____223

"How Beautiful the Feet of Him...that Publisheth Peace"   227
"Caput Mundi" _____228
Christmas 1981 _____230
Mankind at the Crossroads—Nuclear Destruction
    or an Abundant Life _____231
Better Days Coming _____233
List of Contributors _____234
List of Supporters_____235

Our Family Album (photographs)   239

In Hungarian
Gábor Garai

What a language to speak!—
                Incomprehensible to outsiders.
Those who speak like this
              are outsiders everywhere.
Orphan, heavenly nest in a vortex of floods,
turtle-dove's leaf-braided shelter,
                  what power had you
to survive the madness of vultures
                   in brotherless loneliness?
Who brings you an olive-branch day after day?
Who entices you ashore with
                "you'll make it dryshod"?
For you always touched land among blood-creamy rocks,
and craziness goes swirling endlessly about you
as space spins round a point
              in the sealed circle . . .
Sun. Sky. Stone. Wind. Water . . .
              You love me?
                  I love you!

I take you with me like home-baked bread,
I drench you in foreign seas
and lift you clean above the wave-torn seaweed.
A miracle made flesh—my life is your medal:
your people, suppressed a hundred times—who knows how?—survived!
Look at the happier nations gawking at you—
they can't make out one word of the rigmarole.

To me, however, you are living water on the tongue:
you are my religion, and if need be, my mask,
my aerial roots,
           my guard in far-off lands,
my homeward-pointed shepherd-star.

Translated by
Edwin Morgan

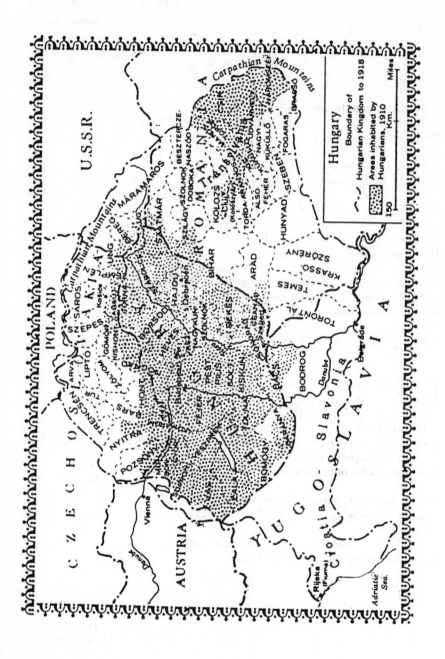

Editor's Note

They came singing, and crying, from the foothills of the majestic Carpathians, from the counties of Abauj, Borsod, Heves, Nográd, Zemplén, Ung, Bereg, and Máramaros.

They came from the boundless plains of Petöfi's native region, the acacia-laden villages of the Great Plains, where "twilight hours perform a magic," and from the areas of Pilis, Szolnok, Csongrád, Hajdu, Szabolcs, and Szatmár.

They said farewell to the gentle hills of Transdanubia, where every stone speaks history. They left the counties of Somogy, Zala, Veszprém, Fejér, and Baranya.

They emerged from the shores of the beloved rivers, the untamed Tisza, the wild Körös, the leisurely flowing Szamos and Maros.

They left the forest-bedecked hills and mountains of legendary Transylvania, the Mezöség, and the fabled counties of Küküllö, Udvarhely, Kolozs, and Hármoszék.

They came from the cities and the towns, driven by hunger, anger and poverty, and a tender wisp of hope that in faraway America, where work is abundant, pay is high and opportunity unlimited, they would eventually earn

11

enough to return to satisfy their hunger for land and live happily ever after. Between 1882 and 1914, close to one and a half million men and women emigrated to the United States from Hungary.

The Statue of Liberty beckoned, and they dreamt of a better future.

Arriving in America they first settled on the Eastern seacoast, in New York and in the neighboring metropolitan areas, in New Jersey and Connecticut.

Many of them were invited or enticed to work in the mines of Pennsylvania and West Virginia, from where very few returned alive and whole.

Still others wound their way into the industrial centers of the American heartland to Pittsburgh, Cleveland, Detroit, and Chicago.

The exceptionally able or lucky ones among them soon began to leave their mark on America. Pulitzer built a newspaper empire. Zukor and Fox established a new industry with a boundless future — movie making. Many talented Hungarian scientists contributed to the development of American technology. In the field of music, the names of Ormándy, Bartók, Szigeti, Széll, Solti, Doráti became household words.

But the majority of the Hungarian immigrants became part and parcel of the great mass of the American working people.

They built their schools and established their cultural and religious institutions, their fraternal organizations, their newspapers.

And some of them felt the gentle glow of that "noble flame" in their hearts that the poet referred to — that urge to do something for their fellow men while engaged in sustaining themselves and their families.

It was such people who, early in this century — in 1902 — established a Hungarian-language newspaper dedicated to the ideals of a more just and humane society, to socialism, and to the task of organizing workers in trade unions to protect their economic and social interests.

This is how our newspaper was born.

* * *

For the past eighty years our newspaper has been reporting to its readers with great regularity — in Hungarian — on the news of the world, the problems of working people.

Now, at the approach of our eightieth anniversary, we feel that it is appropriate to report to the children and grandchildren of our readers, to their non-Hungarian spouses, families, and friends — in English — to give them an inkling as to what our newspaper is all about, to tell them about the substance, the viewpoint, and the tenor of our paper.

This is how our anniversary literary offering came about.

In it we pay tribute, first of all, to the culture of our native Hungary by presenting a few masterpieces of modern Hungarian prose and poetry, followed by an anthology of representative articles, editorials, and letters gleaned from the pages of our newspaper during these past eighty years.

A special section is devoted to our "torchbearers" — outstanding Hungarians and Hungarian Americans — whom we have been honored to count among our friends, readers, and active supporters. It is a particularly great privilege for us to offer excerpts from the autobiography of our distinguished friend Hugó Gellért, Co-chairman of the Anniversary Committee.

Many people assisted the Editor in the preparation of this commemorative volume. My heartfelt gratitude goes to Susan Joseph, for her perceptive comments and her skill in copy editing; to Professor Julia Puskás, for her gracious permission to use extensive portions of her forthcoming publication, *From Hungary to the United States;* to Paul Kövi, for permitting us to include several glorious chapters from his book, *Transylvanian Feast,* in this anthology; and to Hermelie Heimlich, for her patient, devoted assistance as art consultant.

I am greatly indebted to Patricia Austin, Claire Vágó, and Oscar Vágó, for their excellent translations from Hungarian into English.

For their competence and for their tireless efforts in assembling and producing this work, I extend my thanks to Dr. R. Avron Kartyshai; Maggie Block, of Three to Make Ready Graphics; and Ted Reich and Karl Leichtman, of Prompt Press.

I wish to express my deep appreciation to my friends and colleagues for their encouragement, cooperation, and critical reading of key portions of this volume: Hugó Gellért, Paula Gross, Duci Kovács, James Lustig, Margaret Friedman, Árpád Fodor-Nagy, and Clara Reich, of New York; Gustav Jánossy, Frank Jehn, Denis Nánásy, Sándor Rákosi, and Louis Weinstock, of California; Lili Farkas, Julius Macker, and Ernö Roth, of Florida; György Miklós, of Detroit; Zsigmond Krauthammer and Árpád Mezey, of Cleveland; Erna Fodor, Emil Gárdos, Tibor Lieberman, Barbara Striker, Dr. George Striker, and Béla Zenko, of Budapest.

Without the help and constant encouragement of my wife, Fay, this work could not have been accomplished — and if undertaken could not have been finished.

Whatever merit this anthology may possess is largely due to the contributions of all of the above, who were involved at various times, in varying degrees, and at different stages of the production of *This Noble Flame.*

- Zoltán Deák
Fall, 1982

MAGYAR!

ON YOUR FEET HUNGARIANS!

The Horthy Quislings betrayed the people of Hungary to their hereditary enemies—the Germans. The Hungarian government and the Hungarian people are not the same.

The people want to fight against the Nazis. They want to be in the war for freedom.

It is their government that fights for Hitler.

Many of the people of Hungary are already fighting in the snow capped Carpathian Mountains of the North. They are fighting in the sunny wheat fields of the South—in the ranks of Yugoslavia's People's Army of Liberation under the great Marshal Tito. They are fighting to convert their fertile Danube valley from a Nazi "Lebensraum" (Living Space) to a Nazi "Todesraum" (Gravevard).

It is a hard fight. You know what happened at Lidice. You know what happens everywhere when civilian patriots stand up against the tanks and machine guns of mechanized Nazi divisions.

Now it is happening to Hungarians. They need your help.

We are Americans. Our fathers came from Hungary—the land of Louis Kossuth who said Hungary must live in liberty like America or die.

We want Hungary to live. The Hungarian people's fight for freedom is our fight—because every country that fights for freedom guarantees the freedom of America.

The Hungarian people now fighting for their freedom will take heart in the knowledge that they are backed to the hilt by citizens of the great United States who were once their countrymen.

We know the tactics of the ruling clique of Hungary. Our fathers escaped from their tyranny. We can and must make certain that the Hungarian people win their liberty in this war and retain it in the peace that follows.

To do this most effectively we have formed the Hungarian American Council for Democracy and the National Council of Hungarian American Trade Unionists. American Hungarians of all religious and political beliefs are included in these organizations.

We are not alone. Free Hungarians are similarly organized in England, Canada, Mexico, Chile, Uruguay, Argentina, Brazil, and Bolivia. They are rallied around the banner of Michael Karolyi, former President of the Hungarian People's Republic, who was exiled from his homeland because he believed in the ideals of Kossuth and Lincoln—and fought for them.

We stand for a speedy United Nations victory and lasting peace.

We stand for the liberation of the people of Hungary and all the oppressed peoples of the world as agreed at Teheran by Roosevelt, Churchill and Stalin.

We stand for a democratic Hungary in a democratic world.

We stand for a Hungary built on a "good neighbor" policy with her neighboring states.

We want to mobilize every American of Hungarian origin for an all out support of the war and its objectives. If you believe in this—join us.

At this critical time, we call on all American friends of democracy—whether they be of Hungarian parentage or not—to help us, support us, fight with us!

If you are an American of Hungarian origin—join us!

If you are an American of any other origin—sponsor us!

I join ☐   I sponsor ☐

THE HUNGARIAN AMERICAN COUNCIL FOR DEMOCRACY
23 West 26th Street, New York 10, N. Y.

NAME...
                        PRINT

ADDRESS...
                        PRINT

I want to help by contributing $............

Hungarian American Council for Democracy
Béla Lugosi, President.

National Council of Hungarian American Trade Unionists
Julius Emspack, President,
National Secretary-Treasurer, United Electrical, Radio and Machine Workers of America

Send communications and contributions to:

'INGARIAN AMERICAN COUNCIL FOR DEMOCRACY
'ST 26TH STREET, NEW YORK 10, N. Y.   **MUrray Hill 4-3457**

Account audited by Martin Schwaeber & Company, Certified Public Accountants

An appeal issued by the Hungarian-American Council for Democracy, Béla Lugosi President, supported by our paper, urging the Hungarian-American community to aid anti-nazi struggle in Hungary. Summer 1944.

Oh, How High The Sky Is

A Festival of Hungarian Literature

About Hungarians

C. P. Snow

Hungary is a good deal of a mystery to the English-speaking world. There is a vague impression that it is a country which produces a remarkable amount of miscellaneous talent. If you want high class scientists, get them out of Hungary. John von Neumann, Eugene Wigner, Albert Szent-Györgyi, Leo Szilard—two Nobels, one who would certainly have been another if he hadn't died young, not only talent but genius in that group—there are plenty more where those came from. The same with economists, eminent all over the world, ready to produce confident solutions to any problem and contradict each other at the drop of a hat. Films? For years the British film industry was run by Hungarians. Actors? You want a perfect performer for a model upper class Englishman? Better whistle up Leslie Howard, who happens to be a Hungarian. Want a less admirable sardonic Maughamish Englishman? Get George Sanders, who also happens to be a Hungarian.

That impression, though vague, is not inaccurate, as far as it goes. It is perfectly true that Hungary, with a population of about ten million, has produced, and continues to produce, a galaxy of gifted persons quite disproportionate to its size. Compare Canada, with over double the population, enormous natural resources, by western standards well governed. Or Sweden, slightly less people than Hungary, the most orderly of all societies. Neither has developed anything like the number of the Hungarian world figures. Nor has Australia, immensely rich, strenuously competitive when they feel like it (as in athletics and the visual arts).

What is the Hungarian secret? No one has found an answer. The necessity to survive, Hungarians sometimes say, with a cryptic smile—you others don't know what it's like to be a Hungarian. Anyway the English-speaking world looks on, wonders, and envies. When one arrives in contemporary intellectual Budapest, brilliance is in the air. One feels exceptionally dull or pedestrian. It would be nice to be so clever.

And yet. The impression stops short. The English-speaking world seems abnormally remote from the Hungarian reality. This is at least in part because we are so ignorant of Hungarian literature. About science, not so ignorant, or the performing arts. But about the literature, which is the flesh and bone of any society, almost a dead blank. What does a reasonably cultivated English speaker know of it? He will have heard the names of the great nineteenth century writers, Petöfi, Jókai. He might have read a little (in translation, of course) of both. He could be more familiar with Ferenc Molnár, as an accomplished playwright performed in London or New York. Recently, thanks to the devoted work of *The New Hungarian Quarterly*, he has been able to pick up acquaintance with some major senior writers of today—Gyula Illyés, László Németh, Tibor Déry (also known for political reasons, but a writer needs to be read for his literary gift, which The N.H.Q. has made possible for Déry). Some of József Lengyel has been translated. That is about all. You will, of course, find specialists in Hungarian in England and America, but those names would be something like the recognition symbols of a tolerably well read man. They are less than he would have of any other of the high literatures of Europe.

Language may be, and must be, one reason for this, though I suspect not the only one. Obviously Hungarian is not an accessible language to English speakers, or, as far as that goes, to other Europeans. Plenty of English speakers aren't completely lost with Latin or Teutonic languages and the Slav ones are at any rate Indo-European. In historical fact, Russian literature travelled early and fast into English, and there has never been a difficulty of understanding on the level of art, whatever was happening elsewhere. Polish literature has been much better known than Hungarian, and the minority Slavs intermittently rather better. Whatever the complex of reasons is, we missed out on Hungarian, and it is our loss.

It can't be completely remedied. Hungarian friends tell us, and I accept it, that we can't reach the core of the literature unless we read the poetry. But how can we read the poetry? Only a few times in literary history has poetry crossed linguistic frontiers in a form which didn't distort it. Very occasionally, as with Edgar Allan Poe in French, it gained preposterously in the exchange and took on a wonder unknown in the original. Usually, instead of that kind of perverse gain, there is a semi-fatal loss, as with Pushkin or Hugo in English. One of the few translations which seems to go over straight is Shakespeare as done by the brothers Schlegel. All these exchanges are between languages closely related and similar in form. Translating Hungarian poetry must be about as difficult as translating Chinese—perhaps more so, since Chinese grammatical structure is as simple as English.

This article is an excerpt from Mr. Snow's Preface to the book 44 Hungarian Short Stories, *published in Hungary in 1979, by Corvina Kiadó.*

Oh, How High the Sky Is!

Tibor Cseres

Dreams will not come to order. Like clouds they come, and like clouds melt away even within the minute.

But that they do have a meaning beyond this I have known since childhood from the gently warning words of my mother: "Never tell your dreams to strangers."

It is not merely for the sake of proverbial wisdom that I bring up the nature of dreams. If that were my intention I should have begun thus: dream till dawn, milk at morn. Or with that great consolation for all those fallen on evil days: in his dreams even the blind man can see. Or I might have started off with the wise old maxim: the carefree, the good dreams are the ones you forget on waking.

I will not begin this way, and I'm not about to go into the nature of dreams in general; what I have to tell is about one particular woman. About the woman who sang in her sleep.

Her name was Júlia, or Jula, and she had come up to Budapest when she was quite young, at a time when most townsfolk sought the peace of the countryside, at the outbreak of the Second World War.

Jula was a Chango* by birth, an orphan from Moldavia, and had the native habit of lisping her sh's to s's, saying something like "saypees" for *sheepish*. She arrived here very quickly after a few days' rest in Gyergyó where she had stopped on her way from Bucharest together with her girlfriend Anna, my niece. She went into service, just as Anna did, in this other big city, and once here they both sought happiness and prosperity through the labour of their hands.

Now Jula had come so far so bravely not solely out of friendship for Anna; rather it was because of Benci, who was Anna's brother and a cousin of mine.

Benci was a gay blade, adventurous by temperament, and I will never

---

* A small Hungarian dialect-speaking ethnic group largely confined to Moldavia.

18

know what promises, what fine words he had kept feeding her with; but she certainly did not need much luring, her heart being so drawn to him of its own sweet will.

But then soon after Benci got married in Budapest and was lost to view together with his wife, and that severed the love-knot that had been tied between them.

Jula ought to have returned home. But she didn't. There was someone to look after Jula, so she did not have to feel so forsaken by the world. That someone was my niece Anna, who might perhaps have believed herself to blame for Jula's love-lornness.

Anna found for her a boy who worked in the waggon factory; and before the third week was out this lad asked Jula to marry him, the girl's integrity having struck such a dazzling shaft of light into his heart.

And then and there began the role I was to play in her life. Some age-old custom still lingering in Jula's native village requires that a girl should ask the advice and permission of her eldest male relative when she is about to part with her maidenhood.

I was no relation of hers, I was neither mature enough nor had I aged sufficiently towards respectability to be able to offer any one advice. However, she had scarcely any acquaintances apart from me, and for her I was still one of the folk from home and in some way a relative.

One Sunday afternoon she came to call on me in Anna's company, whose intervention, however, she headed off with some excuse, and the request she had to make she put to me herself.

To my mind there was only one question worth clarifying:

"Do you love him?"

Her eyes filled with tears, and she shook her head almost imperceptibly.

"But I do trust him very much," she whispered.

And so it happened that I gave my permission.

As the eldest male relative I was naturally duty-bound to be present at the wedding, which took place in Jász Street in a district called "Angels' Field," the boy's place of residence and one might say his birthplace.

"There'll be music," they told me in advance, "from a 'solitary' record-player."

This piece of news suggested to me what present I should give—the present I was obliged to give both as guest, and relative, according to the tradition of country and town.

My gift was a set of four records of twelve folksongs from Moldavia. Some well-known musicologists of the time had coaxed them by devious ways from the lips of Chango women and had the songs cut into the preserving wax. I cherished the fond hope that the records would be a great joy to the bride.

Well, the wedding feast!

The evening was one continuous tango and czardas. Spirits were running high, and everyone thought the bride's calm self-possession very becoming. For a long time I delayed presenting my gift.

A little before midnight, however, seeing that the bridegroom's patience was running out, I took up position by the record-player and announced that I was going to play my gift records.

The wedding guests were a little taken aback, and so was the bride—and still more so when, in the wake of sultry tangos, the Chango women began to intone their songs full of innocent emotion with all manner of lisped sibiliant sounds.

At the end of each song the singer said her name and age as of the date of performance . . .

The astonishment did not last long, however. People resumed their chatter and laughter during the third or fourth song, though still keeping their voices low apparently out of respect for my person. Also perhaps in tactful consideration for the bride's sorrowful attention.

For Júlia was the only one really absorbed in listening, and her eyes opened wide as she went nearer to the record-player drawing her husband with her: "Come and listen. I know this one, too."

But the bridegroom's attention soon flagged. His mind was already on something else.

So, left to ourselves, the two of us went on listening to all twelve songs, more than once. For Júlia insisted on having some of the verses repeated, either because she remembered some very clearly or others but very faintly.

Due to an oversight the singer's name was omitted after one of the songs. Júlia closed her eyes and said: "It was my dear mother's voice."

I had nothing to say to shake her in her belief.

Immediately at the beginning of another song she exclaimed: "That's my voice. I always start just like that."

The song began like this:

"The hills and dales do sound,
the big clouds do go round,
O, how high the sky, beautiful starry sky."

And as soon as the song ended, she buried her face in her hands and began to sob and never stopped for a full hour.

We all fell silent watching her, and each of us thought that she was crying her heart out at the loss of her maidenhood. I was no exception, though I should have known well enough how some of the songs might have affected her.

That evening stayed in my memory for a long long time, but eventually it dropped out of my thoughts. I even forgot about the records, though they were later returned to me.

"What do we need the records for," said Jula excusing herself in embarrassment, "if we can't play them without that music machine?"

In the year following the wedding she bore twins, a girl and a boy, in Jász Street.

Her husband was conscripted into the army and sent to the front; not long afterwards the news came that he had died, devoured by the ice-toothed great retreat.

The two children were brought up despite the odds, thanks to the goodwill of relatives, the street, various friends and by Jula's hardworking hands.

But then quite a few things came to pass in Jász Street and thereabouts.

The boy went to work as a turner, in what you might call his father's place. The girl—little Jula—finished secondary school and was studying to become a pharmacist. She was about to get married at twenty when she came to see me. She bore a strong resemblance to the Jula of twenty years before, and she put to me the same question and the same request.

"I've been proposed to by a teacher and I need advice what to do."

Cast in the role of eldest relative, I asked the one important question again:

"Do you love him?"

She lifted her head and nodded agreement quickly and firmly, adding that they had no flat as yet but . . .

I put a cousinly hand on her head, and asked how her mother was doing.

The bright and happy face suddenly clouded.

"Mama's often so quiet these days. We never hear her laugh. And when anything bad happens to her during the day, she sings in her sleep at night."

"Whatever does she sing?" I asked.

Little Jula could not say.

"It has a funny tune and mother seems to lisp while she's singing; when she wakes up she doesn't remember or doesn't want to remember anything. She only gets more depressed. Oh, if only she could be got out of it! Really, it's so terrible. And we can't talk about it to anybody. My fiancé doesn't know about it either."

I realized that neither children knew anything about their mother's birthplace, nor about the time before they were born.

"Next time she sings it, try and listen closely, will you," I told little Jula.

Little more than a week before the wedding, to which I had been duly invited, the girl came along with her news.

"She sang it a couple more times. We listened very hard. But we aren't any the wiser. She mumbled about hills and dales, and the words were all full of s's and sh's."

If she wasn't, I certainly was the wiser by the information.

I spent the remainder of the week trying to get hold of copies of the old records. I thought that if the records had been a nice present for the mother they would be for the daughter too. So I made the rounds of all the second-hand music shops in the city.

With some difficulty I did come upon records of some six of the songs, but as they were reluctant to sell them I had tapes made of them. Luckily I'd got the one I most wanted.

"Will there be a tape-recorder?" I asked the bride.

"That's about the only way we'll be able to have music," the teacher's son said.

I did not pay much attention during the marriage ceremony and dinner that followed, but towards midnight I asked for a break between the rock-n'-rolls and cha-cha-chas and time at the tape-recorder.

My finger hesitated a second before pressing the key. I wondered if the

21

company, mostly youngsters, would not burst out cackling at hearing the lisping words of the songs. If anyone sniggered I would have taken a strong line. On Jula's account.

I was going to prevent the scandal of laughter.

"Tell me, Jula, can you still speak Chango?" I turned to the bride's mother, who with all her grief had turned into a working-class woman like any other in Jász Street.

"But of course I do, just a wee bit," Jula said in her lisping dialect, brightening up, "but not as much as of old 'cause folks are few and far between as I could talk Chango with."

The youngsters looked on in silence. Not a single smile bloomed on their faces. And then I let the spool of tape spin away.

And the old Chango women came on with their songs. They lisped and hissed in their heart-gripping, sweet, and beautiful voices, singing about sorrow, woods, brooks and love, and after each song they introduced themselves: the singer was so and so, and they said their age and also the date when the recording took place.

I left till last the two songs that had lacked the singers' names in the original version too.

"My mother's voice," Jula sighed, her eyes in a fixed stare, just like when she had been the bride. With eyes frozen dry she stared at the spinning tape as if refusing to recognize the voice she had heard from that record of old or refusing to believe that the same song was coming from the tape.

Then followed the voice which she had identified as hers when she was twenty.

"The hills and dales do sound,
the big clouds do go round,
O, how high the sky, beautiful starry sky.
Say, my rose my dear, do you love me?
Then if you'd like, my dear,
to pass your life with me,
hold my right hand, and say
that it will be this way.
I love, I do love you, but don't tell anybody
until in holy church together we shall marry.
O, how high the sky, beautiful starry sky,
beautiful starry sky."

At the very first words I expected her to say, "That's my voice. I always start just like that."

But she didn't. She said nothing. Only the tears began to well up and kept flowing without ceasing, without any attempt to hide them. They trickled down into her lap, and she did not lift a finger to crush any of those many pearls.

Never had those youngsters of today seen anything like it. Nor had I. Such a rushing stream of tears.

"She's crying for the village she left behind," a colleague of the bride explained to me, "that's how memories of childhood come rushing into the soul."

I knew well enough, however, that gushing up in this bitter and salty spring were other things besides—love and the first summons of love. Benedek! My faithless, adventure-loving cousin Benci after whom a girl had come wandering from so far and in vain. And also the father of her two children, in whom she had trusted just as vainly, because he too had never come back to her from the war, and whom she had lately grown to love so much in vain. In his dying, you might say . . .

Some six months went by, and I encountered the young wife again. (She hadn't had any occasion to seek the company of the "eldest male relative" since.) She bloomed and shone.

Oh, when should a woman be at her brightest, when should she be in full bloom, if not when she's been married but half a year!

"And your mother?" I inquired, as soon as I had run out of compliments. "Does she still sing in her sleep, when something bad happens to her?"

Little Jula was surprised; this seemed to have been the last question she expected. She shook her head and thought for a minute, like one who did not want to speak untruthfully and who tried to give the matter serious consideration.

"No," she said at last, "no. She hasn't sung once since then."

And I thought to myself, either her tears had finally run dry at the wedding, or lately nobody had done her any injury that rankled in her sleep.

Translated by László T. András
Poem translated by Kenneth McRobbie

1961

Brutes
Zsigmond Móricz

The little dog, the poodle, cocked his ears, sniffed the air, and the next second began to bark viciously.

"What's the matter?" asked the shepherd. The poodle barked even more vigorously.

"Townsfolk?" the shepherd asked.

The dog stopped barking for a few moments.

"Plainsmen?"

The dog began to bark again.

"Well, then, why are you worried?"

The shepherd stretched out full length on his sheepskin cloak, in the shadow cast by his donkey, and paid no more attention to the matter.

A little while later the two sheepdogs also noticed the approach of the strangers and began to bay in deep resonant tones. They made such a deafening racket one would think they were being skinned.

But the shepherd already knew that fellow herdsmen were approaching, the poodle had already told him that quite explicitly.

It was quite some time before the two shepherds astride their donkeys could be made out, riding across the parched plain. They came slowly along on their animals, their two dogs running in and out round the donkeys' legs.

The poodle stood by his master's foot and continued to bark fiercely.

The big sheepdogs gradually subsided after they had recognized the strangers as shepherds. Perhaps they recognized the dogs too.

They were quiet for a minute or two, then fired off another volley, but their heart was not really in it.

Only the poodle refused to give up, and continued to yelp as if someone was slicing him with a knife.

Moricz Zsigmond, greatest Hungarian novelist of the 20th century.

As soon as the two strangers reached the flock, the sheepdogs picked a fight with the oncoming dogs, and all that could be seen was a flurry of snapping jaws and dust and fur. One of the shepherds roared at them from the back of his donkey, even raising his staff and threatening to beat them to death, but then let them be and jogged on towards the sheepskin cloak.

"Greetings."

"Greetings."

The shepherd propped himself up on his elbow and took a look at the newcomers, then shouted to the dogs:

"Get away from there!"

At this the dogs snarled at one another in a somewhat friendlier fashion. One of the guests dismounted and approached, walking bow-legged.

"Good day to you."

"The same to you."

He stood up as a mark of politeness, although the visitor did not deserve the honour because he had shown him ill-will. A little while previously our shepherd had heard at the tavern that the other had said his sheep were the offscourings of the plain. Why should he talk like that about him? He was entitled to graze his flock wherever his agreement with the authorities permitted.

But then one did not immediately show one's feelings and thoughts. He shook hands with them and said:

"You get off as well."

The other shepherd then dismounted and they unbridled and unsaddled the two donkeys. But the donkeys remained standing where they stopped and did not move; only their skin quivered under the sting of the gadflies. At most they flapped their ears.

The two shepherds took their sheepskin cloaks off the donkeys, spread them out on the arid earth, and lay down. They lay this way facing each other, just staring in front of them. They did not speak.

They were all three of them shepherds who were out with their flocks all the year round and never saw the village, unless occasionally to attend a wedding feast or a country fair. They were rugged plainsmen. Around them was the endless sky. That was all, for while an occasional cloud sailed across the sky, on the ground there was nothing but the chirping crickets. And not too far away a twisted wild pear-tree drooped.

The big flock was far off, the boy was with it. The shepherd's small son, a twelve-year-old urchin; all there was of him was a big hat, a small sheepskin cloak, and a bit of curiosity. So he began to drive the flock back, and around dusk he came up with his father.

Even then the men remained silent. A shepherd can spend entire days in silence. When they are together, they are silent together. And even when they go visiting like this, they are no more talkative.

"And what about your woman?" one of the strange shepherds asked.

He was a big, burly man, a tough freckle-faced man with blue eyes and a red moustache. As to the colour of his hair, one couldn't tell, for his hat was pulled low almost to his eyebrows.

The other guest also grunted something. He was a smaller man with a stubby nose and ferrety eyes. He puffed on his pipe, and looked up, but did not say a word.

"She's been here."

"When?"

"Oh, about a week ago."

"When's she coming again?"

"She'll come all right."

"Do you have food?"

"I have some."

"Enough for two weeks?"

"For ten days."

"Ten days."

They remained silent again.

The boy just stood there. He stood and leaned on his crooked staff, silently watching the guests. He would have liked to find out what they wanted, why they had come, but he did not dare to speak. He did not even want to. If they didn't, neither did he. It wasn't urgent.

The sun was setting slowly. It also looked at the three men curiously, it also did not know who they were and what they wanted. It regretted that it was having to leave for the fold with its own flock. Would the secret have been revealed by then?

Well, it wasn't, for the three men just lounged there and smoked, sitting there with crossed legs.

The shepherd only looked around once, and even then he pretended to look at his flock, but in fact he was looking to see whether his staff was within reach.

When the sun went down, life began to stir on the plain. Birds flew overhead, small birds swarming in large flocks. Clouds of gnats rose from the grass. The birds fell on them.

"I say."

"What do you want?"

"You have a belt?"

"Yes."

"I saw it last year at the fair; it's got brass decorations."

"Yes, that's so."

"You ought to sell it."

"Sell it?"

"Yes."

"It's not for sale."

"No?"

"No."

"Why not?"

"Well, it just isn't. I made it for myself."

"For yourself?"

"For myself. And my son."

"And for your son?"

"For him."

"For the two of you?"

"Of course."

With that they sat a while longer.

And it grew dark. It grew dark as suddenly as if somebody had blown out a candle.

"And you don't want to sell it?"

"I said, I didn't."

At this the burly shepherd took up his staff and quietly drew it close to him, as though he wanted to get up. The host shepherd did not move, he just watched like a sheepdog, but he was on the alert.

"That's your last word?"

But by this time the shepherd had sprung to his feet. The other two jumped on him.

Once, twice, the staffs clashed. First the two staffs struck the single staff, and then one staff struck the host's head.

He staggered.

"So that's why you've come?"

But he could say no more; in a second the two brutes had fallen on him and beaten him to death. He lay dead on the ground, yet again they struck him once or twice.

The little boy just stood there beside them and stared. It had happened so abruptly that he could not even move.

"Take off your father's belt," the red-faced man said to him.

The boy just stood there.

"Take it off!"

The boy turned deathly pale, and keeping his eyes on the men went over to his father and removed the belt from his waist.

"Give it to me."

The boy lifted the belt and looked to see to which he should give it. He looked, and was unaware that a staff was being raised behind him to hit him. It was a blow on the head that killed him instantly.

The four dogs, as if they had understood what was happening, suddenly came to life. The two strange sheepdogs attacked the other two, seizing them by the throat. The four torn and bleeding dogs thrashed the ground, hauling and yelping.

The little poodle hurled himself at the red-faced shepherd and bit his leg. The shepherd battered him with his staff and kicked him until the little dog lay lifeless on the ground.

The four sheepdogs were not even visible in the dark, fighting and mauling one another with every ounce of their strength.

The two men remained standing, leaning on their staffs, waiting for the dogs to finish. When their own dogs came back, bleeding and licking their wounds, the red-faced shepherd ordered:

"Start scratching."

And the two sheepdogs started to scratch. They scratched a hole in the earth. But it went too slowly.

The men took short-handled spades from the packs on their donkeys and helped them.

Once the hole was dug, the smaller shepherd dropped the boy's body into it. The man's body, however, was too heavy.

"Use the belt."

He twisted the belt around the dead man's neck and towed him in to the rough trench.

By the time the moon had risen the dead shepherd, his son, and their three dogs were buried. The two men built a fire from dried dung on the grave and fried their bacon over it. They ate their meal with relish.

"Well, that's that," said the red-faced shepherd. "Let's move on."

They began to drive the flock, and the three hundred sheep began to move across the plain, but it was a slow job, because the animals wanted to lie down and rest. They could not understand why they had to continue their wanderings on empty stomachs. But since they had no choice, they went on and on. The four donkeys ambled after them and the two wounded sheepdogs limped after.

The two shepherds walked calmly after them.

Ten days later a tall, dark woman could be seen walking across the vast plain.

She wore a peasant dress of white linen, her sandals were firmly fastened with twine, and she wore a linen kerchief on her head.

She was carrying a pack on her back and walked swiftly, although she had already been walking for three days. Her village was far away, since her husband, because he was grazing his own flock, could not easily obtain the use of neighbouring pastureland.

Her heartbeat quickened when she saw the twisted wild pear-tree from a distance; that was where her husband habitually grazed his flock.

But this time she could not see her man anywhere.

There was no farmstead or village hereabouts within a day's walk. Not a soul anywhere, only the endless plain. If anyone was not in his accustomed place, no one could find him. She found the old place for the fire, and sat for a while beside it.

She wandered all day about the pastures she remembered. But she could find not even a trace of the flock, no fresh trail, no shining little sheep droppings. The dried-up traces were several weeks old. And there had been rain, a storm too, which had washed away most of the traces long ago.

She slept under the great, overwhelming sky and could not understand where her man could be. After a short slumber she set out eastward to find other shepherds who might know something about him.

She reached a pasture where she saw smoke; cheerful smoke rising.

That wouldn't be her man, she knew already from the fire. Her man, poor soul, did not even have a desire to make a fire if he did not need to. He liked everything dry and his food cold. He never made a fire in the morning, he ate his bread, bacon and onions just as they were. He only made a fire around mid-day or at night, to cook a few noodles or a clear soup, and that only for the sake of the boy.

Huge, furious dogs made as if to attack her savagely, but she had no fear of them because she knew their language; she had been a shepherd's daughter and was a shepherd's wife. The dogs barked at her, but did her no harm.

"Good day, good people," she said when she reached the fire.

A great red-faced shepherd and three young herdsmen were standing around it.

"Has anyone seen my husband with his flock? My man is the one who always goes towards the sunset."

"With three hundred sheep?"

"Yes, three hundred. That's him. Curly the Shepherd he's called."

"Well, sit down, good woman."

The woman remained standing for a moment, but since no one seemed inclined to speak she squatted down with the pack on her back, hunched on her heels in shepherd fashion.

"Well, I don't know where your husband went. He headed toward the sunset."

"I wonder where he could have gone."

"He didn't say where he was going, but he went towards Transdanubia."

"Transdanubia?"

"He came by here twelve or thirteen days ago. Said he had to be away for a while, because he was in trouble with the gendarmes."

"Him?"

"Yes, him."

"With the gendarmes?"

"With the law."

"He never mentioned it. Just two weeks ago today I was out here to see him. He said nothing about it."

"He was a close-mouthed man."

"Close-mouthed, but he would have mentioned that."

The red-faced shepherd offered her the fork with which he had been stirring the kettle of stew.

"Have some."

"I've eaten."

"Have some, as if you were eating your own. You're welcome to it."

But the woman only shook her head. She did not reach for the fork, she did not dip into the kettle, although the meat looked good, and there was corn meal. These men were eating well, so early in the morning.

She looked at the flock. They were a mixture of sheep and ewes of Hungarian breed. She just stared and stared, as if she were looking at her own. If her husband had gone, she would have no more sheep, or ewes.

"I even remember," said the red-faced shepherd, "that when he passed here he was wearing a belt. It was decorated with brass."

"That was him," the woman said, "he loved that belt, he always wore it around his waist."

"I asked him for it, but he wouldn't give it to me."

"No, he wouldn't have given that to anybody in the world."

"I offered him whatever he might ask for it, but he wouldn't hear of it."

"Oh, my poor, dear husband," the woman exclaimed, and she clasped her hands.

"Then he said he had to go away."

"Did he mention me?"

"No, I asked after you, but he didn't reply."

"Not a word?"

"He only said you had been here. I asked him when, and he said about a week ago. That's what he said."

"About a week ago? Is that what he said?"

"Yes."

"But then it's only a week since he came by here."

"Could it have been only a week?"

The woman looked over to the young herdsmen, but they knew nothing of him.

"They didn't see him, because they hadn't arrived here then."

"Where were they?"

"Oh, here and there."

"Are they new?"

"New or not new, they weren't with me."

"But still, why did he come then?"

"He just came. He just came by here with his flock, he was a bit listless. There must have been something wrong, because he was very quiet."

"That was him."

She stared in front of her with dry eyes, but her heart felt more and more uneasy.

"Didn't he leave any indication?"

"Indication? What for?"

"Well, the . . ."

She stood up.

"Wasn't the boy with him?"

"Boy? I saw a lad with him, they were together with the flock."

"Yes?"

"He had two sheepdogs, and a poodle."

"That's right."

"Well, why don't you wait for him? Maybe he'll be back by autumn."

"I'll go after him."

"Well, suit yourself. You're welcome to stay here. We wouldn't be put out. You could stay here for a day."

"To Transdanubia, he said?"

"To Transdanubia."

"Then I'm going after him to Transdanubia."

"Always towards the setting sun."

"I'll ask somebody."

With that the woman stood up again, shrugged the pack on her back into place, nodded to them, and went on her way.

The shepherds looked after her a long time. They ate and drank. Wine from a wooden flask. Then they rose and turned to their flock.

And the woman went on and on until she disappeared. She was swallowed up by the vast plain. The sun rose higher and higher in the sky and watched the dark woman in white linen walking on and on across the plain. She just went on and on. She did not even look back towards her home. She just went on and on over the endless plain until she was lost in the distance. She walked until she reached the Danube. She found a boatman to take her over and crossed the river. And on she went.

She went wherever she heard of shepherds grazing their flock.

She went on all summer, went until the first snow fell. She wandered over every pasture, visited every flock and sat down to talk to every shepherd and ask whether he had not heard of a small, straight-backed, close-mouthed man with three hundred sheep.

She went home to her village for the winter. She opened the house with the key which she had concealed under the eaves and passed the winter at home. While she had been away her pig had grown, her hens and chickens had multiplied, because the neighbours had watched over them in her absence.

With the coming of spring she could endure to stay at home no longer. The poodle had a puppy; he was a smart little black dog as well, and she said to him:

"Come on, little poodle, let's go find your master."

She went out into the plain again. She carried what she could on her back and walked again to the place where she had left the shepherd.

She found the great twisted pear-tree again. And there settled down as if she intended to spend the summer there.

She stayed there for two weeks, or three, she did not count the days. She watched the dog. When she ran out of food, she went home again, packed up more and returned. Out to the great plain where another shepherd was already grazing his flock.

The hot days and the rainy days came and went. But she could not tear herself away from the place, she just wandered around in the immense void.

Then one day the poodle found something. He brought a hat.

"My husband's!" she said. "Where did you find it, poodle?"

The dog led her to the place.

The poodle scratched in a bit of smooth sand. He scratched furiously, barking and whining and snarling. He scratched and scratched.

Then he uncovered a hand.

The woman began to scrabble in the sand with her ten fingers, and soon the body of her husband was before her, the flesh rotting. Around his neck was the brass-ornamented belt.

She found her son too. The child lay face down and his big hat was on his head. As she lifted the hat she saw the big wound on his little head. The mother stared at it with dry eyes. Just one blow with a stick and that was the end. He had not suffered long.

She sat by the grave all day. At night she raked the sand back. She made a little mound over the grave and stuck two stakes in it in the form of a cross. Then she walked eastward.

By morning she found the flock.

"Where is that red-faced shepherd," she asked, "who grazed his flock in these parts last year?"

"In Szeged," said the strange shepherds.

"So I thought."

"The gendarmes heard about his tricks and took him away for questioning."

The woman did not stop to rest, she started for Szeged.

She arrived on the third day. She went to the captain of the gendarmes and told them everything.

The gendarmes went out with a horse and wagon taking her along with them.

They dug up the grave, wrote down what they saw. They removed the belt from the body of the dead shepherd and went back to Szeged. The examining judge conducted the inquiry.

He questioned one prisoner after another. Facts began to accumulate and it was clear that the red-faced shepherd had been responsible for a whole series of thefts and murders. There was already enough to send him to the gallows when the examining judge asked him:

"And what about Curly the Shepherd?"

The shepherd did not bat an eyelash.

"Curly the Shepherd?"

"That's what he was called when he was still alive."

"When he was still alive?"

"While he lived he was called Curly the Shepherd. And what happened to him?"

"I don't know him, Sir."

"He grazed his flock beside you, on the puszta of Csobor. Together with his little boy."

"That's possible."

"Do you know him now?"

"If he's the one who went over to Transdanubia."

"It would be very useful to know where he went. To Transdanubia or elsewhere?"

"Well, he visited me on his way there, that's true. He was in some kind of trouble with the law, and he was going toward the setting sun for a while."

"The setting sun or a resting place?"

"A resting place, I think."

"That's what I think too. And you helped him to get there."

"I, Sir?"

"Him and his son."

"Never, Sir."

"Listen, the law has finally caught up with you. You only have this last one to confess. What had Curly the Shepherd done to you?"

"Nothing, Sir."

"Done nothing to you?"

"I had absolutely no quarrel with him."

"Then why did you say in the tavern of Csür that he was grazing his flock where he shouldn't?"

The red-faced shepherd's eyebrows quivered.

"I didn't say that."

"Others heard it."

"Nobody could have heard it."

"They heard it, and you know that very well. To whom did you say it?"

"If I said it, that wasn't why."

"Then why?"

"I didn't say it because of that. A shepherd is allowed to graze wherever his agreement says he may."

"He had three hundred sheep. Where did he disappear with them? He couldn't have disappeared off the face of the earth. Right?"

"Right."

"But if he's disappeared, then his sheep should be around. Were they rams or ewes?"

"Mostly rams, if there were any."

"Of course there were. Were they his own or his landlord's?"

"He should be able to tell you."

"What did he tell you?"

"I never spoke to him."

"Then how did you know?"

"Others told me. I saw them. He grazed his flock beside mine. He wasn't very talkative. He was a close-mouthed man."

"Was he close-mouthed?"

"Yes . . . he was."

"Then too?"

"When?"

"When you clubbed him to death with your staffs. Both him and his son."

"Did he have a son?"

"He had a son. You struck him just one blow on the head and he was finished."

"Don't say those sorts of things to me, please. I never spoke to him, nor to his son."

"If you didn't speak to him then he wouldn't have spoken. He was a close-mouthed man."

"What does Your Honour want?"

"I want you to unburden your soul. One more or less shouldn't stop you."

"I can't own up to something I didn't know."

"Think."

"I've nothing to think about."

"Did you take the spades with you?"

"Spades?"

"On your donkeys."

"Donkeys?"

"Because it was a very clean job."

"I had nothing to do with it, Sir."

"Did you drive off the sheep?"

"I had sheep of my own, Your Honour, I wasn't interested in anyone else's."

"But they were fine sheep. Three hundred. He was a good man, Curly the Shepherd. He got them by his own work, he saved his earnings."

"Maybe. But I know nothing about it."

"Are the sheep with your flock, or have you sold them?"

"Don't suggest such things, I beg you."

"Now listen to me. You're not a child! Anybody who has admitted all his other crimes ought not haggle over three hundred sheep. What's that to you? When you might go before God with a purified soul, do you want Curly the Shepherd to blacken it?"

"I can't help it."

"I could spit in your face, like the face of some snivelling brat. You went there after sunset, hit them on the head, killed their dogs and buried them in the sand,"

The red-faced shepherd grew more stubborn. His burning eyes glared at the examining judge.

"It was none of my doing, Your Honour."

"Get out of here, you brazen-faced . . . I don't want to see you any more."

The shepherd trembled.

"Get out of my sight. You're not a shepherd, you're a thieving blackguard! And you can be quite sure that you'll find no peace on the gallows either."

"I can't confess to what I didn't do."

"Out!"

The shepherd turned and started for the door with heavy steps. But as he gained the door and reached his hand for the doorknob, he staggered back.

His hand could not touch the doorknob. He could not move. He just stared and stared and a small froth appeared around his mouth.

There, hanging on the doorknob, was the brass-ornamented leather belt.

The shepherd slowly raised his hand to his head, then turned.

"Your Honour . . . I confess . . ."

The examining judge did not say a word, but only looked at the man with eyes like glowing embers.

"We killed Curly the Shepherd for his three hundred sheep and two donkeys."

With that he dropped his head.

The examining judge looked at him for a long time, then rang the bell.

Two gendarmes entered.

"Take him away. Give him twenty-five strokes of a cane."

The shepherd dropped his head and went out through the door, a broken man.

"Thank you, Sir."

The judge looked after him and reflected:

"Brutes."

1932

Translated by Gyula Gulyás

Vision in Union Square

Dr. Béla Pogány

I have to cross Union Square on my way home from the office of our newspaper. The park is usually populated with an odd assortment of people, mostly elderly. Most of them seem to be unemployed, vagrants, with a generous sprinkling of beggars. Then there are people who just seek rest in summertime in the shade of trees and dreamily watch the playful variations of the shadows of the trees. Quite frequently I see elderly people holding a piece of dry bread in the water fountain to soften it in the water so they can suck at it in their toothless mouths.

The other day, as I was hurrying home in a downpour, I found the square almost completely deserted. On one of the benches, however, I saw an old man sitting all alone. The downpour had cooled the air and it was almost chilly. The leaves on the trees were already beginning to fall, and I could almost hear them dropping on the wet pavement. I had an umbrella in my hand.

As I got near the man I saw that his grey hair was water-soaked. He was asleep, and it seemed that he sank into himself. His cheekbones were markedly prominent and they indicated that he was either a seriously ill man or a starving one.

He sat there with his hands in his pockets, slightly leaning to one side. The collar of his torn jacket was turned up. His worn, porous clothing seemed to soak up the raindrops as if it were the soil itself. The raindrops gleamed on it for a moment and then disappeared, and the jacket seemed to remain dry. His haggard face hung immobile. Maybe the man is dead, I thought. Maybe he has already merged with nature, maybe the earth has already claimed him and is waiting to completely absorb him amid the yellow tree leaves, the dancing raindrops.

37

In the silence softly punctured by the sound of the rain, I found the sight heartrending. Suddenly I panicked. My god, I have to save this man, he is dying. If someone falls into the water, one does not stop to think whether he was a good man or an evil man, a criminal or an apostle; one only sees a man sinking and one has to act to save him.

What shall I do? Solitude, desolation, the presentiment of death hovered above the man seated under the gorgeous foliage of trees. And as I was standing there impotent, helpless, I couldn't take my eyes off the old man. I saw a vision. I saw myself dying there in the old man's place. It is me sitting there, defeated by life, abandoned by my fellow men. I am dying there. Why did I deserve that fate? All my life I fought for others, I always wanted to do the right thing, the noble thing. What did I do to deserve that fate? Yet at the end I was abandoned, neglected; nobody cared for me, nobody wanted me and I am struggling homeless without a roof over my head and finally I have surrendered. I am awaiting my fate, my end, on this water-soaked bench under the glorious foliage of summer trees.

And if I still should have enough strength and I could still open my eyes and saw a man standing in front of me, what would I say to him? Maybe I would say: My friend, you are still living, you are working, you are still young. Give me your money so I can hold onto life for a while longer.

And then, recovering, I took a few steps toward him, thinking that I would put a few dollars in his pocket. But then I stopped. I realized that in the United States one must not touch a sleeping person. Misjudging my act, they might think that I had tried to pilfer the last few dollars from a sleeping, helpless old man.

What shall I do? Shall I wake him up and with a touch of sentimentality give him a few dollars, thereby redressing the scales of moral order and justice in this world? I heard people approaching and I walked away helplessly, shamefacedly.

Maybe this was the man who used to soak his dry bread in the fountain. His face haunted me for days. To this day I think of him with unrelenting anguish. I can't understand it, that after all the horrors I have witnessed or read about — the horrors of war, of death camps — the suffering of a single person still can create such ache in my heart. What a peculiar instrument the human heart is, that it can bleed for the hurt of one man as much as that of millions. Or is it because every human being represents all mankind?

Oh, let us not abandon the old men, let us save them in their day of anguish. What is the use of culture, of civilization, what is the whole order of society, if we cannot resolve this everyday horror of our daily lives?

1952

Dr. Pogány was a member of our editorial staff.

REBELLION RIDES THE OCEAN...

Föltámadott a tenger...

Rebellion rides the ocean,
The ocean of mankind,
Affrighting earth and heaven,
The maddened waves a leaven
To terrify the mind.

That carmagnole, you see it?
You hear that roundelay?
For you who might not know it,
The time is ripe to show it:
The way the people play!

The ocean howls, it rages,
The ships are flung about,
Till naught but hell avail or
The masthead and the sailor
Be brought to utter rout.

Roar out your rage, you deluge,
Roar out your raging fume,
Show low your deepest fathom,
Throw high on clouds at random
The fury of your spume,

Inscribe upon the heavens
For all eternity :
«Above, though rides the galley —
Below, though waters rally —
The sovereign is the sea!»

Pest, 1848.

–Sándor Petőfi

The Family Hearth
Imre Dobozy

Esther had put the children to bed and was just going to wash up when her husband stepped in the kitchen. He was unshaven, grimy and unkempt, his face contorted with strange grimaces and his clothes exuding unfamiliar odours. He threw his hat on a distant chair and shouted impatiently as if he had left home that very morning.

"Here I am! . . . Got something good for supper?"

Esther just stared at her husband—at his crumpled loden jacket, which hung on him as if it had been pitched there with a fork; his restless, thin face marked with unruly lines, his hungry, glowing, beady black eyes, his reddish hair which hung in sweaty wisps on his forehead; and his narrow chin which he thrust into the air sharply and stubbornly even when he was smiling. She just stared and said not a word, and not because her husband had come unexpectedly either. Truth to tell, she never expected him, and yet his arrival never caused her surprise.

Esther had long regarded their life together as a repetition of rare meetings which had savoured of the accidental, which could be borne only without desire and expectation, sadly and sternly, and with untiring forbearance.

She did not think of her husband, she trembled neither for him, nor because of him. If he came, he was at home, if he did not come, he was somewhere else. That was how she trained herself, that was how the pain of loneliness mellowed into dull resignation. Yet she loved this man. Somehow, for some reason, she loved him all the same, silently and aimlessly; or perhaps she loved merely the dreams of her girlhood, which, although they were never fulfilled, were nevertheless sweetly and movingly beautiful . . .

"It's been six months since you went away . . ." she said at last, not in reproach to be sure, but as a simple observation on the passing of time.

Tóth looked at his wife. He grinned awkwardly, and his eyes avoided her scrutiny in confusion. But this unconscious embarrassment, this painful and visible little twinge of his hardened conscience, did not last long. Tóth took out a cigarette, lit it, and now, looking his wife in the eye, he asked curtly:

"So what?"

His wife slowly turned away. She threw some twigs on the fire and busily blew at the rosy embers. Even the sooty mouth of the fireplace seemed to echo swiftly and derisively, "So what? So what?"

True, she could not have expected anything else. When her husband had first set out a good six months after the wedding, saying that he would have to look for a job because they could not eke out a living from three acres of land and a tiny vineyard, she had, in her fear and childish obstinacy, begged him not to leave. She'd be willing to do anything, but she did not want to live alone, she could not bear it. And they were going to have a child and the child would look for its father every day with its inquiring eyes . . . Then her husband had interrupted her roughly: "So what?" . . . And the next day he left. From then on Esther knew that she was present in her husband's life only like a lamp: if it was needed it was turned on, if not, it was turned off . . .

Later she discovered that it wasn't even for the sake of earning money that her husband would leave home. His blood drove him. His roving, vagabond, restless and greedy nature drove him from region to region,' in pursuit of new lands, new roads, occasional jobs and occasional loves . . . By autumn, when the weather turned biting, he usually found his way home. He was think, unkempt, weather-beaten and surly. On these occasions he would bring a little money which he would slam on the table. Then he made himself at home, scrubbed himself clean and gradually became corpulent and heavy. But only until spring. Then he would be off again and melt into the great big world. He would vanish and would not even bother to write. Esther often thought to herself that if she should once begin to cry and sob away all her loneliness, her nights of worry, her eternal and bitter struggle for the two children, the flood of tears would wash away the foundations of the house. But she did not cry. There was no one to listen.

Her husband squatted down beside her. He rubbed his stubbly face against her cheeks, placed a smacking, loud kiss on her ear, and asked her:

"Aren't you even glad?"

He laughed hoarsely and pinched her breast.

"I'll scrape the hair off my mug in a jiffy . . . and I'll be as handsome as they make 'em. You'll feel like having me then, I'll bet."

At such times, during the rare discordant momemts of his rough advances, Esther usually felt a girlish fullness of the heart. In the great inner silence which she had imposed on herself, her heart would begin to sing. She could forgive everything, and she wanted to be good, hoping that something of her goodness would rub off on her husband.

But now she waited in vain for that inner sound. She remained calm and even strong somehow. It did not occur to her that she had gradually severed the remaining weak threads of her former capricious and loose dependence on her husband and was now able to stand on her own two feet even if her husband did not come home for years on end. Nothing occurred to her, she merely sensed that the ususal emotion failed to come over her, and when she straightened up, flushed from blowing the fire, she stood there like a rather chubby, but very sweet and tranquil statue.

By now Tóth was rummaging in the cupboard for his razor. But all at once he stiffened, like a dog picking up a scent. For some time he stared uncomprehending at the neat rows of cups and glasses as if he were seeing them for the first time. Then he reached deep into the cupboard and took out a large china bowl that he did not remember having seen before. He turned it about, looked at it, and put it back. But he did not say a word. He fished out some other dishes from the cupboard and then replaced them. Suddenly he slammed the door of the cupboard and, turning around, began to examine the kitchen. He noticed everything. The new cloth on the table, a new cardigan on the hanger, a sack full of nuts in the corner, a new alarm-clock on the window sill, the signs of an unpretentious prosperity within the old bounds of the familiar and monotonous poverty.

His face convulsed in an angry twitch.

"You!" he said to his wife and slammed the razor-strap he held in his hand on the table.

He scrutinized his wife closely only now. She was not as she had been. She was not as careworn and timid. She had filled out, she looked calmer and perhaps even prettier; she had virtually blossomed like a flower. Her forehead was smooth, her usually dishevelled hair that used to look like a stack of hay was now neatly combed. There was no trace of the former long-suffering meekness in her eyes. Her glance was indifferent, a little lazy and almost satiated.

Tóth bit his lips. He swore to himself. Somebody had entered this woman's life . . . At the building sites where he worked, he had known lonely women whose natural reserve had been worn down by loneliness and who gladly threw themselves into, or rather fled into a man's arms for a kind word, for a caress. You didn't even have to call them, you only had to listen skilfully and cleverly as they complained of their loneliness. But his wife, who had been left very much to herself and was love-starved, showed no desire to throw herself into his arms and take sure refuge in his embrace.

He stepped up to her.

"Speak!" he said, cracking his fingers in rage.

"What about?" she asked.

She did not understand her husband's anger, nor was she afraid of him.

"You whore!" he yelled. "D'you think I'm blind? But I'll get it out of you!"

Esther turned pale. No . . . her husband didn't know what he was saying. Perhaps he was drunk. Or perhaps something was the matter with him. Or maybe he wanted to leave her for ever, and had come home only to pick an ugly and unbearable quarrel. She did not know what to say. She stood by the fireplace, stunned as if she suffered a stroke. Her husband grabbed the razor-strap from the table, swung it, and screamed so that his thin face writhed from the roots of his hair to his pointed chin:

"Who did you lie with, you bitch! Who consoled you while I was away? Answer me!"

The shouting awoke the children. They dared not open the door but they peeped in, clinging to the curtain. They did not recognize their father through the close weave of the cotton fabric. They could only see the blurred image of a man who was threatening their mother in the kitchen. The older child tore open the window of the room and jumped out, his short underpants a white patch in the darkness. He waited a little, then, terrified, rushed to the neighbours for help.

Esther threw up her arms to shield herself.

"Don't you dare . . ." she said dully. "Put down the strap."

"I'll kill you!"

"Don't . . . What do you want? What should I talk about? I'll tell you everything, everything . . . but stop this . . ."

"Who's your lover?"

"You mustn't say things like that about me . . . God will punish you if you say such things . . ."

"Do you deny it?"

He raised the strap in a towering fury. It was the rage of the swindler who, screaming for revenge, all at once, feels that he too has been cheated. As if it had not been he who had left his wife for long months, alone amid grinding worries with the children, but someone else; as if it had not been he who had tumbled with any woman who came his way, living totally for his wanderlust, roaming from bed to dreary bed in whisky-soaked passion. Now he wanted to administer justice, to beat and lash, to see red stripes on the woman's white skin, to hear her repentant wailing. He wanted to tear the whole world apart.

Esther backed away.

"You've never hit me before," she pleaded. "Your heart has never let you do it . . ."

"His name! I want to hear his name!"

"But whose? What do you want of me?"

"Stand still! You wretch! . . . You'll tell me yet!"

At that moment the neighbours arrived. The Halász family, all three of them. The old man led the way, his clothes slung on unbuttoned, his son behind him and last came the old woman, wailing bitterly although she could not see what was happening in the kitchen:

"Oh, my God, Mother of Jesus, the things a body lives to see, they're killing each other . . ." Her husband did not even speak to Tóth, but snarled at his wife: "Shut up, you, or I'll make you!"

With that they invaded the kitchen, just in time. Nothing had happened yet. Esther was white as a sheet, terrified, but as yet unhurt.

Tóth's anger turned against the intruders.

"Get the hell out of here!" he screamed. "What do you want here?"

By now the neighbours from down the street had also come, with their two strapping young boys, one of whom was swinging a cudgel as big as a fence-post. Hardly had they squeezed themselves into the kitchen, when still others came, three at a time, and yet others, as if the whole end of the village had been ordered here to put out a fire. They came with picks and clubs and pushed and squeezed their way inside, so that Tóth, driven into a corner, was unable even to move an arm. He shouted:

"Get out! Get out!"

Nobody said anything. Nobody moved. Stern eyes watched him. Only the heavy breathing of the people and the ticking of the new alarm-clock could be heard.

There was silence for a long time, a heavy, pregnant silence. Then old Halász spoke up:

"Put down the strap."

Tóth did not put it down. What he held in his hand, what he did with the strap, was none of their business. This was his house and it was none of their business even if he beat his wife to death. He did not put down the strap, but gripped it hard. These people will leave sooner or later, they'll get tired of the spectacle, and then, then he would give her what for.

But they did not leave. Those further back began to press and push those who were inside, the ring around him was getting tighter, the Halász boy was pushed against Tóth until their chests touched. And then someone from the back spoke up, deliberately and with disgust:

"You tramp!"

Tóth flared up.

"Who's that?"

Madari, a dark-faced, sinewy, sullen peasant raised his arm.

"Me," he said. "Don't worry, I won't run away . . . But listen here, if you lay a finger on your wife, you'll regret it."

"That's my business," said Tóth.

Madari elbowed his way forward. This sullen man flew into such a murderous rage that his face turned almost black. He shouted so hard that he snapped out the words.

"You tramp and bitch around . . . and leave your wife and two kids to howl in misery . . . That's our business."

"What do you mean *our*?"

"Ours, the co-op's! The Petófi co-op's! We took her in . . . She has bread and peace of mind . . . If you've come home just to make trouble, get out!"

He came forward, shoved the Halász boy aside, grabbed Tóth's arm, and held it in a tight grip.

"Drop that strap. Or else . . ."

Tóth would have raised his arm, but he could not. In Madari's merciless grasp he felt his arms, shoulders, even his heart, grow numb. It was impossible to bear the terrible grip of this dark-faced peasant. Slowly, Tóth let the strap slip from his hand, and as if his strength had left with it, his body crumpled.

Madari did not say another word. No one spoke, everyone just stood there in threatening quiet for a long time. Then, as they gradually began to withdraw from the kitchen, they winked to the woman as if to say, don't worry, we'll be back if you need us.

Esther picked up the strap from the floor and hung it in its place. She said nothing. Somehow, she was even sorry for her husband. But when he sat down on the chest and put his head in his hands, she could not remain silent.

"I'll make your bed here," she said, "in the kitchen."

Tóth looked at her.

"We'll see," he said gloomily.

But he already knew that he would sleep in the kitchen, and that he would not cross its threshold after the light had been turned out, perhaps for a very long time to come. He would not have the courage. And as he stretched himself on the bed made on the bench, staring through the window at the darkness outside, a quiet, long unfelt, painful fear crept into his heart. It was the kind of fear that used to disturb him when as a child he had done something wrong and was scolded, "either you mend your ways or you leave this house . . ."

It was long past midnight when he finally fell asleep.

1961   *Translated by John Brown*

Adventure in Uniform

Sándor Hunyady

When the war broke out, I joined up as a second-line reservist in the Fifty-First Regiment with the grey facings. True, I had not been given the volunteer's braid, but none the less I was very nicely off. My unit was stationed in Kolozsvár, where I had been born, and I knew half the town. I was a journalist and had joined the regiment almost straight from the editorial office. My sergeant called me "Mr. Editor." My whole military service consisted of getting into my uniform twice a week, in order to present myself for appearances' sake, at company headquarters. Otherwise my life went on as usual. I wore civilian clothes most of the time, and through the windows of the café I would watch companies marching to the station on their way to the front.

I am not saying all this just to boast. The older I get, the more ashamed I am of having cheated myself out of my share of suffering when everyone else was suffering. But it is part of the picture that the reader should know what an irresponsible puppy and how far from being a fine soldier I was on that summer Sunday afternoon when this story began.

Yet I had a fine martial air at that moment. I was wearing typical private's uniform, with heavy laced boots and tight-fitting blue trousers. Round my waist was the regulation belt, with the double-headed eagle on its brass buckle. I had just left the barracks; my day's service was done. I was hurrying home to my rooms to change back into civvies and to go to the theatre, where I was courting the second *soubrette*.

As I said, it was a Sunday afternoon. The street was crowded with promenading servant-girls in their best clothes. Kolozsvár is a verile catchment area for all the folk currents of the neighborhood. And the small groups of Székely, Rumanian and Hungarian girls sauntering along arm in arm gave the servants' parade the iridescence of a peacock's tail. Each village was represented by its own characteristic dress, by the characteristic colour of the hair, figure and temperament, by its ribbons, skirts and kerchiefs. What gaily swarming crowds! How brightly the clean-washed, eager faces shone! Everybody was in a hurry to cram as much happiness as possible into an afternoon that was passing far too quickly.

Many of the girls looked at me invitingly, some of them smiled at me, a few even accosted me. Indeed, why shouldn't they? I was twenty-two years old, and in my private's uniform and iron-heeled boots I must have looked exactly like any other peasant boy from one of the neighbouring counties. I found it all very amusing. I felt like a prince in disguise. I winked back at the girls and even pulled their pigtails. I behaved just as a private should who is out for a bit of a Sunday adventure. I scored victories and suffered setbacks. The girls joggled me, trod on my feet, pinched my arms. The wide-rolling river carried me gaily along amidst its little eddies.

Suddenly the tide swept me up to a tall girl from Kalotaszeg. We bumped into each other. I looked at her. She was a lovely creature. Clean as fresh linen and slender as a birch sapling.

I caught her arm.

"Where are you off to?"

"I'm off to find a sweetheart," she answered flippantly.

I drew her toward me.

"Then you can stop right now, because I'm doing the same."

The girl looked at me. It was an honest, serious, scrutinizing look, as if I were a chicken or cabbage she considered buying at the market place. Finally she nodded.

"All right. Let's go together."

A wave of pride rushed over me. Deep within me I felt a strange warmth spreading, the legacy of a million years. The spark in her touched off an answering glow in me. I was filled with a sense of triumph, and at the same time of tenderness, of melting devotion. And I knew that she felt the same about me. We walked on silently through the jostling crowd. Our mood was touched with a new gravity. My hand was scorched by the touch of her strong elbow as I cupped it in my palm to prevent her being whirled away from me.

She really was a lovely girl. Chestnut hair, grey eyes. Her soft light-brown skin seemed to be too taut for her full face. It stretched tightly over her nose, her lips, her chin. I was inclined to think that she could hardly shut her eyes, the little muscles round them were so elastically resistant under that clear complexion.

When I first accosted her I had been perhaps a bit familiar. But after a few minutes of silent walking, I involuntarily spoke to her more tenderly, with greater respect. And I saw with surprise that this serene young peasant girl responded at once to my new approach. She too dropped her flippant tone and asked me with simple directness where I came from. Was I from Kolozsvár?

I told her I came from Szilágy County. I even invented a name for the village: Pokozd.

"And you, I see, come from Kalotaszeg," I said to her. "What's your name?"

"Vilma Jakab. And yours?"

"Sándor Nagy," I lied, for I was in no doubt that the girl would leave me flat and run off angrily if I told her I was not of her own class.

As we strolled on she told me that the place where she worked was in Bocskai Square, and that her master was some kind of civil servant. It seemed to be a decent family. Still, she didn't know the place very well yet . . . She had only come up to Kolozsvár from her village two weeks ago.

"I'm free till eight," she told me, "but then I have to go home. They will be having supper at home tonight. Not that they couldn't manage without me. It's just a cold supper. Sausages."

Each Sunday this peasant promenade follows the same precise course, reminiscent of the march of ants along the ground. The colourful stream flows first through Honvéd Street, then up the right-hand side of Main Square; from there it continues through Union and Bartha Miklós Streets towards the Szamos river and turns again along the right-hand side of the avenue. The right-hand side is crowded, thick with dust, loud with noise, and one is bumped and pushed along continuously under the ancient trees; the other side is almost completely empty. Only a few people stroll there in the shadow of the trees opposite. I thought this was just a matter of custom, so I said to the girl:

"Let's cross over to the other side. What's the use of getting squashed in this crowd?"

The girl stared at me.

"Sándor! Don't you know that we are not allowed to go over there? The policeman would chase us back. That side is reserved for the gentry."

Of course I didn't know. Gentleman idler that I was, how should I have known the extent of the stupidity and insolence reflected in such police orders?

The blood rushed to my head. Without thinking I mumbled to myself furiously.

"What a damned shame. I'll have to write something about it."

"What did you say?" the girl asked fearfully.

I evaded a direct answer.

"Damn them, it's a dirty trick, not to let one walk where one wants to! Why are those people over there better than we two?"

The girl did not have the slightest notion of socialist ideas. She simply shrugged her shoulders.

"I don't know why you should get so angry about it. We can go down there if you like, where the geese and ducks are, we won't find many people there."

But I was furious. It suddenly occurred to me that I couldn't take her to the Kiosk, a "first-class" restaurant either. The waiters would promptly inform us that it was no place for privates and servant girls. Impudent swine! For the first time I was feeling on my own hide what the arrogant measures taken for the convenience of my kind of people meant to others.

There was a little amusement park along the avenue, so we went there for want of a better place. We rode on the swings. We weighed ourselves. We looked at the Tattooed Lady. We took turns hitting the test-your-strength machine. When I paid, I changed a five forint piece.

The girl stared at me and the coin.

"Where did you get so much money?"

"My father has quite a bit of land and we are also part-owners of a threshing-machine," I lied to her, quite fluent by this time. "Five forints are nothing to me."

But the girl did not let the matter go at that: "We also have land and a house. But my father would kill my brother if he threw away good money the way you do . . ."

By now I had completely forgotten that I was due at the theatre. I had forgotten the *soubrette* and my own position in civil life. Deep down in my heart I was wishing that the Szilágy County background I had invented was true and I myself really a peasant boy who that Sunday afternoon had found the one true love of his live realized in this fresh, lovely, natural young girl.

It was an afternoon of perfect bliss. There was only one dangerous moment in it. A bow-legged, pockmarked old cavalry corporal tried to take the girl away from me. First he walked up and down before us like a dog in heat. Then suddenly, he picked a quarrel with me, claiming I hadn't saluted him properly. He made me stand at attention and gave me a thorough dressing-down in front of the girl. He had the authority, for he was a corporal and I was a mere recruit. I tried to put up with his insults patiently, but felt my face turning pale and the muscles of my right arm quivering with a desire to pull out my bayonet and plunge it into this yellow-toothed, tobacco-smelling vile rat.

The tension between us was growing more dangerous every moment. By now our eyes were flashing out something quite different from what we were saying. I don't know what would have happened if the girl had not intervened, if she had not drawn her arm through mine in a gesture of profound solidarity and turned humbly, yet very firmly to the corporal:

"I know quite well why the honoured corporal is badgering this young man. Please leave him alone, sir. In any case you won't be able to separate us anyway, because you see we are from the same village . . ." And she squeezed my arm to her side.

The corporal stood quite still for a few seconds, staring at us very hard as if calculating inwardly whether it was worth his while to risk a row. Then, perhaps a spark of humanity sprang to life in him, or he saw something hard and determined written on both our faces; he put his sword firmly under his arm, turned on his heel and went off in search of new conquests, venting his anger in a single sentence:

"Damn both of you and your village as well!"

When the danger had passed, we walked on quietly side by side for a while. It was she who at last broke the silence. Quietly, tenderly, wisely she spoke her mind:

"You see, Sándor, that is why you ought to try and get a promotion. If you had had even a single star on your uniform that corporal wouldn't have dared to be so insolent towards you. Because people only dare to be as mean as that with those who have nothing and nobody in the world. One doesn't need to have much, just a few pitchforks of hay, and people will immediately overlook this and that, and be nice to one, for they'll reckon 'who knows when we'll need a bit of his hay . . .'"

Plenty of my girl friends had tried to inspire me to greater ambition in the past. But I had always resisted their attempts. Yet there was so much selflessness and tact in this girl's attitude, such wisdom in what she said, that I felt like kissing her hands.

Our arms round each other's waist, we walked on in silence—private and servant-girl—amidst the gradually dispersing crowd, as dusk began to envelop us.

When the church clock struck half past seven, and the girl began to talk of having to go home soon, I said to her with a heavy heart:

"It won't be easy to part from you, Vilma . . ."

She considered a while, then looked up at me and said:

"We don't have to part. You can come up to my room. You will have to wait while I serve supper. Then you can stay with me. But only come if you don't have to go back to your barracks before morning, I wouldn't want the porter opening the door for you in the night and asking you whom you'd been visiting."

Plain talk indeed! A frank invitation to a night of love. But it was not said lightly. She spoke simply and without beating about the bush. As of something natural and human, a part of life as simple as breathing.

"Thank you very much," I answered gratefully. "Luckily, I can stay out all night, the sergeant is a pal of mine."

We started off quietly toward Bocskai Square.

On the way the girl told me that her employer's name was Ferenc Bodrogi, she did not know where he worked except that it was in some kind of an office. He had a wife, a son and a daughter. His son was away at present in the y. They lived at number four on the third floor.

Her explanation first startled me, then I very nearly burst out laughing. I knew the family extremely well. Bodrogi was an engineer at the gasworks, I had gone to school with the son and had even flirted with the daughter. I had been to their home quite often. It was strange for me to have to enter the familiar gate and go up the dark and narrow backstairs, only lighted on the second floor by a very small gas lamp.

When we reached the third floor the girl searched in her skirt for the key to the kitchen and unlocked the door. I knew the kitchen quite well too. Sometimes, when the bell was not functioning at the main entrance, I had knocked at the back door and come in that way. There had been a little Rumanian servant girl in the house before. She had been rather pretty too, and I remembered pinching her cheeks.

Vilma now turned the light on and took off her shawl. I stood on the threshold of the open door and wanted to go in after her.

She turned toward me.

"Stay outside on the balcony for a bit, Sándor, till the family has gone out or gone to bed. One of them might come into the kitchen. There's no need for them to see you. They might not even like your being here."

'They certainly would not,' I thought to myself as I stepped out on the narrow open balcony. It was quite dark by now. Lamps shone brightly in the doors and windows looking out to the balconies which ran round the inside courtyard of the huge block of flats on each floor, and you could see shadowy figures moving about in the kitchens. Somewhere a servant-girl was singing. Another soldier, presumably on the same errand as myself, loitered on the first floor balcony, leaning against the iron railing.

50

It was a hot summer evening. 'The smell from the courtyards of houses like these is certainly pretty awful at this time of year,' I thought to myself as I sat down on a dustbin, between a cold flat-iron and a paper-sack containing charcoal.

Vilma was busying herself in the kitchen. She got the plates, forks and knives ready, sliced the bread and put a clean napkin in the bread-basket. She peeled five pairs of sausages and sliced onions to go with them. From the cupboard she took out some cherry-strudel—obviously left over from lunch. She called to me through the open door of the kitchen:

"Will you have some, Sándor?"

I would have liked to, but Vilma was unable to bring me anything for in the door leading to the flat appeared the daughter of her employers. There was a time when I had found little Piri attractive. I had particularly admired her skin and her hair. Now I no longer liked her face, It was much too hard. I was annoyed, too, at her not returning Vilma's friendly "good evening" when she came into the kitchen. From the dark balcony I noted the boredom with which she went up to the table and idly picked a cherry out of the strudel.

My blood boiled to hear her talk to my Vilma as if to her slave.

"Bring in immediately the supper, Vilma. We're going to the cinema. When we're gone, you can put the table in order, do the beds, and then you can go to bed yourself, we won't need you any more tonight. Only don't forget to wake me tomorrow at seven, and clean my tennis shoes."

When the young lady had flitted back into the flat, Vilma came out into the passage for a moment and said:

"Isn't she pretty? Her name's Piri."

The bell in the kitchen rang impatiently. Vilma carried the sausages and onions out and left the kitchen empty.

I could follow every step of the girl in my thoughts. I could visualize the dining-room, the dinner-table, the settee, the clock, the pictures on the wall.

She went on hurrying to and fro between kitchen and dining-room. They rang for water. They rang for salt. I heard her turn on the tap. When, at long last, they were through, Vilma came out to the railing and shook the crumbs from the tablecloth. Then Piri appeared once more. This time she had her hat and coat on. She measured out sugar and coffee for the next day's breakfast from the cupboard. Then she left without saying goodnight.

The main door slammed and I saw the family I knew so well go down the stairs.

At last the girl called me in.

"Go into my place while I put the kitchen in order, will you?"

What she'd called "my place" was a tiny room, or rather a cubby hole, ventilated through the kitchen. There was barely enough space for the iron bed and the single chair, on which stood a tin wash-basin. The girl's coloured skirts and cheap blouses hung from two nails in the wall. At the head of the bed stood a small painted wooden box, the kind peasant boys take with them when they go to do their military service. On that wooden box lay a Roman Catholic prayer book, which had been stuck full of holy pictures with paper-lace edges. The Holy Virgin wore forget-me-not blue veils, the pictures of Christ were pale and waxen, with blood dripping from under the crown of thorns.

I sat down on the bed and silently watched Vilma putting the kitchen in order. Outside the heavy summer smell from the yard had appalled me. But in that windowless little chamber I thought I was breathing in the light smell of village soil. The smell of a peasant house with an earthen floor. Perhaps it was not just a fancy, perhaps she has brought that far away fragrance with her clothes.

"Aren't you coming?"

"Right away. Just let me wash my hands properly," she replied, "I've been slicing onions, you know . . ." And she went to the tap by the wall, where she washed her hands thoroughly with a big cake of crude laundry soap.

At long last she came into her tiny cubby hole.

"Get up, so that I can make the bed."

I rose, took her by the waist, and drew her to me . . . I have had plenty of adventures with women. But never before, or since, have I felt such purity, such dramatic strength in any embrace. My own strength was as nothing compared to hers as she put her muscular arms round my neck. She took my head in her hands and looked straight into my eyes.

Softly she said:

"It's all because of your eyes. That's why you're here. I loved your eyes the moment you first spoke to me . . ."

Well, this adventure turned into a genuine love affair. We met on three consecutive Sundays and there was a holiday in between when we were together too. Four times in succession, and each time I put on my private's uniform and played the peasant boy. Or rather I didn't even play the role. I simply behaved naturally, in harmony with my happy mood. I only had to take care not to talk about things that might awaken the girl's suspicions. And in fact our conversation was much more interesting than is usual on such occasions. And that by no means because of my intelligence; it was due to the wealth of her emotions, her utter sincerity, her remarkably expressive and colourful language.

On the fifth Sunday afternoon I did not go to our usual meeting-place in front of Hintz, the chemist's, on the Main Square. Why did I stay away? I can't remember. Perhaps I had something to do, perhaps I simply overslept. The fact remains that I did not go, but kept my civilian clothes on all day and at about seven o'clock that evening I chanced to pass the chemist's shop.

She was still standing in the doorway of the Hintz house, motionless, a shawl round her head and shoulders, waiting. One could see, by the way she stood, that she has been there for hours. Her face was earnest and sad. There she stood, looking out into the rain from the entrance. For it was raining and growing dark. So she did not recognize me in my suit and rubber raincoat. Indeed, she hardly looked at me. She was expecting somebody quite different—a young soldier in a blue coat with belt and boots.

As I walked past, my heart gave a big leap. But I did not want her to see me in my elegant clothes. Besides, I wasn't alone. A colleague of mine hung on my arm, for we had only one umbrella between us. We were discussing the war, and were walking fast because of the rain.

But when we were about three blocks away, my throat grew suddenly dry. I thought of Kipling's native girl who waited for forty years at the crossroads for her unfaithful British soldier. I ran all the way back to the chemist's shop. But she was no longer standing in the doorway. Poor girl, she must have just left. It was half past seven by that time, and she had to go home to lay the table, serve the supper.

I cursed myself. My heart ached. I loved that girl.

On the following Sunday it all came right again. We met as usual. I lied to her about having served a day's detention in barracks. We walked together, we rowed on the tiny lake by the avenue, and fed the swans with breadcrumbs. And at night we again lay together in her little room, in the narrow iron bed, clasping each other closely in the earth-scented dark. Suddenly the girl laid her head on my breast and whispered:

"How long can we be like this? One of these days you'll be put into field-grey uniform like the others and I'll see you marching to the station with flowers in your cap . . . And when that happens, I'll drown myself in the Szamos . . ."

I very nearly gave myself away at that moment. I should only have had to turn on the light and show her my hands: 'Look how soft my hands are. Open your eyes at last: do peasant boys have hands like mine?'

But I did not have the courage to do it. I was afraid of making her unhappy. I felt she would not take what had happened between us as a joke. But I also knew that the truth was bound to come out. I simply could not go on cheating this pure, kind-hearted creature who had given herself to me so completely, so unreservedly, without any thought of what people would say if they found out, without fearing shame or unhappiness. Once she had said to me very simply: "If I have a baby I can never again go home. My mother would shut the door in my face."

I don't know exactly how I conceived the miserable idea that it was much better to let her find out about me by herself, without my telling her. Just let her see me in my true light and draw her own conclusions, so avoiding a big scene. I could always add further explanations later.

It was a stupid idea. Today I can find no excuse for my accepting old Bodrogi's invitation to supper. Why did I have to do such a thing? Perhaps it wasn't I that did it, but the devil, who sometimes gets the upper hand in us.

The old gentleman found me at the café.

"Come and dine with us tomorrow night, young man . . . my son's back on three days' leave from his unit."

I dressed with meticulous care for that supper. I had a fine beige summer suit, and that is what I put on. I looked at myself in the mirror and saw an exquisite dandy.

I rang the front door bell. Piri opened the door to me.

"Well, here you are at last! Nearly half an hour late."

We had a quick nip of rose brandy. Then we sat down to table. I was placed next to Piri. I had a vague idea that they might not be disinclined to offer me her hand in marriage. Only, of course, I would have to pull myself together, take the bar exams or get a teacher's diploma.

The hostess called through the door:

"You can serve, Vilma."

Everybody was jabbering away around me. My friend was telling me about artillery training, the hostess was complaining about the market prices and the engineer was analysing the situation at the front.

Piri put her hand on my arm.

"What's the matter with you? Why are you so nervous?"

It was at this moment that the girl came in. She was carrying a big platter of stuffed eggs. She was standing quite close to the table by the time she saw and recognized me. Her face first turned as white as a sheet, then it changed to a flaming red. She did not say a word, she even looked quite composed. But I sensed her deep pain as her arm and elbow trembled when she offered us the eggs.

I could not look at her as she carried the platter round the table. I just stared in front of me. There was complete silence. When she reached my side and offered me the food, I whispered:

"Good evening, Vilma."

"Good evening," she answered dully, an empty look in her eyes. And again I sensed that she had to summon all her peasant strength to keep from fainting there beside the table, with the dish in her hand.

Miss Piri began to giggle:

"So you know each other, do you?"

And with ingenious feminine intuition she added:

"Perhaps from some soldiers' ball?"

Everybody broke into laughter, amused at the incongruity of such a ridiculous supposition. The girl herself, her expression set and cold as stone, walked mechanically round the table offering the food. When nobody took any more, she went quietly out of the room. Her hands were full of dishes, and she pushed down the door handle with her elbow. Then she closed the door again very softly from the outside.

We ate and ate. They spoke to me, but I did not answer. I did not even understand what they were talking about. With all my heart, with all my mind, I was in the kitchen, seeing the insect powder strewn in the corners, the entrance to Vilma's tiny room with the narrow iron bed, the nails in the wall, and the gay clothes hanging from them. At the table my hosts scolded me for being so absent-minded. In my confusion I muttered something about a sudden toothache, and Mr. Bodrogi advised me to apply some rum. His wife rang the bell hanging above the table for the next course. She rang once. She rang twice. She rang a third time. Nobody came. Finally, with a look of annoyance on her face, she got up from the table and went out into the kitchen herself.

There was a long, painful pause. I felt my heart throbbing in my throat, but I lacked the courage to dash out into the kitchen and find out what was happening there. What could have happened? From out there one could hear a low, subdued discussion, followed by ominous silence. Finally the door opened and the hostess reappeared, holding the second course in her own well-manicured hands. She sat down in her chair, her face red with anger.

"That girl," she said, "has suddenly gone mad. She says she won't stay another minute. She's given back her pay. She put it down on the table and declared she'd rather throw herself out of the window than come back into this room. Have you done anything to this girl, Sándor?"

They all stared at me.

"Me? I didn't do a thing," came my cowardly denial.

Nobody was laughing now. The dining-room was charged with a sense of calamity. We ate in silence. Everyone felt that something serious had happened. Suddenly Piri jumped up and, on the pretext of going for the mustard, ran in to the kitchen, as if unable to control her excitement and eager to satisfy her curiosity. But she was back again in a minute.

"The silly girl has already packed all her things. She's given me back the key to the kitchen. Here it is."

And she put down on the table the little key I knew so well.

"Has she really gone?" I asked in a low voice.

"She is just leaving," Piri answered sharply, looking straight into my face with malevolent curiosity. Suddenly all the restraints of patience, good manners and friendship which bound me to these people snapped. I threw my napkin on the table and jumped up. Without even an apology, I ran out like a lunatic. I raced along the passage and down the stairs, taking the steps three at a time. I caught up with her just as she was stepping out into the street. She had her shawl on and was carrying her heavy wooden box in her right hand. Her shoulder sagged under its weight. I sprang in front of her, all out of breath. She stopped. She looked at me with a warm gentleness, without reproach, as though she were saying good-bye with her eyes.

"Vilma, my darling," I stammered and tried to take her left hand in mind.

She put it behind her.

"Let me go—sir," she said softly, but with such indescribable firmness that I had to step aside. Once more she looked at me. Then she turned her head away and stepped out into the dark street carrying her green wooden box. I never saw her again.

1930   Translated by Zsuzsa Madarassy-Beck

The Importance of Learning Foreign Languages
István Örkény

I don't speak German.

Somewhere between Budionny and Aleksaevka we had to push a few pieces of heavy artillery up a hill, for they were sinking fast into the mud. It was my turn, for the third time, to push a huge field gun, and the son of a bitch started rolling back just when I thought I had made it to the top. So I pretended I had to go to the toilet and sneaked away.

I knew my way back to camp. I cut across a huge sunflower field and soon reached the stubble. The rich black soil clung to my boots as the lead weight must cling to deep-sea divers, when they descend to the depths. I must have been walking for about twenty minutes when I ran into a Hungarian sergeant and a German officer whose rank I couldn't figure out. Running into anyone, let alone these two, on that flat terrain was in itself an incredible stroke of bad luck.

The German was sitting on a small folding chair, his legs spread wide apart, and from a container that looked like a tube of toothpaste, he was squeezing some kind of cheesespread on a slice of bread. The Hungarian sergeant was standing, smoking a cigarette. When the German saw me, he motioned me to stop.

Was sucht er hier?

"What're you doing here?" translated the sergeant.

I said I lost my unit.

Er hat seine Einheit verloren, said the sergeant.

Warum ohne Waffe?

"Where's your gun?" the sergeant asked.

I said I was in a forced labor camp.

Jude, said the sergeant.

Even I understood that. I tried to explain that I was not Jewish, but for being the local distributor of a leftist newspaper, I was assigned to a special forced labor company.

Was? asked the German.

Jude, the sergeant said.

The German got up; he brushed the crumbs off his jacket.

Ich werde ihn erschiessen, he said.

"The major will now shoot you," translated the sergeant.

By now I was drenched in sweat, and beginning to feel sick. The German screwed back the cap on the tube of cheesespread and took out his gun. Perhaps if I spoke German, I could have explained to him that I wasn't wearing a yellow armband; therefore I couldn't possibly be Jewish.

Er soll zehn schritte weiter gehn.

"Move on ten paces," said the sergeant.

I moved ten paces and was ankle-deep in mud.

"That's enough."

Gut.

I stopped. The major aimed his gun at me. I can still remember how all of a sudden my head felt terribly heavy and I thought my insides would burst. The major lowered his gun.

Was ist sein letzter Wunsch? he asked.

"What is your last wish?" the sergeant asked.

I said I had to move my bowels.

Er will scheissen, the sergeant translated.

While I was relieving myself, the major leaned on his gun. As soon as I straightened out, he lifted it.

Fertig? he asked.

"Finished?"

I said finished.

Fertig, the sergeant reported.

The major's gun must have had an upward aim because he seemed to be pointing it at my navel. I stood motionless for about a minute. Then, still pointing the gun at me, the major said:

Er soll hupfen.

"Start hopping," translated the sergeant.

After I had hopped for a while, I had to crawl. Then he ordered me to do fifteen pushups. Finally he told me to make an about-face.

Stechschritt!

"Goose-step" came the translation.

Marsch!

I tried to march but it was no use; I had trouble enough walking, let alone goose-stepping. Balls of mud were flying over my head. I was proceeding at a maddeningly slow pace, sensing all the while that the major was aiming his gun at my back. To this day I could tell the exact spot where the gun seemed to have been pointing. If not for that sea of mud my ordeal would have lasted a mere five minutes. This way, however, more than a half hour had elapsed before I could bring myself to drop on my stomach and look back. . . .

I don't speak any Italian either; unfortunately, I have no ear for languages. Last summer I was in Rimini, Italy, on a ten-day organized tour. One evening, in front of a luxury hotel called Regina Palace, I recognized the major. But I was out of luck. If I had gotten there a minute earlier, I would have knocked his brains out. As it turned out, he was just getting on a red glass-topped bus with several other people and didn't even recognize me.

Lacking the necessary command of foreign languages, all I could do was yell in my native Hungarian: "Stop! Don't let that Nazi pig get away!"

The doorman, a tall, robust Sudanese, shook his fingers at me and motioned with his head: scram! I couldn't even explain to him what had happened even though he probably spoke French and English, as well as Italian. Alas, I only speak Hungarian.

This brilliant piece by the noted Hungarian author was published in our paper in 1981.

The Circus

Frigyes Karinthy

No doubt, it was a passionate yearning that drew me to the circus, but perhaps I longed just as much to play the violin. I got the violin first, however, and I was not taken to the circus; so this may be why, from time to time, I kept now and then dreaming of the latter. Once I saw that circus far away, behind the hills, and I felt as if somebody were leading me there by the hand. Another time I was standing in the very middle of a great unknown city; yet there it was—the same circus, the same entrance, and the lobby with doors opening in opposite directions. This time I might even have had a ticket and gone in, but at this point, my dream became confused, and again I was left outside.

At last, I dreamed the dream out to the end. There I was standing at the entrance, behind the box-office, and a limping, bearded, excited man, the manager of the circus, stood next to me, drawing aside the gaudy-coloured curtain with one hand and gabbing loudly: "Come in, gentlemen, come in, this way, please, just step in, the show is about to begin, this way, this way, please!" People were streaming in, no end of people—a motley crowd, domestics, soldiers, well-dressed women, well-shaved men—pushing one another, laughing and chatting at the top of their voices. I knew very well that the manager would spot me immediately. He noticed me indeed and, grabbing my arm, asked angrily: "Hullo, hullo, have you got a ticket? If not, out with you!" My heart died within me, I began to stammer that I had no ticket, that I did not want to enter as a spectator anyway, but here, look at my violin, I want to . . . and I perately showed him my fiddle, which I was carrying under my arm. He bent down close to my face and waited angrily till I had finished stammering that I had no ticket but had composed a song, all by myself, on my fiddle, and if he would but let me in, I should play it to the audience. At this he laughed so loud that I could see right down his throat, like into a deep, deep tunnel, and then he said roughly: "Young fellow, you are off your beam, your head is surely full of steam." I found this a very witty piece of poetry and saw that the manager was flattered by my involuntary acknowledgement. He gave me a pat on the back and told me to wait a moment, something could be done about it perhaps, anyway we would talk it over.

Later on he actually came into the dark gangway where I was standing all a-tremble, and said with a patronizing air that fiddling was just gobbledygook. I understood immediately that he had not much confidence in my prowess. I protested vehemently, whereupon he became serious and told me, well, all right, we might as well have a try, but first he had to speak to the superior military authorities where I could get a stamp at an imperial and royal hoity-toity. Till this was arranged, he would like to show me the whole circus from behind the scenes—the actors, the animals, everything—so that I should have an idea what it was all about and what the audience wanted.

My heart beat with joy and happiness at the thought that I was in on the show at last; nevertheless, I was scared, too. Tightly pressing the violin under my arm, I endeavoured not to forget the melody. The manager led me past many many curtains on which all kinds of pictures were painted. High above, men in red garments were working. I expected to see actors and lady riders now, but no! a broad, high staircase came next. The manager scampered up the stairs so quickly that I could hardly follow him. Then we passed through rooms hung with velvet drapery. By mistake I opened a door, through which poured a deafening din, and I saw a swarm of human heads inside. The manager shouted at me to close the door immediately. That was the audience, he said, waiting for the performance, and it ought not to see what was going on here. Then he opened a small iron door. An enormous, semicircular hall spread out deep below us. In the middle of this magnificent hall with its fountains and palms, a good-looking man with taut lips and wild eyes was in the act of strangling a woman. Her throat merely gave forth heavy, rattling sounds. It was horrible to behold. I began to scream and curse, and demanded that the woman be freed from the man's grip. But the manager held me back.

"You fool" he said, "don't you see, these are my actors, it's only a play; besides, they are not human beings at all, they are only wax-dolls, like in a wax-cabinet." I looked more closely and saw that the woman's face was quite unnatural and that her eyes were of glass.

I was ashamed and began to speak of something else, but my heart was still throbbing wildly. Now the manager led me into a big, untidy room, where gaudily dressed boys and girls with made-up faces were sitting on benches like in a school-room. This was the school for clowns. I too had to sit down on a bench, and the manager called one pupil after the other to the teacher's desk. One of them came up walking on his hands and intermittently striking the floor with his head. He had to repeat this act. Then the manager called a tall man who drew out a knife and ripped open his own breast. Lungs and blood and guts streamed from the wound, and the man collapsed with a loud groan. The manager nodded approval.

"That's good," he said, "they'll like that."

The suicide went back to his place, took needle and yarn from his bench and sewed up his breast, hissing and grimacing all the while. Now I saw that his chest was stictched together in ever so many places.

He was followed by others who distinguished themselves in a variety of ways. There were ventriloquists who imitated human and animal voices with such admirable accuracy that I could hardly believe my ears. One of them impersonated a child so perfectly that tears rushed into my eyes when his voice became that of a dying child; but looking into his face I saw with amazement that his eyes and mouth remained motionless. Another one created the illusion of a crying and scolding woman. He was succeeded by other imitators of women's voices; lewd, hoarse laughter struck my ears, and I saw threatening eyes glowering in the darkness.

Then the manager glanced into a book and called me by my name. I rose from my bench, his eyes measured me from head to foot, and he shot this question at me: "Well, what can you do?"

I pointed to my violin and again stammered something about the melody I had composed. A burst of laughter rang through the room, and the manager furiously banged his desk.

"Do you still want to annoy me with that damned fiddle of yours?" he asked. "What rubbish!"

I wanted to tell him that the melody I had composed was quite exceptional, and that I should like his permission to play it. However, he hailed one of the boys and ordered him to show me the musical instruments.

I was taken to another room. Enormous engines and tools stood there, each representing a musical instrument. Gigantic trumpets emitted a deafening thunder when the bellows, to which they were attached, were compressed. Triangles as large as a room were sounded by means of steam hammers. On top of an enormous kettle-drum trained elephants moved in a circle, beating the drum with their feet. There was also a prodigious organ driven by an electric machine which simultaneously operated thirty pianos and a thousand steel-whistles, ranging in size to the bulk of a factory chimney. The conductor was standing on a high bridge; as he threw out his arms, a single chord blared forth, producing such a blast of wind that I thought I would be swept away. Before each musician there was a keyboard like that of a type-setting machine. They were all wearing spectacles and kept peering at the score.

Giddily and my ears roaring I now found myself in another room where the manager already was waiting for me. I told him I had seen the musical instruments but did not know any of them and was unable to play them. He shrugged his shoulders and said he regretted very much, but in this case I was a goner. Then we were standing before two doors covered with curtains, which led into the theatre. Through one of them the actors, wearing a thousand masks, were hurrying towards the stage. Each time the curtain flapped, the twinkling of varicoloured lights could be seen. I wanted to go in, but the manager told me that as I did not know anything, it would perhaps be better if I visited the mortuary first.

We entered the other door. A dark gangway led down to the cellar. Flickering gaslight was hissing far away, in the dense and foggy shadow, niches opened on both sides. Grimmy-faced servants in white aprons were moving in and out. I was seized with fear and did not dare to look in. At the end of the gangway the manager stopped and talked to somebody. I looked around surreptitiously; all along the wall long tin tables were lurking, on which naked corpses were lying in rows: old people, children—I even caught sight of preserved parts of long-deceased bodies. A suffocating, heavy smell of formalin streamed out of the depths. I espied yet another completely dark gangway leading downwards. The manager was speaking about me; he seemed to be recommending me to the doctor with a view to my staying there. The doctor was looking in the direction of the dark gangway.

At this, I implored them not compel me to stay there; I told them I would rather—if there were no other choice—learn something which would enable me to appear on the stage. They wagged their heads, and the doctor remarked that only acrobatics would do as the audience was already impatient.

Now they took me high up, into a kind of attic. Through little vent-holes I could see the town way below. Long, narrow ladders were leaning against the walls. Ropes, bars and nets lay strewn about, and youthful acrobats, in pink tights, were practising on the ladders. A ladder was placed before me, and I was told to climb up. As I reached the top, the ladder was swung out over the street—I held on tight and looking down could see the whole town with people running about the streets like ants. Then, screaming faintly, I lost consciousness.

But there I was again, and for many a week and month I continued to learn and practise. Up and down the ladder I climbed, and when this went fairly well and I was able to stand on the very top, they reached up a chair which I carefully balanced on the highest rung and then climbed onto myself. Later on, we did the same with two and even three chairs. What seemed like an age, went by in this manner.

And then, at long last, I stood on the stage—but my face had become thin and wrinkled and caked with rouge, like those I had seen at the beginning. It was as though I had been with the circus for many, many years, and I knew every nook and corner in it. I was wearing pink tights, and I prowled about in the semi-darkness of the side-curtains in a state of great fatigue. Perspiring servants were running about with carpets. I heard a continuous wearisome humming, but I was too tired to want to know what it was. Suddenly a sickeningly bright light broke in upon me—and before my eyes the velvet curtains parted. Beyond, a sea of hands came into view. There was a brief clapping, followed by an expectant, whispering silence.

There I stood, all alone, on the carpet in the broad, white light of the stage. I ran to the centre with noiseless steps, the cone of the searchlight following me everywhere. With snakelike movements I bowed repeatedly towards the boxes, on either side. Then I got the ladder and quickly, without making a sound, and so easily that I did not even feel my body, I climbed to a height of four storeys. Up there I cautiously crawled still higher up a single thin pole, swaying a bit, until I got my equilibrium. Next, a table with iron feet, placed on the end of a pole, was reached up to me. I grabbed the table and supported two of its legs on the top rung of the ladder. Then climbing upon the table, I stood up straight, carefully keeping my balance. Now three chairs were set one above the other, and I could hear a contented murmur from below as I climbed up the structure. The legs of the last chair pointed upward, they quietly swayed to and fro, as with bated breath I set an enormous cube point downward on the end of one of the legs. The whole construction was lightly throbbing under me as if the beating of my pulse were running right down to the lowest rung of the ladder. Then slowly I crawled up it. I reached the pinnacle and relaxed. Hot drops of sweat slid slowly down my face. All my muscles were taut as a bowstring, and trembling. I waited till the structure stopped swaying, then, in a deadly silence, I straightened out, opened my robe, and drew out the violin . . . With a tremulous hand I laid the bow across the strings . . . now, groping with my foot, I cautiously let go of the pole . . . bent forward . . . balanced for a few moments . . . and, making use of the silence of terror which tore open the mouths and gripped the hearts in the depths below me, slowly and quiveringly I began to play the melody which long, long ago had resounded and sobbed in my heart.

1915

Translated by György Welsburg

Whitman's Trumpet Hangs on a Dusty Wall

Péter Moór

A weary wayfarer, I. And tongue-tied.
A bearded babe whose step-ma lost patience with the need for new
    words and rhythms.
A bearded son too clumsy for baby-talk of sweet and serene
    mother . . .
A weary wayfarer on the brim of the Melting Pot.
A voice impaired by the Cauldron's eternal steam-stream: whose
    images are misty (with a chronic mist) unborn, fidgety
    creatures, hypersensitive vines creeping cowed on the
    crackling concaves of the Melting Pot:
I cannot wring heart-strings!
    This people is tapped insistently by the great hand of the
        ominous hour,
    Lord, you have given them a commander, valiant and
        worthy of a great people of valour—a great
        commander and a good provider!
    Now give them a prophet-poet equal to our times!
    With hearty songs and rhythms thunderously
        reverberating!
    Who can ride a storm of a hundred manes
    Waving now like the foam of California,
    Again, like the Oklahoma dust
    Gold wave,
    Grass wave,
    Wheat wave,
    The steely waves of timbers
    The fiery waves of Pittsburgh steel
    The oily waves of Texas
    A mane, waving a hundred ways,
    A thousand ways as America waves . . .

O Lord, send them, now, one of Whitman's breed:
A singer of hearty songs
A wringer of strings of hearts
Thunderously reverberating
Who can ride the storm of a thousand manes . . .
A great itinerant songster.
(Not a weary wayfarer)
Zestful and a jester,
A riproaring six-footer
Always on the road
Always on the go
Everywhere present
All-wakeful and ever-ready . . .
A true son of his country
A true father of all the sons of his country
Who can mount a storm and ride it
Who can weave the waving mane
The thousand-shock mane of the storm now called America.
Who will weave this mane in a single epic
A great scout:
Who sows a deed and reaps a song
Who sings a rhyme and deeds quicken.
Who can weave a story or a song
Out of the Gold Dust
The Dust Bowl,
The Gold Rush
And the Oil Rush
One great good song:
Of Colorado, Oklahoma, Texas . . . of Pittsburgh
All and sundry—
Who can resing a bighearted Democracy
With emotion, with gusto
Protectively and exhortatively
(con affetto, con fuoco!)
He is deep as the Pacific
And tall as Mt. McKinley!

For, O Golden Guild of the Golden Quills:
It is not true that the Moon is like the pale cheek of a
    lady about to die . . .

Or a little princess with feet of silver
Or a brass farthing—
The thirtieth silver piece of Judas, perhaps!
But not red like a rose aglowing.
It is crimson like blood, Yes!
Steaming, hot blood!
Like blood in the blood bank
Like blood spilt generously on the bank of a Chinese river,
    a Singhalese river, a Russian river.

A river of blood makes the Moon so red
The dead so pale
The rivers so red
So gruesome the tale— . . .

The voice of the prophet-poet of 1942—
Is not the optical appraise of the metallic properties of our
    heavenly satellite.

No! No!

It is the triumphant echo of a valiant horseman steering
    the thousand-thunderous mane of a tempest . . .

Péter Moór, noted author and poet, was on the staff of our newspaper for several years following World War II.

The Torchbearers

Hungarian Americans in the Service of Progress

The Eternal Task
Gyula Illyés

With these mortal eyes
to learn what I am here to do,
the job that waits for me to do it,
for which somewhere,
a peasant, hoeing, sends me this
glass of wine,
a worker touching down his soldering-iron
sent light
into my room,
to find with mortal eyes
the eternal task:
Make the future speak!
—already it is quarreling with death,

skillfully, intelligent,
bustling, with
authority.

To do the job
well, to our liking
—yes, like good
love-making.

Almost stroking its face
in gratitude.

To leave it there,
to look back a few times
on the one who lies there satisfied;
she keeps my riches,
conceiving my future,
the meaning, maybe forever, of all
I was here for,

mortal, imperishable.

HUGO GELLERT

REMINISCENCES

–EXCERPTS–

For Hugo Gellert

Out of Hugo's art we rise
    in living history,
proud and upright, forging on
    for bread and liberty.

His working man and woman
    in bold, decisive line
sweep across his canvas
    in masterly design.

Sharp with cunning, Hugo's hand,
    he does not spare the devil
be he John D. or J.P.,
    money lords of evil.

His homeless, hungry, naked child
    in a wilderness of stone,
her eyes condemn a heartless land
    as she walks her mile alone.

His laborers, Black and white
    in stern solidarity,
power joined, their vision clear:
    as equals to be free.

For Hugo's monumental art,
    for his gentle, modest way,
in the People's name we cite him:
    HONORED ARTIST OF THE U.S.A.!

Edith Segal

Prague, April 2, 1981

The World Federation of Trade Unions, representing 190 million workers on five continents and dedicated to the unity and solidarity for peace and progress of all workers of all nations and creeds, adds its voice to the many honoring an outstanding American, Hugó Gellért, distinguished artist, fighter for human rights and for international friendship, defender of culture and human freedom, in celebration of his seventy years of work as an artist in labor's cause.

A humanist in the traditions of Daumier and Siqueiros, Gellert has taken his stand with labor in his life as well as in his paintings and lithographs. It was Gellert who headed the artists' Action Committee when the mural "Man at the Crossroads" by the great Mexican painter, Diego Rivera, was destroyed by order of Nelson Rockefeller.

Now, 47 years later, Man is still fighting his way beyond that crossroads, having suffered a war produced by fascism which cost 60 million lives. Through these years Hugo Gellert has been and remains an artistic craftsman of superb quality and a staunch fighter for the life and hopes of humanity as the proper subject of art and a tower of strength to those of his fellow artists who also fought against the dehumanization of "non-objectivity" which was imposed on US artists by every gallery, every critic and all media accessible to the control of monopoly capital.

Fraternally,

Ibrahim Zakaria
Acting General Secretary

Europe Summer of 1914

In the Spring of 1914 my studies in New York at the School of the National Academy of Design came to an end. At the commencement exercises I received a couple of medals—one for etching, one for composition—and a cash prize for painting the human figure.

That money was just about enough to pay the fare to Paris, where I wanted to study for a year at the Julian Academy. At that time, it was the thing for aspiring young artists to do.

Arriving in mid-June, I found the Academy was closed, to be opened in October. I decided to use the time until then to visit my relatives in Hungary.

Having very little money, I started out on foot. I slept in the fields, bathed in brooks, and lived on milk, bread, fruit, and cheese obtained at farms, as I walked across France. As often as not, the peasants refused to take money. Once a week, I had a hot bath and a good meal at some hotel.

One morning, at dawn, after walking in the cool of the night, I came to a village. In a courtyard at the well, stripped to the waist I washed myself. Hardly had I finished, when a door opened and an old lady sat down on the doorstep to peel potatoes. I made a drawing of her. Closing my sketchbook, I heard a voice behind me: "Don't go away, stay for breakfast." It was the voice of a man, who seemed to be in his mid-thirties. Then with quick steps he walked into the house.

Later, he came back leading a little girl of about five. "Would you make a drawing of her?" he asked. "Gladly," said I, and picked up my sketchbook.

As I finished, he grabbed my paintbox and tote bag and bade me follow. He led me into the house, to a neat and tidy room. A bed in it had red striped feather bedding piled up to the ceiling. "Today is the 14th of July, Bastille Day, our national holiday," he told me. "Be our guest and sleep here tonight."

Men began to gather in the courtyard. From behind the house they brought forth carpenter sawhorses and long planks, making huge tables. Benches were placed beside them and the tables were set. More men came, some with their wives and children.

My host appeared in a resplendent uniform. He was the chief of the village Fire Brigade. With him was his wife, the little girl, and the old lady, who was his mother. All the others were members of the Fire Brigade and their families.

We had more than a good breakfast. It was a hearty meal. Then, after clearing the tables and washing the dishes, all to the fair grounds! Merry-go-round, village band, dancing. We spent the day there . . .

Back in the house we had cold chicken and wine, cake and black coffee, then to bed. The feather bedding was changed to snow white.

Bidding farewell to my host and his family next morning, I felt I was leaving old friends. I wonder how many of those marvelous, friendly, virile Frenchmen lived to celebrate July 14 the next year. . . .

On reaching the border at Strasbourg, I rode to Munich by train. From there to Vienna, thence down the Danube on a boat. It was a wonderful journey: beautiful scenery, Gypsy music, and pretty girls. At dusk, as we stepped off the boat in Budapest, the news vendors were shouting: "War breaks out! War between the Austro-Hungarian monarchy and Serbia!"

At first, everthing seemed to be calm and quiet. Then, as Germany joined the monarchy and Czarist Russia and France and England declared war on them, the atmosphere became tense.

Visiting an uncle, in Budapest, a telegram was received from the Ministry of War. My poor uncle's ruddy face turned ghastly white, as he, with trembling hands, opened it.. .

Luckily its contents only informed him about the transfer of his elder son, from the Serbian to the Russian front, and that his train would stop at the Eastern Railroad Station in Budapest, where he might be met.

I got there early and, while I was waiting, a young man began to talk to me. Under the stress that was increasingly being felt, he opened up and told me about himself. He had been a theological student, hoping to join the priesthood of the Roman Catholic Church, when he met a pretty girl, whom he married. That was the end of his priestly career.

Talking about the war, remembering 1905, I ventured to say that a revolution in Russia was likely. He didn't agree. He said the Russians were a fanatically religious people.

A uniformed railroad man was alternately weeping and shouting angry words to the crowd surrounding him. He had lost five of his brothers on the Russian Front. He was rebellious!

It was the first time I had seen a mature man weeping. His rebellious grief for his brothers awoke sympathy and admiration for his courage. He made a deep impression on me.

My cousin arrived on a freight train. He and his mates remained aboard. We talked to them through a huge opening on the side of the freight car. Their stay was brief. A whistle-blow, the choo-choo of the engine, and my cousin and his companions were gone. . . .

I received a letter from my father. He was worried lest I'd be carried away and join the war. Nothing was further from my mind. I didn't like what I was seeing and I was no friend of the military.

My father, a tailor, as a young man served three years in the army of the Emperor. During that time, whenever kith or kin visited him, they found him behind bars. The reason? This is an example: Busy on a uniform for a superior officer, he had to meet a deadline. He was ordered to stay in the barracks during the late Autumn maneuvers, while the other soldiers were out in the rain. Towards evening, expecting his mates to come back drenched to the skin, he thought he'd build a fire in the stove of the barracks. He walked over to the stables and picked up a fistful of straw.

Coming back, he met a young officer. "What's that in your hand?" he asked. "A bit of straw, Herr Lieutenant, to start a fire for my mates to dry themselves, when they return."

"Don't you know that straw is Crown property?" shrieked the officer and twisted my father's left ear, bursting his eardrum.

Then my father was put behind bars for appropriating "property of the Crown."

Back in New York, during the Winter of 1915, I heard that my cousin was crippled in the war. His feet froze in the Carpathian Mountains. Not long after that, he died.

John Reed and "The Masses"

I was working in the lithograph house of Rusling Wood, designing posters. One day the boss called me to his office. He told me that, the season over, he would like to keep me, but I must take a cut in pay. I said I would not work for less. Then he said he was sorry, but he would have to let me go at the end of the week.

Jobless, the following Monday, I delivered a couple of drawings to The Masses, a radical monthly magazine of art and literature. When I came home, a telegram awaited me: "Come back to work— Rusling Wood."

The next day I showed up at the shop. The boss told me that he had received a large order for a poster I made for "Ferris Seeds," and an even larger one for a window display I designed for "Royal Grape Juice." Now, he said, he could afford to pay me at the old rate and I could start working at once.

After I was fired, I told him, I had made plans for myself. I was willing to work for him three days each week, but I must have the rest of the time for myself. If that met with his approval, I'd start working again.

"Oh, no!" said he. "That won't do! I must have your undivided interest!"

The Masses did not pay for contributions but was against the war. It had a

"The masses of workers are not only capable of
great dreams but have in them the power to make
dreams come true."

John Reed

large format and I liked the works of its artists and writers. I made antiwar cartoons at that time for the Hungarian workers' paper, *Elöre*, but my contributions to *The Masses* were "purely artistic" designs. Art Young, in his book, *On My Way*, said they were "decorative delights."

After my first drawings were printed, I was invited to the monthly meetings of the contributors. At these meetings, drawings and writings about which the editors disagreed were reconsidered.

At my first meeting, Floyd Dell read a poem. It was voted on and accepted. Thereupon and irate voice shouted: "Phooey, bourgeois bunch, they vote on poetry!"

We were petrified. Floyd was the first to regain his presence of mind. "But, Mr. Havel," he said calmly, "you, too, are an editor of *Mother Earth*. Don't you ever make any decisions?"

"Yes, yes" was the answer. "We, too, make decisions, but we don't abide by them. . . ."

Hypolite Harvel was an anarchist writer and a nice fellow, as I later found out.

At one of these meetings I met a youth with an infectious smile. His name was Mike Gold.

I first met John Reed when I delivered a drawing at *The Masses* office one day. Charles W. Wood, a frequent contributor, who worked on the staff of the *New York World*, the Pulitzer paper, was also there. Horace Traubel, the poet and disciple of Walt Whitman, though he had no connection with *The Masses*, had a desk at its office. They were lively talkers and I enjoyed listening to what they had to say.

One day Jack Reed declared that he was looking for a job. To me, that seemed incredible. He was the ace reporter. His report on the Paterson textile strike and the great pageant he conducted at the old Madison Square Garden, with the participation of twelve hundred of the strikers—whom he had brought to town—were sensational. In a setting created by Robert Edmond Jones, his Harvard classmate and outstanding innovator of stage designing, Jack reproduced the picket line and the police attack against the strikers. One of them was killed. Then followed the funeral of the victim, in which Elizabeth Gurley Flynn, Big Bill Heywood, and Carlo Tresca repeated their funeral orations. These were impressive performances that greatly moved the huge audience of twelve thousand. (Bobby Jones was a union brother of mine. He died in 1954.)

Jack Reed's reports of the Mexican Revolution against Huerta, in which he marched with the army of Pancho Villa; his report of the Ludlow massacre of miners and their families at the Rockefeller-owned coal mines; his reports from the European battlefronts during the first year of World War I, were all carried by the most influential publications of that time.

But as it became more evident that great preparations were afoot for the entry of the United States into what Jack Reed called the "traders' war" and "not our war," his forthright antiwar stand made his writings less and less desirable to the publishers of those periodicals.

Shortly after the outbreak of the war in Europe, the British ambassador and J. P. Morgan Jr. met in the Morgan Library in New York. Mr. Morgan pledged his "power and force, financial and commercial, actual and potential," to the British government. "The matter of contracts and commissions and profits could be taken up later."

We did not know it then, but from that day we were in the war. Nonetheless, "He kept us out of war" was the slogan of the reelection campaign of Woodrow Wilson in 1916. And the clamor of electioneering had hardly died down when preparations for the war to make the world safe for democracy and the war "to end all wars" were in full swing. But not without resistance. Antiwar demonstrations flared up all over the country.

In a great demonstration, here in New York, I was marching with Arturo Giovanitti, the poet-writer of *The Masses*. My brother Ernest was arrested. Taken to night court, he refused to pay a fine, saying that his arrest was a violation of his constitutional rights. His fellow demonstrators, who would not leave without him, paid his fine.

In the Senate, Robert M. LaFollette led "the band of willful men," as Wilson called them, who valiantly fought against U.S. entry into the war.

The Elöre

The workers' press of Hungarian America attained great influence during the First World War. For its courageous antiwar stand the *Elöre*, the Socialist paper, well deserved the large following of its worker-readers and the respect and support of a goodly section of the rest of the Hungarian community.

The Elöre Cultural Club (established in 1909) also helped to enhance the paper's popularity and to extend its material base. It so happened that Andor Garvai, well-known Hungarian playwright and journalist, was stranded here at the outbreak of the war. He worked for the paper and became the soul of the Cultural Club. He was a warmhearted, outgoing man who inspired enthusiasm for the arts.

Lajos Egri, whose one-act plays were performed by the Club even before Garvai's arrival and who published a small book of verse, was now working on three-act plays that were later produced on Broadway.

Kálmán Márky and Rezsö Stark were our best actors. They had a great share in the success of the performances.

I planned and painted the decorations. I shall never forget Ferenc Ecsedi, the best carpenter in the world, who with the greatest dedication sacrificed his Sundays for stage building and constructing scenery. Unfortunately, I no longer remember the names of the many splendid women performers. Only their beautiful faces appear before my mind's eye . . . . But their images and deeds will remain with me, as long as I am aware of myself.

The plays were shown in New York, then in the New Jersey towns in which large Hungarian communities existed. The scenery was placed on a truck. At times only the driver and I, at other times some of the performers as well, rode with the props. But normally the cast went by rail.

Garvai directed all the plays and, as master of ceremonies, was also without equal. Between the acts, while we transformed the stage, he amused the audience.

During those hysterical days, Giovanitti's home was invaded by two Secret Service men. His wife, Carie, was alone when they came. They ransacked the place and found a manuscript in Arturo's writing desk. It was a translation of some of the works of Bocaccio.

Holding it high, one of the two shouted: "Who is this man, Bokaksio?"

"He is an old Italian poet," was Carie's answer.

"I don't care how old he is," bellowed the bull, "where is he?"

On a bright afternoon in the Spring of 1917, Arturo and I spent some time in Bronx Park. St sunset, on our way out of the park, we heard the newsboys cry: "Revolution in Russia! . . . Revolution in Russia! . . ."

I became so excited, I zig zag jumped the park benches the full length of the walk.

That night I went to the Hungarian Workers' Home and, in celebration, I walked up to the bar and ordered a glass of beer.

The chief of the printing press of the Hungarian paper *Elöre* was also having a drink. "You are unusually gay, my young brother," he said to me. "Haven't you heard?" said I. "There is a revolution in Russia!"

My Brother Ernest

Ernest was drafted and on October 10th, 1917, he arrived at Camp Upton. The following is an excerpt from his diary, dated October 12, 1917.

"They requested me to state my views, and ordered a stenographer to take down my words. I was asked if it was on religious grounds that I based my objections. I replied that I was a conscientious objector—that I am opposed to war—that I regard all wars as futile as far as settlement of any principles is concerned—that I considered the present war the logical result of the mad ambitions for commercial and territorial expansion on the part of the ruling classes of all of the European nations involved—that wars are possible only through the control of the political machineries, and all channels for forming public opinion by those unscrupulous minorities—that wars will cease when the masses will take an intelligent, active interest in politics—that I deplore our entrance into war. . . ."

On October 20th, Ernest came home on a two-day furlough. Going back he took his violin "to entertain the boys," and a few books "to have something to read, if they put me into the clink."

Shortly after, Ernest was transferred to Camp Mineola, L.I., where I visited him several times.

A good friend, a young girl, asked me to take her autograph book to him. When it was returned to me, this was written in it:

"Fully to believe in a principle and to have the will to abide by that principle at whatever cost—can anything greater fall to the lot of anyone?

"If my physical strength should break in the ordeal of my moral strength, I want no tears. The tribute I crave is a smile reflecting my own happiness—that ecstacy experienced by all who have fitted themselves as vanguards against oppression."

Mineola, Nov. 2, 1917,   Ernest Gellért

"The above was written in a sudden outburst of heroism at the appearance of the blessed food which all devout Christians include in their prayer. Since that event, however, two full days have passed—and now I am willing to amend the list of acceptable tributes to include a dish of gulash or some other like delicacy."

Nov. 4,   Yours, Ernest

On one of the visits Ernest showed me a newspaper clipping. It showed Lenin's ten-point program which began with, "Peace, Bread and Land. . . ."

It was the first time we heard about Lenin.

In February 1918, the first issue of *The Liberator*, the successor to *The Masses*, appeared on the newsstands. It carried the first eye witness accounts of the Russian Revolution, by John Reed. I made the design for its cover.

On April 8, 1918, Ernest died at Fort Hancock, N.J., in military confinement. We were informed that he committed suicide, shooting himself with an army rifle.

When his body was sent home, a bullet hole was in the chest. The barrel of an army rifle was so long, that anyone's arm was too short to reach the trigger, when the rifle was directed at one's own chest. Therefore, we were told, he had reached the trigger "by means of a stick."

But he was confined, and he never had a rifle. And going to the mess hall and the lavatory—the two places he was allowed to go—he was always accompanied by a guard. And what is more, the stuff he was made of was not for suicide. . . . Ernest was 22 years old.

Drawing Mayakovsky

Sent by the *Sunday World* to make a drawing of Mayor Walker, I arrived around eleven o'clock. I was ushered into a waiting room filled with men and was offered a seat.

The first one called, I found myself in the Mayor's bedroom. He, in his pajamas, posed for the drawing. When I had finished, he asked if he could do anything for me.

Whenever I passed City Hall Park, I was always annoyed by a statue of a rather fleshy man with a foot resting on the throat of a woman. It was called "Civic Virtue."

"Please don't put up any more statues like "Civic Virtue," I said.

The Mayor promised and we shook hands on that. Then he presented me with a pack of cigarettes. "Kosher, made in Ireland," was printed on them.

It was exactly noon when I reached the office of Governor Al Smith, in Albany. I told the receptionist that I had come to make a drawing of the Governor for the *New York Sunday World*. He told me he was instructed not to disturb him, as he was busy with a Senator. He asked me to sit down and wait.

A whole hour passed. Then the phone rang. The receptionist lifted the receiver, hung up, and left. I walked up to the door behind his desk and opened it. There was the Governor with another man.

"I am sorry to disturb you, Sir," I said in a loud voice, "but I have to take the 2-o'clock train back to New York to meet a deadline, and I have to make a drawing of you to take back with me."

"How long will it take to make the drawing?"

"Oh, about five minutes," I blurted out in my anxiety.

"All right, if it only takes five minutes," he said. "You don't mind if I continue to talk to the Senator?"

"Of course not."

Seated with the sketchbook in my lap, I got busy.

Suddenly, I heard the voice of the Governor: "This is the longest damn five minutes! . . ."

I glanced at the clock on his desk: I had taken exactly seven minutes.

I closed the sketchbook, and got to my feet. "All right, I'm finished," I said, and walked toward the door.

"Hey," shouted the Governor, "won't you show me the drawing?"

"No," said I. "Anyone who thinks seven minutes is too long to sit for a portrait does not deserve to see it!"

I caught the two-o'clock train and delivered the drawing on time. It was printed in the paper that Sunday, and the following Monday I went to the office for my next assignment. One of the reporters told me breathlessly: "The Governor phoned. He wants your drawing . . ." He was gasping as I shouted: "Does he? He won't get it!" And I ran to the "morgue," where the used works were stored, and asked the young attendant for the drawing.

"The Chief was here this morning and took it," he told me.

So, the Governor got the drawing. . . .

Vladimir Mayakovsky, the great Soviet poet, visited the United States. Mike Gold interviewed him for the *New York Sunday World* and I made a drawing of him. While I made the drawing, he told me that he dined with an American couple in a Greenwich Village restaurant where candles were burning, though they were well equipped with electric lights. He thought that was ridiculous.

I tried to explain that in a humdrum existence, where the electric light is commonplace, the soft light of candles may become a romantic symbol.

In the Soviet Union at the time, they were straining to extend electric power throughout the country. Mayakovsky was very much a part of that effort, and so candles made no sense to him.

He must have told David Burliuk about this, because Burliuk phoned and invited me to "a little get-together." Mayakovsky was there. At this "get-together" Mayakovsky made a drawing of me.

Burliuk, like Mayakovsky, was a Russian futurist poet-painter. I was greatly impressed by Mayakovsky's deference, addressing him: "My Master." Burliuk's works in this country were colorful paintings, peopled by peasants and embellished by domestic animals, nostalgic of his homeland.

On several occasions Burliuk asked me to make a drawing of him. I told him to come to my place to sit for it. He never came, so, to my sorrow, the drawing was never made.

"The New Masses"

Back in 1922, Floyd Dell and I met with Charles E. Ruthenberg and turned *The Liberator* over to the Workers' Party.

The absence of the magazine was keenly felt by us. About a year or so later, I bumped into Scott Nearing at the corner of Fifth Avenue and 14th Street. He greeted me with these words: "If you fellows want a monthly magazine, I can get the money for it."

"If you'll get the money, we'll have the magazine," was my answer. And we shook hands on that. But I added: "Mike Gold is visiting the Soviet Union. We'll have the magazine as soon as he returns."

Mike Gold came back. He was steamed up about Meyerhold's Theatre, which he'd seen in Moscow. He was interested in theatre and theatre only . . . we had a tough time talking him into joining us on the magazine.

Before long, he organized the new Playwrights Theatre, with John Dos Passos, Francis Edwards Faragoh, Jo Bassie, and John Howard Lawson as founding members.

Dos Passos asked me for an exhibition to "dress up the lobby" of the theatre. I gave him twenty paintings and drawings. Someone broke into the lobby and stole the whole exhibition.

* * *

On May 1, 1926, *The New Masses* was on the newstands. It was a large-format magazine, with color on the cover and some inside pages as well. We paid for contributions—a little—but not for long. The fund soon left the baby out in the cold. The format shrank, first the color, later the pay for contributions faded away . . . we were back to "normalcy."

81

But pay or no pay, there was never a dearth of good drawings. An impressive list of contributing artists included Peggy Bacon, Phil Bard, Cornelia Barns, Maurice Becker, George Bellows, George Biddle, Abe Birnbaum, Don Brown, David Burliuk, Alexander Calder, K. R. Chamberlain, Jean Charlot, Glenn Coleman, Miguel Covarrubias, Stuart Davis, Adolf Dehn, Fred Ellis, Al Frueh, Wanda Gag, Hugó Gellért, J.H. Glintencamp, William Gropper, George Grosz, Xavier Guerrero, Ilonka Karasz, I. Klein, Walt Kuhn, Yasuo Kuniyoshi, J.J. Lankes, Louis Lozowick, Reginald Marsh, Jan Matulka, Julian De Miskey, José Clemente Orozco, Anto Refregier, Philip Reisman, Louis Riback, Diego Rivera, Boardman Robinson, A. Ronneback, Renee Ruellan, William Siegal, John Sloan, Otto Soglow, Moses Soyer, Raphael Soyer, Hans Stengel, Harry Sternberg, Maurice Sterne, Albert Sterner, Beula Stevenson, Rufino Tamayo, Abe Walkowitz, and Art Young.

The John Reed Club was formed by *New Masses* artists and writers. Joe Pass gave the club its name. The club provided a forum and conducted an art school. Later a musicians' section was added. On May Day, the decorations, banners, and a good-sized contingent of artists and writers were provided for the parade. Branches of the club sprang up in the large industrial sections of the country. A national convention was held in Chicago, where a delegate's car was stolen. He reported his loss to the police. "That's no good," said a knowing Chicago artist. "You must report it to Al Capone's gang." The car was returned.

* * *

I was asked to decorate the Workers' Cafeteria in Union Square. I planned a decoration for the full length of the hall, eighty feet long. On the opposite wall, which was broken by two doors, I planned a decoration twenty feet long, to include the figures of John Reed, Charles Ruthenberg, Karl Marx, and Lenin. Another, six feet by six feet, wasnof Sacco and Vanzetti.

The long decoration showed workers in mines and in steel mills, and women picketing; also the *Daily Worker*. These were my first murals, and probably the first working-class murals in the United States.

Imre Bálint, the secretary of the Anti-Horthy League, was a member of the painters' union. Himself an artist, he was to gild the metal ceiling, making it richly decorative in red and gold.

Meeting with Hungarians in Moscow

In Moscow (where I went in the hope of having my *Kapital* illustrations published) I met some wonderful Hungarian men and women. They made it easy for me to overcome the hardship of not speaking Russian. János Mácza, the art historian, and his wife; Béla Uitz, the artist, and his wife; Antal Hidas, the poet-writer; and Béla Illés, the writer. Through them, I met Béla Kun, and his wife; Andor Gábor the poet-satirist; and Pál Hajdu, and his wife.

I often think of them with much gratitude for helping to make my first visit to the workers' State such an exciting experience. To paraphrase the ancient Latins: "I (too) came, saw and learned." I spent a hot August day with Máté Zalka, the writer, who, like Béla Kun, fought through the Civil War against the counterrevolution. But not a word was said about that during the entire day.

He brewed tea in a samovar, served it in glasses, Russian-style, and talked about writing and a bad movie he saw. He spoke so emotionally about the bad movie that I remarked: "If I'd let myself feel as bad about every bad movie I've seen, I wouldn't be alive."

"That's very well," said he. "You live in a capitalist country, where movies are made for profit. But here no excuse exists for making bad movies."

A decade later, we heard much about General Lukács, who organized and trained the International Brigade of which the American Abraham Lincoln Battalion was a part. That gallant fighting force joined the Loyalist Army of Republican Spain in confronting the fascist hordes of Franco.

Only after he fell in battle, leading his Brigade, did we learn that General Lukács was Máté Zalka. . . .

The Anti-Horthy League

At the dissolution of the Austro-Hungarian Monarchy, in 1918, Count Michael Károlyi became President of the Hungarian Republic. The peasants called him "the Count who gave the land," for he distributed the land, first of all his own estates, among them. But after the Russian Revolution of the workers and peasants, the Hungarian bourgeois Republic was born too late. Károlyi himself was aware of that when he handed the Government over to Béla Kun.

Béla Kun and thousands of Hungarian soldiers, who were prisoners of war in Czarist Russia, joined the Red Guards and helped to defeat the counterrevolution. Then they went back to their own country and formed the Hungarian Republic of Councils.

That Government, however, was short-lived, because the Allied Powers, including the United States, saw to it that it should be ended. With their backing, Admiral Horthy, of the Austro-Hungarian Navy, was put on horseback. He rode into the war-ravaged country, and the first fascist state came into existence.

Those who were able to, fled the country. Many came to America and joined the Hungarian working-class movement. Its paper, the *Elöre*, was enriched by the contributions of the newcomers and their devotion to the welfare of working men and women, who form the majority in this country, as well as in the entire world.

On a Sunday afternoon in 1927 when Wanda Gag happened to visit us, the phone rang. Emery Bálint, George Austin, Louis Köves of the *Elöre* and a couple of other people were waiting at the railroad station. I drove down to get them. They told me that plans were afoot to organize the Hungarian workers against the Horthy Government and to curb the influence of its agents in the United States. They wanted to know if I would accept the chairmanship of such an organization and if I would be willing to work for its objectives. My answer was: "Yes."

Meetings were held and an organization, the Anti-Horthy League, was established. It was the first antifascist organization in the United States.

The fascist Horthy Government of Hungary, in need of a loan, looked to the bankers of Wall Street. But it was felt that a little preliminary preparation was a necessity.

To that end, with the connivance of a reactionary Hungarian newspaper, they cooked up the idea of putting up a statue of Lajos Kossuth, the leader of the glorious Hungarian Revolution of 1848-49.

That Government, which drowned in blood even the slightest efforts at reform in Hungary, was to create a Kossuth Monument in New York City!...

We of the Anti-Horthy League exposed their hypocrisy and rallied the Hungarian workers against them.

The statue arrived in New York, with three hundred so-called "pilgrims." They landed at a lower West Side dock. We were there, several thousands strong, awaiting them.

The photo bulb of a news photographer exploded with a bang. The police thought we had thrown a bomb, and attacked . . . In the confusion that followed, the "pilgrims" were herded into cattle pens, lowered in the elevators to the waiting busses, and whisked to the hotel, where they had reservations.

But our people awaited them there too. The "pilgrims" were so panicked that they abandoned their luggage in the anxiety to reach safety in the hotel lobby.

Then came the great day—the unveiling of the statue, at which Mayor Walker, and Count Szechenyi, the Hungarian Ambassador, were to officiate.

Three hundred "pilgrims" were marching on Riverside Drive, in the resplendent attire of the Hungarian nobility: feathers in their hats, swords dangling at their sides. . . . An impressive sight! All under the protection of New York's finest.

Charles Yale Harrison, a veteran of World War I and later author of the book *Generals Die in Bed*, made arrangements with an ace pilot of the war to fly us to the unveiling ceremonies.

I made a leaflet with drawings, showing how Horthy had transformed the gallows into a statue of Kossuth.

We arrived in New Jersey with a bundle of the leaflets to meet the pilot. A few of the leaflets had nothing but, "Greetings to the Mayor" printed on them. Those were on the top of the bundle. We showed one of them to the pilot. . . .

He led us to a small monoplane. It was so little, I doubted it would lift the three of us. Its sides of canvas were flapping in the wind . . .

Harrison and I were seated afore with the bundle of leaflets between my legs. The pilot turned the propeller, jumped in to sit behind us, and we were flying toward the afternoon sun . . .

I carefully lifted all the "Greetings to the Mayor" leaflets off the pile and stuck them into my pocket.

We were at about the middle of the Hudson River when the pilot told me to let go the first handful of leaflets. They fell a little short of their destination. A few seconds later, another batch hit the bulls-eye.

We flew in and circled above, distributing pamphlets. When we had no more, the pilot asked, "How about giving them the airman's salute?" I hadn't the faintest idea what the "airman's salute" was, but I said, "All right!"

We swooped! Scattering the crowd of frightened people. I, too, was scared out of my wits . . . "Do you think the Mayor liked that?" asked the pilot. "Oh, he must be delighted!" said I. Then he swooped again, a third time . . . The policemen on top of the surrounding buildings were looking on helplessly . . . After that, we crossed the Hudson, flying back to where we had come from. On taking leave of the pilot, he asked, "Do you think we'll get publicity?" "You'll get plenty of publicity, you'll see!" I told him.

On the way to the Manhattan Casino on East 86th Street, where a mass meeting was arranged for that evening, I picked up a newspaper. In it I read that I had been arrested. I felt like Mark Twain, when he read about his own demise: Reports of my arrest, too, were "exaggerated." But what worried me was that I also read that the pilot might lose his license for violating the flying code.

At the meeting, which was jammed to standing room, we assumed full responsibility for the flight, telling the newspaper reporters that we had tricked the pilot by making him believe that he was greeting the Mayor.

After the meeting, I phoned the pilot. I talked with his wife, who informed me that her husband had gone to look for a lawyer. I assured her, "He has no cause to worry. At the meeting we stated to the press that we, and we alone, were responsible for the flight." To top it all, Mayor Walker—probably remembering his promise to me about statues—when told about the warrant to arrest me, said, "Leave him alone, he's had too much publicity as it is. Don't give him any more."

At the meeting, we also declared that if President Coolidge receives the "pilgrims," as was announced by the newspapers, we shall be forced to picket the White House. And we sent notice to that effect to President Coolidge.

But the President was to receive them and so, we, too, arrived in Washington. The "we" included Livia Cinquegrana, musician; Telcs, the son of the well-known Hungarian sculptor; Imre Bálint, writer and secretary of the Anti-Horthy League; and myself, its president.

Armed with picket signs, we marched through the gate onto the White House grounds . . . An excited reporter ran after us, "Don't go in there, you might get twenty years for it," he warned us. "Picketing outside is just as effective."

We thanked him and accepted his advice. We were picketing *outside* the grounds. The police came and arrested us.

One of the unfortunate "pilgrims" enacted in mime what they would do to us were we in Horthyland: they would hang us from lamp posts . . .

After that, even the policemen were on our side. They obligingly held our picket signs for the photographers to take good pictures of them. They hauled us into the "Black Maria" to go to headquarters for booking. There, each of us put up ten dollars, for appearance in court on the following morning.

But we decided to forfeit the ten dollars and, much to the surprise of the "pilgrims," we rode back to New York on the same train with them.

A Literary Debate with Ezra Pound

Around the end of 1926, Brancusi held an exhibition. I wrote a brief review of it for *The New Masses* of January 1927:

"When we are no longer children, we are already dead," wrote Brancusi in the catalogue of his New York exhibition.

I believe I have heard that before. The eternal wonderchild of some immaculate conception—the artist. Walking through this life innocent, starry-eyed. . . . It is about time the artist—like every other human being—grew up. Imagine the builder of the Brooklyn Bridge announcing: "I am a child." Or the man who conceived the plans for the Hudson Tube—or a scientist. Why then is the artist so boastful of his immaturity? If art is the great thing it is cracked up to be, how then do its high priests expect it to be the sputterings of infants? Is it that the diaper affords an excellent protection for their desire to remain vague and noncommital, and thus enable their creations to become "timeless" (pure, above the battle, etc.)?

There is at least one definite principle of Art and that is that it's bound to time and space—and one cannot dodge this. Those who try to get around it only cause their works to be stillborn.

One of the pieces of the exhibition is marked "*Portrait (1916)*." What is it that Brancusi worked on in 1916 during the war in Paris? What had he to say? He cut a huge phallus into marble—that is what he had to say! Men are slaughtered, men are crazed . . . the artist, the divine, toys with the phallus . . . It is Art, it is pure, it is beyond good and evil . . . Hurrah, long live Art!

Brancusi is a great craftsman. No one I know of has a better understanding of the possibilities and the limitations of the materials he uses, be it stone, bronze, or wood. But he satisfies himself with his equipment as an end. It is only the means.

Hugó Gellért

Ezra Pound sent the following protest:

Rapallo, Italy
8 Jan. 1927

Dear Gellért
You're bughouse.

First place: why the HELL should Brancusi, a Roumanian peasant by birth, take sides in a war between German Empire and two Capitalist arms firms?

Second place: There never was an artist less addicted to "art for art's sake" than Brancusi. The mystical residue, or "fonds" in him, is a great embarrassment to his aesthete admirers.

Third place: Are you sure he did do a marble phallus? There is a g.m.p. by Gautier, done in 1913, after which Gautier put his anarchist-syndicalist propaganda in his pocket and went off to get shot.

Fourth place: Art is part of biology. Do you expect Ehrlich or any other biologist, after looking down his microscope, to fix up his findings in accord with some socio-political program?

Do you heave rocks at every electric light bulb, just because Edison doesn't paste a Bolshevick label on each one?

Brancusi is trying to save the world by pure form. You may disapprove of messiahs; but you should not mistake them for aesthetes.

It is the artist's job to make something that will be enjoyable even after a successful revolution.

A Czecho-slovak who had spent a good deal of time in jail for political, anti-Austrian activity, once said to me: Yes, we wanted freedom; now we have it, we find it would be a good thing if we also had a little money.

The next step is to feel that there are few good jobs, like, let us say, the Odyssey or something of that sort, either done, or in the process of being done.

Or, as above, the electric light bulb is not an end in itself, although it was the end of a set of researches. Neither is the work of art an "end" in itself, though it is the end of its maker's job. It has no political opinion.

Ezra Pound

Answering Pound, the two opinions were printed side by side in the March 1927 issue of *The New Masses*.

Dear Pound:
1. Forgive me. I did take it for granted that Roumanian peasants were humans and that it would disturb them to have other humans murdered.

87

2. As you like it: "One should not mistake Brancusi for an aesthete
. . . he is trying to save the world by pure form. . . ."

3. I am sure that the marble I spoke of was Brancusi's. I am not sure
it was a phallus. One can never be sure of a work of art. Maybe it was an
impatient worm, tired of waiting to become a butterfly, just about to
crawl out of its cocoon.

I can't admire Gautier's gesture. Whatever he did put into his
pocket, he certainly did not go to get shot. He thought he would do a
little shooting himself. He realized there was a war; some credit is due
him for that.

4. You would be surprised, it is not only possible for biologists and
sociologists to work hand in hand, but most desirable.

What funny notions you do have. Why should I throw rocks at
anything useful?

The artist's job is not to pray for pie in the sky. If the revolution is
worth hoping for, it is worth working for. Yes Sir!

I am afraid your Czecho-Slovak friend got too old in those Austrian
jails. He must be a social democrat or something. Does he think that
with the overthrow of the Hapsburgs the last battle for "freedom" is
won?

The old mother is shrieking with birth pains. The Odyssey of today
must be on its way. It is not coming from Rapallo. It must be made by
guys who are trying to find out what the damn thing is all about and who
are not running away from it.

True, the electric light bulb is not an end in itself. But its creator
had the end in view: to make light.

Brancusi's pure form leaves us in darkness.

Hugo Gellért

P.S. Come World War II and the Sage of Rapallo, guided by his superior
wisdom, joined the followers of Mussolini.

Touring the Country with Count Károlyi

Early in the Spring of 1930, Michael Károlyi
arrived in New York. The men of letters of this city, headed by Theodore
Dreiser, gave him a rousing reception. It was followed by huge meetings of
Hungarian workers in New York City, in several towns in New Jersey, and the
Pennsylvania steel and coal country. After a gigantic meeting of Hungarian
workers held in Los Angeles, in Hollywood, Charlie Chaplin entertained

Károlyi in his home and invited him to his studio. The "Movie Industry" held a party in his honor in a large open area; studio owners, directors, actors, and actresses all were present. One of the members of the famous musical Strauss family of Vienna was also there.

Then, on to San Francisco! The plane which was to fly there, after taking off, turned around to return to its starting place. The pilot received warning of a storm ahead. Later, when the plane resumed its flight, an unforgettable sight greeted the eyes: a rainbow encircled the horizon. Its brilliant colors formed a ring all around, where the sky and the earth met.

At Berkeley, faculty and students filled the auditorium to hear Károlyi. Then another huge meeting of Hungarians in San Francisco. At the end of that meeting, a young woman came on the stage. I had known her in New York, more than a decade earlier. She was then a bright young girl, who had led a successful strike in the shirtwaist factory where she worked.

She told me that she now owned a restaurant in San Francisco and came to ask us to have dinner at her place at least once while we were in San Francisco. She gave me the address and I promised to do my best to have Károlyi visit the restaurant.

This meeting was held toward the last days of April. On the way to the hotel where we were staying, Károlyi said to me, "How about visiting Tom Mooney on May Day?" "A wonderful idea!" I exclaimed.

On the next day, Károlyi had an appointment at the *San Francisco Call-Bulletin*, to meet its owner, the young Hearst. While Károlyi was so engaged, I told Freemont Older, the editor, about our desire to see Tom Mooney.

He immediately phoned San Quentin prison and arranged the visit for us.

Came the great day! We had no sooner arrived at the prison than Tom Mooney, all smiles, was ushered in and was left with us in a large room bathed in sunshine. We spent the entire morning with him. While he and Károlyi were absorbed in animated talk, I leisurely made a drawing of Tom.

The following day, May 2, I took the drawing to Freemont Older and left it with him. On the third of May, it appeared in the paper.

Capone: "Us fellas gotta stick together"

Ln May 1932, in an old mansion on 53rd Street, the Museum of Modern Art was to open with an exhibition of mural decorations. The museum provided the theme, "The World Today," or something that meant the same. Twenty artists were invited to exhibit. Three of the works made sharp comments on the prevailing state of affairs.

One of the Vanderbilts, a young man, got himself a job as reporter on one of the Hearst papers. He interviewed Al Capone in a Chicago jail and Al Capone told him, "Us fellas gotta stick together." So, "Us Fellas Gotta Stick Together" became the title of one of the murals.

On May 2, 1932, this report appeared in the *New York World Telegram*, under this headline, "INSURGENT ART STIRS UP STORM AMONG SOCIETY. Murals for Modern Museum rejected as offensive, then accepted. Linked Hoover to Al Capone. Caricatured Ford, Morgan and Rockefeller—Mrs. John D. Jr. on the Board."

Three murals submitted by young artists for the opening exhibition at the new building of the Museum of Modern Art, 11 West 53rd Street, have been the subject of lengthy conferences involving families among the most socially prominent in New York, it was learned today.

The murals, first rejected as offensive caricatures of contemporary individuals, later were accepted.

Individuals caricatured include Henry Ford, John D. Rockefeller, J. P. Morgan, and President Hoover, all of whom are portrayed with "Scarface Al Capone," under the caption, "Us Fellas Gotta Stick Together."

Mrs. Rockefeller Neutral

As the controversy progressed, it developed that the advisory committee of the museum, headed by Nelson Rockefeller and Mr. and Mrs. John D. Rockefeller, Jr., took the part of the three artists whose work was the center of the storm, while the majority of the more venerable trustees opposed hanging the murals.

Mrs. John D. Rockefeller, Jr., a member of the Board, is understood to have maintained an attitude of neutrality.

Hugo Gellert, who painted the "Us Fellas Gotta Stick Together" mural, and William Gropper, who painted another disputed mural involving Mr. Morgan and Ambassador Andrew W. Mellon, confirmed the existence of a controversy about their work.

Artists Threaten Revolt

The tide finally turned in their favor, they said, by a revolt among the other artists invited to contribute murals. Soon after receiving the notices of rejection, they said, they told the others of their fate and eight or ten declared they also would withdraw if the murals of Gellert, Gropper and a third, by Ben Shahn, dealing with the Sacco-Vanzetti case, were not hung.

The exhibition was to open to art critics today. Tomorrow there will be another private showing, and Wednesday, the general public is to be invited.

Gellert's mural depicts Tom Mooney in jail. Over him are deputy sheriffs and police throwing tear gas bombs. Higher still, are mountains of money bags, with Capone and a machine gun on top.

Behind Capone stand Mr. Ford, Mr. Rockefeller and Mr. Morgan, with Mr. Hoover just behind Mr. Morgan's back.

The Gropper mural ("The Writing on the Wall") shows Mr. Morgan and Mr. Mellon. Nearby are two pigs eating ticker tape. A line of militia protects the group.

Shahn's mural depicts Sacco and Vanzetti in their coffin with various persons who had a part in their conviction and death, standing nearby.

It was Reginald Marsh who organized the artists who threatened to withdraw their works.

"Billions for Jobs, not war" An internationally honored poster by Hugo Gellért. 91

Bartók the Man
Gabriel D. Hackett

W hen one looks at Bartók's portrait, what one sees is a face of deep seriousness without sternness. Great dignity, a searching look. Two steel-blue eyes with an expression of no nonsense, no compromise. Judging from the almost monumental, sculptor-carved head, one imagines a tall body, instead of the lean, almost fragile physique he had to put up with all his life. That's why almost all of his portraits have been cropped to show the genius' head only. And as the years went by and his fame grew, this artistic idealization continued. On the late posters, postage stamps, drawings, his forehead was almost bigger than the rest of his face.

Bartók himself would be the first to smile at his "Parnassus." Not because he ever underestimated his own value or importance. He was aware of it sooner than anybody else, but because he was too modest, too intelligent to give it more than a minute's time. The neglect and cheap irony of the Hungarian critics, all lackeys of the reactionary Horthy regime, naturally annoyed him but never stopped him. He just shrugged and remained himself.

He was, and had to be, the "man" in his family from the age of ten. His father died early and he grew up, loved, cushioned but also spurred on by three women: his energetic mother, his adoring aunt, and his sister, all of whom burdened him with limitless expectations. Hardly shedding his knee-pants, he was the "talent-in-residence" of this family and, serious boy that he was, under tremendous moral obligation to live up to all the expectations. His letters bear witness to this: to his constant seriousness, his sense of duty. Still, all this did not prevent him from having a wide horizon and a vivid interest in the world around him. He was as contemporary as the times themselves. He had an interest in everything: arts, natural sciences, folklore, politics. The

so-called "narodniki" movement of the Russian intellectuals of the turn of the century reached Hungary, too. Hundreds of young men and women turned to the people — some in politics, others in the arts. Bartók and Kodály, in Hungary, did so on a musical level.

Bartók's hatred of reaction and superstitions was proverbial. The past should be researched, evaluated, not imitated. "God," he kept explaining to his little son, Peter, "is Nature itself. We all are a part of it. Nothing really dies, or what dies is not lost. It only changes into something that's still useful for Nature. Grass is greener in the cemeteries." . . . If he had what could be called a religion, it revealed itself in two things: in uncompromising, ethical honesty and in merciless objectivity. For these principles he was ready to risk his whole position, his future existence. In 1919-20, in the worst years of the Hungarian "white terror" and maniacal redbaiting (actually the grandfather of all European fascism), the regime went after the scalps of two fine musicians: Zoltán Kodály and Béla Reinitz. Bartók, ready to lose his job as a professor at the state-owned music university, stood up for his two friends. He reasserted his stand a few years later when the first black shadows of Nazism started spreading over Hungary. Americans who are free to sign protests or petitions without fear don't know what a chance one took in doing the same thing in Horthy's Hungary.

When the Germans overran Austria, Bartók canceled his contract with his old representatives, the Universal Music Company of Vienna, and made a new contract with a British outfit, Boosey and Hawkes. And, finally, in 1940, when there remained no other way to express his disgust and hatred of Nazism, he decided to leave his motherland.

Before leaving, he made up his last will and wrote into it the following codicil: "As long as Hungary is ruled by the present regime and any street is named after them [obviously meaning Hitler & Company], I forbid any street or institution to be named after *me!*" With this behind him, he left the country, along with his wife, Ditta, and, later followed by his younger son, Peter, arrived in New York. . . . America, sad to say, was not yet ready for Bartók. The country was first on the eve of, than in the midst of, a deadly world war. Its attention was not concentrated on outlandish modern music, presented by a little-known, overly modest composer. The few music experts who knew Bartók were aware of what value the country had received. But there were just too few of them. *Newsweek* printed five lines, calling Bartók "a chieftain of modern European music." Bartók just nodded. This was nothing compared to the shoulder-patting style of the Budapest press.

His integrity often hurt his own elementary interest. When his friends saw that his recordings did not sell well enough and his little research job at Columbia University did not bring enough to assure a proper living, they tried to help him through a naive stratagem. But this was not so easy with him! They practically had to go as far as to fake the bookkeeping of his record publisher and introduce nonexistent sales in order to make him accept the money. He protested: "How is this possible?" Finally, always suspicious, he agreed to take the money. Shall I say that the publisher did not have to wait long for his dollars? But Bartók was no longer alive.

No less a battle was won by two other friends of his: Ernö Balogh, pianist, former pupil of Bartók, and Rudolph Nissim, an official of ASCAP, the great U.S. musical organization.

Membership in ASCAP was limited to U.S. citizens and no exception was known. Yet Nissim and Balogh cajoled and convinced the leadership to create such an exception and to "adopt" Bartók. Once again it was Bartók who made himself difficult. He wanted no "charity"! Finally, he gratefully accepted the honor. It was just in time. Not much later he fell ill with his fatal blood cancer, and ASCAP paid every medical and hospital bill of his for three years and buried him in the organization's own cemetery, where he still rests today. In today's terms, ASCAP spent nearly $100,000 on a man who was all but unknown to the majority of its own members.

Another real Bartók story was the case of young Peter's military service. Only U.S. citizens had an obligation to serve, if called. Nobody would force Peter to take part in the war. Bartók and Ditta, however, felt that — at a time when millions of American boys fought in the fetid jungles of the Solomons, New Guinea, Guadalcanal — it would be unethical to take advantage of such a loophole. And they convinced young Peter to go and volunteer in the Coast Guard.

Bartók's personal habits were simplicity itself. While he did not walk around in a wrinkled old sweater like Einstein, he kept on wearing, for years on end, summer or winter, the same old heavy, Hungarian-made suits you can see him in in his photos, as well as the same old black hat. He had strict rules about how many cigarettes he permitted himself a day, how much Ditta could spend a day on food.

People talking too much annoyed him terribly; he called them "floodmouths." He became most irritated, however, with the literary "bluestocking" ladies, always overenthusiastic without knowing a bit about his music. He was even more irked by the sudden onslaught of little-known Hungarian musicians who called themselves his "best pupils" and suddenly materialized out of the woodwork in order to establish their credit for the future. News went around that he would not live long.

As he liked to be alone, to ponder, even some members of his family were too much for him, occasionally. His favorite private "watering place" was a small German-American tavern-and-grill, next to the Bronx terminal of the D train, which he daily used. There, in the very last booth, half hidden, he sat alone, having a bottle of beer and a double knockwurst. All that on his way home, where his wife anxiously awaited him with a fine homemade dinner — and lots of chitchat. Around seven he would finally show up and say that he had no appetite, thanks Ditta dear.

When he already knew that he would soon die, it was not fear that moved him but that lifelong sense of duty. He would not just die without first living up to his promises and finish two large pieces he planned, one of them the famous Viola Concerto. Unfortunately, Death worked faster.

He often talked about "America!" He loved and respected this country for everything that is good and great in it. But this did not blind him. He had, when he cared for it, a great sense of humor. He observed and pilloried the vulgarity, double standards, publicity hunting and pointed out the inner contradictions between the noble principles of the Constitution and the sometimes unseemly practices of everday American life.

He spent his last vacation in a summer house that ASCAP rented for him at Saranac Lake. Behind the villa there was a small one-room log cabin. In it Bartók locked himself up all day and composed every waking hour, in haste, with high fever. The door — even the windows — could not be opened because the room, tables, floor were full of small pieces of paper: all musical shorthand—notes, motifs, a few bars. The smallest draft would have disturbed them. In thick cigarette smoke the race with Death went on. Maybe Mozart dictated his Requiem with such a last rush of strength.

September came and he became weaker and weaker. They decided to return to their Riverdale home and a few days later to go to the 57th Street Physicians' Hospital for yet another checkup. Resignation showed on Bartók all over. "What a pity," he said to a friend, "to leave while I still have my baggages full." He meant plans, of course. Unfulfilled plans. "Just a thorough checkup!" said the friend. Bartók just nodded.

They were all ready to start for the hospital when a taxi stopped in front of the house. One of those "best pupils" arrived, along with a photographer. He had just learned that Bartók was back and his condition was grave. Parbleu, he could not allow him to die without first having had his picture taken with the master!

In the hospital, when he was already in half coma, his lawyer arrived, in similar haste, and asked him to sign a new, "modernized" will. He was too weak to sign his name. His physician, his wife, and his son, Peter, came and went, in and out of the room. A few old friends arrived too, but they were not admitted. They congregated in a group outside, with ashen faces. A young little doctor on the floor came by. He stopped and asked: "Say, who the heck is the little old man they're making such a fuss about?"

Nobody took the trouble to explain. Bartók himself would have only nodded. Through the door suddenly came Ditta's hard sobbing. We all knew what it meant.

An Evening with
Béla Bartók
Duci Kovacs

When we talk of collections of folk songs, we rarely give a second thought to how and whence folk song collections are acquired. What procedures do the musicologists follow to search out and assemble the hundreds or, perhaps, thousands of folk songs and ballads that passed from mouth to mouth when written music was a rarity?

Collectors and researchers of folk songs like Béla Bartók and Zoltán Kodály knew what to look for and where to find what they were looking for. Often it was a long, tedious and painstaking task, as we shall see.

I was privileged to know the Bartóks. Mrs. Bartók was a friend of mine and I was a frequent visitor to their modest apartment in Riverdale, New York.

One evening, after I had dined in their home, Bartók asked me to sit beside him at their grand piano. There was a faint smile on his magnificent face — already pale to transparency because of his fatal illness, of which he knew nothing, nor did any of us.

He played a few notes of a song, and asked if I were familiar with the tune. I was not. Whereupon he turned to me and told this story.

During his years of researching and collecting a great number of Hungarian folk songs, Bartók and his entourage had visited many villages, listening to the songs of the peasants, herdsmen and others, young and old, recording their songs on a simple phonograph. Bartók sought out anyone who might know still another old song, or another version of one. He related, "One day, we were working in a village, and had exhausted all available sources. But we had heard about one very old song that only one woman in the village knew or sang. This woman, we were told, was out in the field, working. We packed up all our notes and equipment, and took off to find the woman. We finally found

97

her working in the field, but she refused to sing for us. All the rest of that day was spent in coaxing and pleading with her, but to no avail. After the day's work was done, the woman tied her bundle to the end of her hoe, as did all the other women, and started to walk home to the village. Frustrated, we followed her back, disappointed that we had failed. As the woman walked, her hoe swaying from side to side with its burden (with a gently swaying gait), she suddenly started to sing "the" song, and she sang all the way home.

As he finished, Bartók faced the keyboard, and sang "the" song in his thin voice, accompanying himself with unembellished simplicity.

Béla Bartók on
New York's Kossuth Radio

Jozsef Kovacs

O ne could write at length about the contacts between Béla Bartók and progressive Hungarian-American groups and their press, the *Magyar Szó*. At this time I want to mention only two incidents.

The first is Bartók's appearance on the New York Kossuth Radio. This radio program was one of the results of Hungarian-American united efforts during World War II and was initiated by the *Magyar Szó*. It operated under the direction of Eugene Práger. Bartók, as is well known, lived in dire circumstances, but accepted Práger's invitation to play for his program. Bartók selected his "For Children" piece. Thanks to Práger's foresight, the whole program was taped and is now one of the treasures of the Archives of the Hungarian Radio. This event took place in the fall of 1944.

The other event occurred after the end of World War II. In the spring of 1945 the temporary Hungarian National Assembly invited Béla Bartók to participate in its deliberations. Elections in those difficult days could not be held; that is why the National Assembly decided that until formal elections could be held, the assembly would include as many of the nation's finest representatives as possible.

When the news of Bartók's invitation reached New York, Péter Moór, a member of the paper's editorial staff, visited the then already ailing master. We learn from this interview, which was published in the *Magyar Szó*, that Bartók received the invitation with great satisfaction and was preparing to take his place in the assembly once in Hungary. This fond plan of his, together with many others, was never realized. He succumbed to fatal illness in September of that year.

On the Causes of Wars

Professor Albert Szent-Györgyi

I was born and brought up in a feudalistic world. It was deeply ingrained in us that dying for the king is the greatest honor. I was in the third year of my medical studies, and was completing my compulsory military service, when World War I broke out, in which I wasted five years of my life. In the third year of the war I could clearly see that we had lost and our lives were being sacrificed senselessly by a few war criminals in high position. I became deeply disgusted with military life and saw no merit in dying. I thought I could serve my country better alive. At the same time I was overcome by a burning desire to return to science. So one day, on the Russian front in Poland, I took my gun and shot through the bone of my left underarm. This was very difficult to do, not because I would have been hanged on the spot if discovered, but because this was contrary to what was ingrained in me.

After healing of my wound I received my medical degree and went back to the army where I was placed in a bacteriological laboratory on the Italian front. Here I stayed a short time only, because in the hospital to which the laboratory belonged, a doctor from Vienna made dangerous experiments on Italian prisoners, saying that they were "only" prisoners. A feeling of human brotherhood began to develop in me and I was so much outraged that I reported this to the army. However, the doctor had two stars more than I and so I had to be punished. For punishment I was transferred into the swamps of northern Italy where life expectancy was very short, owing to the raging tropical malaria. Fortunately, a few weeks later, Germany and Austria collapsed and I could go home.

Before going on I would like to discuss that war briefly, because the present situation is very similar to that which brought about this war. In those days the Austro-Hungarian empire, which included present Czechoslovakia and part of Poland, was very powerful and rich. South of it lay Serbia, a small, mountainous and poor country, the only exportable product of which was hogs, which could be transported only over Hungary, Serbia being separated from the sea by mountains. The Austro-Hungarian empire cut off this lifeline by forbidding export through Hungary. The Serbs became resistive. To intimidate them our army organized big military exercises at their border, and to make these more impressive, our archduke attended them with his wife. While driving through Sarajevo, a Serbian student shot them both. This was a most welcome opportunity for the militarist cliques in Vienna, Berlin, and St. Petersburg. A war is the most desirable condition for generals, politicians, and suppliers of the army. So my government served an unacceptable ultimatum to Serbia. But war could be declared only by the emperor who was an old man and wanted to die in peace. To solve this difficulty, our secretary of defense, Count Berchtold, put before the emperor fake telegrams according to which the Serbian army broke into Hungary. This left no alternative to the emperor; he had to mobilize. Berlin followed suit and so did the Russian Czar, and World War I was on. It is said that wars are due to the bloodthirsty nature of man. This is a lie. The reason for World War I was the existence of small groups which profited by the war. This is how it was, how it is, and how it will be, while what great masses of men want is only to live and let live.

1979

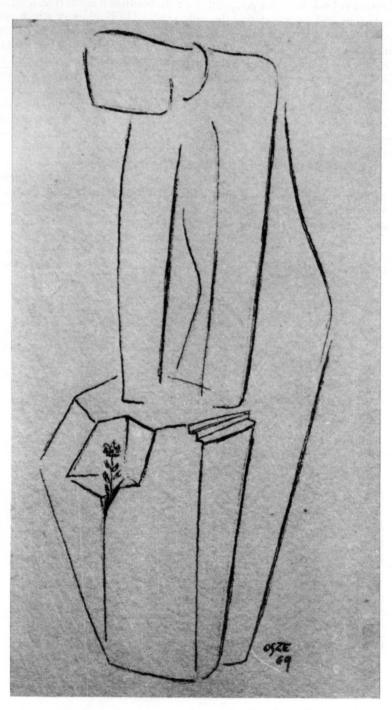

"*The Miracle of the Rock.*" *A drawing by András Ösze.*

András Ösze, world-renowned sculptor, a dedicated friend and supporter of our newspaper.

András Ösze

William Juhász

A great Hungarian artist whose work includes church art, but who would not restrict his themes to the representation of religious teaching, is András Ösze, who now lives in Florida. Ösze tries to embrace the universality of life itself; in every manifestation of life he endeavors to find, and then depict, its essence. His work is religious in the universal sense, whether he portrays the destitution of a Latin American peasant or the nobility of a suffering soul. This quality is further evident when he uses seemingly senseless linear rhythms to suggest the unique relations among created things. The great periods of our civilization have always produced religious art which truly represents the whole panorama of life. . . .

András Ösze was born in 1909 in Nagykanizsa, Hungary. Arthur Elek, an eminent Hungarian art critic who greatly appreciated his work, was one of his first discoverers. In his early youth, Ösze participated in major exhibitions and attracted considerable attention. . . .

His statue of a small child building a church stands in the garden of MABI [a former Hungarian medical insurance organization] in Budapest. It conveys to us the reality and the truth inherent in tales and fables. In the cemetery of Farkasrét, also in Budapest, we find his statue of Árpád Tóth, one of the most sensitive lyricists among the new Hungarian poets . . . .

In 1946 Ösze, having been awarded a scholarship, went to Rome with his wife, a sympathetic supporter. The years he spent there— strenuous years lived in poverty—resulted in the further simplification of his art. He endeavored to confine himself to the essence of things, to find the truth through the language of forms. In the historical atmosphere of Rome, he executed a fountain of noble and classical simplicity.

In 1949, choosing the émigré life, András Ösze went to South America. After some difficult years, he established himself as a teacher in São Paulo, Brazil. However, his art, which is as uniquely Hungarian as it is universal, was not truly appreciated. The reason for this can be found in the fact that it is concerned mainly with the oppressed, the "little men," though not in the strictly political but, rather, in the universal sense. His Brazilian experience greatly intensified his artistic outlook. During his peregrinations in Peru and Bolivia, he became acquainted not only with the folk art of the descendants of the ancient Incas but also with the people themselves who have, notwithstanding their apparent simplicity and passivity, remained the creative carriers of their ancient heritage. While in Latin America, he also came to understand the suffering and humiliation of the suppressed Negroes and their culture, also the depository of an ancient heritage.

Ösze transmuted these experiences, during his Brazilian sojourn, into metal, terra cotta and stone statues. It was there that he discovered that the unique shaping and roughing of metal pieces produces completely novel color and surface effects. Two of his series—"Poverty" and "Slavery"—represent very distinctly the artistic efforts of this period. Ösze's "acceptance" of folk culture, of the fate of the simple and the "small" people, as a religious and sincerely human outlook, must be emphasized. For these reasons, his Brazilian years caused his art to mature.

In 1958, Ösze came to New York, having been invited as an art teacher. He was confronted by new problems so severe as to hinder his adjustment to the unfamiliar conditions of life he found in this city of exceedingly advanced technology. These conditions had proved difficult for Béla Bartók, who was his ideal. It is no wonder then that he followed in Bartók's footsteps. Although in a foreign land, he wanted, above all, to remain faithful to that inner truth which he had chosen to serve without any compromise or any regard for the fashions of the times or the "market."

To be faithful to oneself does not mean always expressing oneself in the same way. In this direction lie the stagnation and rigidity that attend preoccupation with form at the expense of content. It is this very condition that Ösze has fought unremittingly by searching for new forms to represent those intense, inner manifestations of life which he himself has experienced. The personal struggle he has undergone during his residence in New York has affected the character of his work. . . .

Among Ösze's larger creations in plastic art, mention must be made of his model of a Bartók Fountain, which combines the symbolic function of the columns of the Hungarian peasant house with the characteristics of a memorial. The reliefs of this fountain depict Hungarian folk-dance scenes. Only negligence could have prevented the realization of this memorial to our universal musical genius.

Ösze is one of those "non-modern" sculptors who aspire only to realize their artistic aims. Success and recognition have visited him clearly against his own wish. It is of interest to note in this context that the *Christian Science Monitor* has classified his sculptures, shown at the YMCA exhibition in Boston, with those of Klee, Kandinsky, Moholy-Nagy and George Grosz—the international pioneers of modern art—who have also exhibited there. . . .

András Ösze is a member of our 80th Anniversary Committee.

Autumn's Branches
Mihály Tompa

Now fade all of earth's gallantries
from autumn's branches. Softly blown
the yellow leaves drift mutely down
in eddies of the evening breeze.

Is not the falling of the leaf
fit reason for the forest's grief?
No dew, no song, no heat of sun
can hold it when its day is done.

While still in my leafy prime,
my branches blossom with fragrant breath,
roar not, oh, Boreal blast 'of death,
too soon will autumn come with frost

when love and joy and hope are lost.

If no chance, or power can reprieve,
a sleep shall on my eyes be laid,
In painless peace my life shall fade,
and perish like the forest leaf.

Translated by
Anca Vrbovska
(Member, National Press Committee)

The Art of Julius Zilzer

Prof. Alfred Werner

Conceivably, there is no halcyonic period of unlimited calm and bliss — there never was one. The Psalmist spoke the truth when he summed up man's life as an agglomeration of "labor and sorrow." Yet built into every sane person is a mechanism that defies Fate, as it were. Aware of all obstacles, we struggle to make this a better world, for ourselves and for those to come after us, and to decrease, and hopefully even eliminate, pain on our uncertain path through life. There are many who maintain that man's worst enemies are neither earthquakes nor storms, neither fires nor floods, but the demons implanted within him. Psychoanalysis has probed into the darkness of the Id by the method of free association, by making the individual on the couch say whatever enters his head without regard to the importance or unimportance of the proferred material.

But, without the benefit of a theory, artists have been availing themselves of this procedure from the very first artist of the Stone Age. Goethe, in his play about the Renaissance poet Torquato Tasso — who is torn between his desire to abandon himself completely to the worship of his Muse, and the necessity to yield to the rules of a strict and often seemingly heartless society — has his unhappy hero exclaim, "Und wenn der Mensch in seiner Qual verstummt, Gab mir ein Gott zu sagen, was ich leide." Here Tasso acknowledges, gratefully, that he is more fortunate than the average mortal since unlike him who must suffer in silence, he, Tasso, can express his woes in the language of poetry.

Like so many artists before him, Zilzer could express in pictures the fright, the scare, the alarm that was stirred in his soul. In this series of prints many phases of the bewilderment that all but the most insensitive must feel, are enshrined — and tamed, temporarily at least. They are like wild animals which the dompteur has managed to lock into their cages so that we can look at them, briefly, shudder at the sight of their enormous teeth, yet feel unthreatened, protected by the iron bars. The artist, to be sure, is not allowed to

"Continuity" By Julius Zilzer.

keep these beasts incarcerated forever; he must let them out, so that they can roam the fields and the woods, terrorizing all who meet them.

But we, the spectators, were at least permitted to glimpse our dangerous antagonists, thereafter to be able to recognize them at once from a distance. It will be up to the individual to act, upon such a confrontation, in the manner his characterological set-up compels him to: he can try to flee, or to kill the monster, or, perhaps, even come to terms with it. And he can teach his children — see *Continuity* — how to cope with the adversary, for old age has the advantage of experience, to which the artist will add the bonus of articulateness, of persuasive eloquence.

Julius Zilzer was a reader and a friend of our paper. His illustrations appeared frequently in our yearbooks.

Albert Einstein's letter of appreciation to Julius Zilzer, Hungarian-American painter, a friend and contributing artist of our newspaper.

Robert Capa

The death of a militiaman. (1937)

You Are History

Ernest Hemingway

Our newspaper was the only Hungarian publication in the United States which early on recognized the world-historic significance of the Spanish people's fight against Franco fascism. We realized at the start, in 1936, that what was happening in Spain was fascism's dress rehearsal for World War II. We wholeheartedly supported the Spanish Republic's fight for democracy. We organized a nation-wide collection campaign for medical aid to the Spanish people. A member of our Editorial Board, Paul Somogyi (son of Béla Somogyi, the martyred editor of the Budapest *Népszava*), joined the volunteers fighting for democratic Spain. He was wounded in battle and died a year later in the United States. Two other readers of our newspaper, István Cserni and Dénes Kozma, following Somogyi's example, went overseas to fight for the Spanish Republic. Cserni died on the battlefield. Kozma was wounded in action, but recovered, returned to Canada. He remained a loyal reader and supporter of our paper until the end of his days.

Indelible in our memory are these three fallen heroes. In their memory and in honor of the more than 3,300 American anti-fascist volunteers who joined the 15th Brigade, known as the *Abraham Lincoln Brigade*, more than a thousand of whom have fallen in battle; the volunteers from Hungary who joined the 13th Brigade, the *Dombrowski Brigade*, under the leadership of General Lukács-Zalka Máté; as well as all the heroic young volunteers from other countries, we offer the following eulogy written in 1939, by Ernest Hemingway.

The dead sleep cold in Spain tonight. Snow blows through the olive groves, sifting against the tree roots. Snow drifts over the mounds with the small head-boards (when there was time for head-boards). The olive trees are thin in the cold wind because their lower branches were once cut to cover tanks, and the dead sleep cold in the small hills above the Jarama river. It was cold that February when they died there and since then the dead have not noticed the change of seasons.

111

It is two years now since the Lincoln Battalion held for four and one-half months along the heights of the Jarama, and the first American dead have been a part of the earth of Spain for a long time now.

The dead sleep cold in Spain tonight and they will sleep cold all this winter as the earth sleeps cold with them. But in the spring the rain will come to make the earth kind again. The wind will blow soft over the hills from the south. The black trees will come to life with small green leaves, and there will be blossoms on the apple trees along the Jarama river. This spring the dead will feel the earth beginning to live again.

For our dead are a part of the earth of Spain now and the earth of Spain can never die. Each winter it will seem to die and each spring it will come alive again. Our dead will live with it forever.

Just as the earth can never die, neither will those who have ever been free return to slavery. The peasants who worked the earth where our dead lie know what those dead died for. There was time during the war for them to learn these things, and there is forever for them to remember them in.

Our dead live in the hearts and minds of the Spanish peasants, of the Spanish workers of all the good simple honest people who believed in and fought for the Spanish Republic. And as long as all our dead live in the Spanish earth, and they will live as long as the earth lives, no system of tyranny ever will prevail in Spain.

The Fascists may spread over the land, blasting their way with the weight of metal brought from other countries. They may advance aided by traitors and by cowards. They may destroy cities and villages and try to hold the people in slavery.

The Spanish people will rise again as they have always risen before against tyranny.

The dead do not need to rise. They are part of the earth now and the earth can never be conquered. For the earth endureth forever. It will outlive all systems of tyranny.

Those who have entered it honorably, and no men ever entered earth more honorably than those who died in Spain, have already achieved immortality.

John Albok, Outstanding Hungarian American photographer, a devoted friend of our newspaper.

John Albok

"Buy a flower!"

Dancers under a cloudless sky.

The audience at a March 15 celebration organized by our newspaper in the early 1950's.

Three Hungarian Giants of Science

Dr. János Nagy

Throughout the world there are many giants from Hungary. Most of them, including perhaps the most precious ones, came to the United States after the First World War.

From among them I chose three: Theodore Kármán, John von Neumann, and Eugene Wigner, who in the field of real physics have created so many unique and lasting advances. These giants were rather short in body, but, as they say in my old country, "man is not measured by a yardstick."

When they were asked how come there are so many Hungarian-Americans with outstanding qualifications, they all answered the same: it is the result of the high standard of the Hungarian secondary educational system.

The oldest of the three was Theodore Kármán. He was born in 1881, in Budapest, where he got his schooling; he graduated from the "model high school" founded by his father; later on, he received his mechanical engineer's diploma from the Technical University in Budapest. During the First World War he served as an artillery officer, and it was in this period that he laid the scientific foundation for helicopter construction, upon which the development of the industrial production of helicopters was based. With his numerous treatises he created the scientific foundations of aerodynamics. After the war he was professor at the University of Aachen, Germany; then in 1930 he was invited by the president of the California Institute of Technology, where he taught and led the experimental laboratory until his retirement. The American scientific world lacked the very things in which Kármán excelled: theoretical thoroughness and imagination. President John F. Kennedy awarded the first National Scientific Medal, the highest civilian award of the United States, to him in 1961. But Kármán was proudest of all that he was called "the father of the air and of flying."

* * * * *

John von Neumann was born in 1903, in Budapest. He graduated from

117

Theodor Karman

Jenö Wigner

John Neuman

the Park Allee evangelical high school and received his diploma from the Technical University in Budapest, where he also received his doctorate in mathematics, in 1926. In the same year he obtained a diploma in chemical engineering from the Technical University in Zurich. For a short period he taught at the University of Göttingen. At the age of twenty-three he wrote his paper of fundamental importance on quantum mechanics, which later became the foundation of atomic physics. When in 1933 the Institute of Advanced Study was formed, he, along with Albert Einstein, was among the first to become a member.

He soon became a recognized world authority on electronic brains—the computers. A further aim of his was the regulation of meteorology. His interest in and knowledge of mathematics was uniquely broad. After a very successful lecture, in 1955, he was asked whether, with the present development of technology, humanity would survive. He answered that survival of humanity depends on the maintenance of the fundamentals—patience, elasticity, and intelligence.

* * * * *

If, for any reason, someone would ask which of the three Hungarian giants was the most remarkable I would choose, without hesitation, Eugene Wigner. Like Neumann, he graduated from the Park Allee high school, but in a grade above him. He received his doctorate in chemistry in Berlin, in 1920. He promptly switched to theoretical physics. He settled in Princeton, where he was a student of Einstein's too. Together with Neumann, he took part in the establishment of the Manhattan Project, but did not participate in the actual development of the bomb. Of this he said, much later: "Do I feel any regrets in my conscience for having taken part in the building of the atom bomb? No, I do not. The nuclear chain reaction would have been invented anyhow, and I shudder at the thought that it could have been invented first by a more aggressive nation, not by us." When he received the Nobel Prize in physics in 1963, the prize committee summed up his achievement: "He contributed greatly to the development of the theory of quantum mechanics, to the theory of solid matter, and to the theory of nuclear chain reaction." He retired in 1971, after teaching theoretical physics for forty-one years, which is unique in the history of American higher education.

To the question of when was the beginning of the atomic age, he answered, "I do not know what is meant by atomic age. I hope that we will enter into a more humane age, that there will be ever more possibilities for the enhancement and satisfaction of human understanding, affection and happiness. It is a great error to think that material possessions are the most important. There is need for spiritual possessions too for human happiness."

The Review of Modern Physics, America's leading scientific periodical, commenting on the role of natural scientists of Hungarian origin, notes that the effect of these Hungarian scientists on American intellectual life is such that, in the future, one whose achievement is especially outstanding will be honored with the title "Honorary Hungarian."

One of our three Hungarian giants gave to the world supersonic flight and space flight; another the fast computers; and the third laid down the foundations of modern physics, upon which the world of physics can build its further wonders.

Leo Szilard

For those who know him, it is impossible to conceive of the mercurial, quixotic, feather-ruffling scientific genius as a man who can just sit and think. Szilard thinking is another form of matter in motion. He is also a man who has led a life of not-so-quiet desperation in the past 20 years. He and Enrico Fermi, who made the first atomic bomb possible, never originally intended their scientific work for military use. Szilard, from his early student days in Berlin, regarded the liberation of atomic energy as the liberator of humanity from poverty and an end to war. But when he confirmed his theory in March, 1939, "That night, I knew the world was headed for sorrow."

He felt we had to produce atomic bombs during the war because Hitler might do it first. But Szilard was against dropping the bomb on Hiroshima. He has worked actively in the post-war years for a policy of civilian control at home and international control within the UN to reduce tensions with the Soviet Union.

But the scientists who have called for an end to the cold war have generally not been given much of a hearing in Washington. Szilard's own voice had been reduced to a whisper—until he announced that he had cancer. Suddenly, that made his views newsworthy—as if his warnings of world destruction had not been important before. His voice was heard often in the land, by way of newspaper interviews, TV programs and a book of short, ironic Swiftian essays called "The Voice of the Dolphins."

Szilard's main contention is that the U.S. and the USSR share one basic interest—they both must avoid atomic war. He believes the Soviet leadership is as sincere about this as our leadership is. He thinks the main reason we can't get anywhere is because neither of us trusts the other. He thinks there are some things we can do on our own to make the Russians move toward a relaxation of tensions. He does not agree with Edward Teller's view that the Russians intend to destroy us when they can.

"I myself believe that we are headed for an all-out war and that our chances of getting through the next 10 years are slim," Szilard tells his college audiences today.

"I personally find myself in rebellion against the fate that history seems to have in store for us, and I suspect that some of you may be equally rebellious," he adds. "The question is, what can you do?"

What Szilard has done is start a peace lobby from his apartment in the Dupont Plaza Hotel in Washington. He wants to involve scholars and scientists in a wide-ranging program to bring the cold war to an end, phase by phase. He doesn't expect full agreement on all his views. But he wants everyone—ordinary citizens—who is willing to contribute and work toward such a peace lobby to write him at his hotel.

Szilard, who was born in Budapest and then studied and taught in Berlin until Hitler came to power, has lived in America since 1939.

1962

Dr. Szilard, co-worker with Fermi, was among the first to suggest an atomic bomb and get the proposal to Roosevelt. A Hungarian physicist, he was vocal for science's freedom from the military and for internationalization of atomic energy.

Hungarians in the
Labor Movement

Our press, its editors, and thousands of its readers participated in all the great labor struggles of the past 80 years, particularly in the great coal strikes and in the auto and steel organizing drives. There were 2,000 Hungarian pickets in the great copper strike of 1913 in Michigan and Illinois. In the historic Passaic strike our editors were in the strike leadership.

But it was in the great organizing drive in the thirties, in the basic industries, that our newspaper, its editors, its readers, and its friends made the most outstanding contributions toward expanding the trade union movement, and through that to strengthening the economic and political foundations of American democracy.

As a result of the leadership qualities and organizing abilities of such people as Louis Weinstock, Julius Emspak, James Lustig, Paul Dömény, Louis Antal, Ernö Roth, Alex Rosner, Frank Somlyó and others, the ranks of American organized labor have increased by hundreds of thousands.

The role of our paper in this historic advance by American labor was officially acknowledged at the time of the thirty-fifth anniversary of our paper, in 1937, by two outstanding leaders of the great organizational campaigns of the period, John Van Bitner and Philip Murray:

February 4, 1937

To: The Editor, *Uj Elöre*

In the name of the Steel Workers Organizing Committee, I greet your paper now celebrating its 35th anniversary.

We congratulate your newspaper for the magnificent cooperation and effective help that it gave us in organizing the unorganized workers of America's basic industries.

We are looking forward to working with you not only for the organizing of all workers hitherto unorganized, but also on the wider field of defending the freedom of this country against its rapacious enemies.

Fraternally yours,
John Van Bitner, Director
Steel Workers Organizing Committee

To: The Editor, *Uj Elöre*

The fact that your newspaper recognized early the importance of the movement organized by the Congress of Industrial Organizations is positive proof of the wisdom of its editor and a compliment to all of its readers.

Philip Murray, President
Steel Workers Organizing Committee

My First Strike

Anna Minarik

I started to work at the Johnson and Johnson textile plant in New Brunswick around 1903, when I was fifteen. I was tending six machines, even though most of the other workers handled only four. One had to be an acrobat to deal with six of those monsters. I could do it because I was young and strong and nimble. We worked thirteen hours every day, except Sunday, and our alertness couldn't slacken for a moment, because the machines would immediately get tangled up and it would take hours to straighten them out.

There was no resting while tending the machines. We couldn't sit down even for a second. Only when we heard the factory siren could we stop, but by that time our nerves were near the breaking point. If we were lucky and the machines "behaved" themselves, we could stealthily eat an apple while tending the looms, making sure, however, that the foreman, a brutal character named Mr. Maundley, did not notice. We couldn't even hide the core of the apple because he was always watching us. Most of the time when we ate an apple we had to swallow the core too, so as to do away with the incriminating evidence.

Most of my fellow workers were approximately the same age as I. The average life expectancy of the women working there at that time was not more than thirty years. There were absolutely no health-protection devices, and there was a constant cloud of dust in the plant, so that tuberculosis germs attacked the lungs of the workers with lethal regularity, and at a very early age. It was the policy of the company at that time to buy a steamship ticket back to Hungary for any worker whom they noticed had acquired the deadly illness. This way, the company avoided any responsibility for the worker's illness and death.

We worked six days a week, thirteen hours a day. One day at lunchtime I bemusedly said to my friend, "Wouldn't it be nice if we only had to work ten hours?" To my amazement, in half an hour the whole plant was talking about the ten-hour day. Next day we sent a delegation to the management that we would only work ten hours a day. The management shut down the plant. A long, bitter strike followed, but finally the management yielded. I am happy that I did my share to advance the cause of America's working men and women.

1949

Organizing the Copper Workers
Louis Fodor

W e started organizing the mine workers in the copperfields of Illinois in 1913. We started, of course, with the Hungarian miners, but soon the Finnish and Croatian miners also joined us in droves.

The mine owners were enraged. They knew the miners were being organized. They wanted to nip the struggle for unionization in the bud. In the No. 4 mine at Kearsarg, they arrested two workers whom stool pigeons reported to the management. But by that time 70 percent of the miners were in the union, so we went on strike demanding the reinstatement of the two workers.

While the struggle went on, the reactionary Hungarian newspaper reported that the governor was ordering out the National Guard because the strikers had dynamited City Hall. That, of course, was a lie.

The news outraged the workers. We held a mass meeting at which the reactionary paper was denounced. Scores of Hungarians canceled their subscriptions and I went around and urged them to subscribe to our paper. I obtained sixteen subscriptions at that time.

The year ended in a great tragedy, however. Our union decided that it would hold a Christmas celebration at which we would give holiday gifts to the children and to the striking workers. Some five hundred people filled the Italian Hall. Suddenly, a demented stool pigeon of the mine owners cried out "Fire!" in the hall. A tremendous panic broke out, and eighty-five people died. The next day the sheriff visited the organizers' office and said that the county would bury the dead at its own expense. We told him to get out: you killed our people, we will bury our dead.

There were not enough hearses in Calumet City on the day of the funeral, so we carried the coffins on our shoulders to the cemetery.

A New York newspaperman took pictures of the funeral procession. That night an unknown person broke into his room, stole the films, and broke his camera.

1945

Louis Weinstock
Mitch Berkowitz

T he enactment of unemployment insurance as part of the Social Security law capped a determined struggle by American workers to expand their rights. Louis Weinstock, along with Elmer Brown of the printers' union and Harry Bridges of the West Coast longshoremen, led a national movement to win labor's support for the passage of these two historic measures.

Weinstock was born in Hungary and emigrated to the United States after the First World War. By the early 1930s, he was leading a rank and file movement among New York painters to oust corrupt union leaders closely associated with the notorious Lepke-Gurrah gang. At the same time, Weinstock was battling Bill Green and the American Federation of Labor leadership, who opposed unemployment insurance as "a dole." At an AFL meeting in the early '30s, which unemployment-insurance supporters were not permitted to address, Weinstock managed to gain access to a huge overhead chandelier and deliver, via an improvised "air mail," an impassioned plea for unemployment insurance on leaflets floating down to the assembled unionists.

In that same year, Weinstock's rank and file movement succeeded in expelling the corrupt leaders from the painters' District Council 9, and Weinstock himself was elected secretary-treasurer, its highest officer. Under his leadership the union took on new direction. Democracy was re-established, wages were increased, organizing was actively pursued, and large numbers of black painters were recruited into the union. The first welfare fund in the building trades was set up; it has since become the model adopted by unions across the country.

Despite constant attacks on him as a known Communist—attacks by employers, the press, and the government—Weinstock was repeatedly returned to office by members of his union. At the height of the cold war and McCarthyism, Weinstock was jailed for three years, along with other Communist leaders, on a Smith Act conviction. Further persecution by the now-defunct Subversive Activities Control Board resulted in a five-year sentence that was later overturned by a unanimous decision of the Court of Appeals—but only after Weinstock had served one and a half years.

In 1945 he participated in the founding convention of the World Federation of Democratic Trade Unions in Paris. Four years later he was back in Paris as a delegate from his union to the historic 1949 World Peace Congress.

Weinstock's life, a veritable litany of modern American working-class achievement, has also been characterized by a constant, affectionate identification with the progressive Hungarian-American community and its newspaper, the *Magyar Szó*.

Mitch Berkowitz worked in the fur and printing industries, and is an active trade unionist.

Louis Weinstock, outstanding Hungarian-American labor leader, a devoted friend and supporter of our paper with his wife, Rose Weinstock, former member of our editorial board, Harry Bridges, outstanding labor leader, and Admiral Dawson, West Coast progressive leader.

James Lustig and the Great Phelps Dodge Strike of 1946

Bert Eckstein

J ames Lustig was born in Budapest on November 2, 1902. From his early youth he was active in the progressive movement. Soon after arriving in America in 1921, he joined the editorial staff of the *Uj Elöre*, then consisting of John Lassen-Lékai, Dr. John Gyetvay, Louis Bebrits and others. Later, Lustig spent some time in Canada and helped to establish the progressive Hungarian newspaper, *Kanadai Munkás*, in Hamilton, Ontario. At present he is a member of our board of editors and the Secretary of the 80th Anniversary Committee.

During the early 1930s he was among those who helped organize the millions of workers in the basic industries in this country. He is a charter member of the United Electrical, Radio and Machine Workers of America. He was a prime mover in the successful effort to organize the workers in the electrical industry in the New York-New Jersey region. First he became an organizer of the local, but soon advanced to district representative of District 4 of the UE. He was instrumental in negotiating the best agreements with large corporations—including Ford Instruments, Ingersoll Rand, Bockton and Dickenson, Hatfield Wire, Liquidometer. But, beyond any doubt, his greatest achievement in the UE was the strike he led against the Phelps Dodge Corporation. We give here a synopsis of that historic strike.

World War II had just come to an end. The United States, Britain, the Soviet Union and the heroic underground resistance in the Nazi-occupied countries of the world had halted fascism in its drive for world conquest. There was new hope for world peace and progress.

The labor movement in the United States, recognizing the just character of the war, had voluntarily sacrificed its right to strike. Big business, on the other hand, had reaped tremendous profits at the expense of the workers through government giveaways, cost-plus production, and so on. After four long war years of low wages and long hours, the Congress of Industrial

Organizations (CIO), after negotiations failed, decided to strike for higher wages and improved working conditions. In January of 1946, strike struggles took place in the steel, auto, and electrical industries, led by the relatively young industrial unions, the United Steel Workers, the United Auto Workers, and the United Electrical, Radio and Machine Workers. Within two and a half to three months, these strikes were over with an 18½¢ per hour increase and renewed union contracts. Big business challenged the strength of these young industrial unions and the CIO prevailed.

The Phelps Dodge Copper Products Company, a division of the Phelps Dodge Corporation, was struck on January 4, 1946, by Local 441 of the UE; this strike continued for nine months. Copper bosses generally and Phelps Dodge in particular have a history of notorious antiunion activity. Our plant in Bayway, New Jersey, with two thousand production workers during the war, was the largest single copper fabricating plant in the world. The workers had joined the UE before the war, and our union Local 441 was recognized as the official legal bargaining representative by the NLRB. The company never accepted this. Only when the courts insisted was some agreement reached, but the company immediately violated every provision, bribed some of the activists in the new local with promotions to foreman, and so on. As soon as we entered the war, the company declared that the agreement had ended and that management no longer would even meet with representatives of the union. But the mood of the country was one of cooperation to win the war, and the newly created War Labor Board ordered the company to meet with the union and live up to the former agreement as long as the war emergency continued.

Bayway is the waterfront section of Elizabeth, New Jersey, on the Kill Van Kull waterway. The Phelps Dodge plant had a large dock on the waterfront where all the copper ingots from its large refinery in Texas as well as from its Chilean operation were transported by barges.

The Bayway area near the plant was a predominantly Polish community, which in 1946 was mostly foreign-born. The tube mill, while it was located in Plainfield, had predominantly black workers, with all-white supervision. In addition to this, because of manpower shortages during the war, the company had regular busloads of newly hired black workers come in daily from Harlem, on all three shifts. Thus our two thousand strikers were evenly divided, black and white, each with about the same seniority on the job. This was a very unusual situation in 1946, since in most plants minority workers were the last to be hired and the first to be fired. The UE policy of rank and file control of the union and of no discrimination made possible the closest working unity between blacks and whites during the strike. This unity was a bulwark of our strength.

From the very first day the strike began, Jim Lustig, UE district organizer and the leader of the strike, recognized that this would not be an ordinary labor conflict. The workers in the plant jumped the gun and went out on January 4, several days before the date set. We learned later that Wylie Brown, the president of Phelps Dodge Copper Products, had bragged over lunch at the New York Athletic Club with the president of Westinghouse that he would show him how to run a strike—that when he got through with the union, the starving workers would come crawling on their bellies, begging for their jobs.

The company, during the next nine months, sent more than thirty letters to the families of the strikers. At first management threatened the loss of jobs if the strikers didn't return to work at once. It continuously attacked the leadership of the union, called them Reds who were interested only in promoting strife. When the other strikes were settled, the company offered an immediate 18½¢ increase if the men would return to work at once. When all this failed, in the eighth month of the strike, Wylie Brown offered a bribe to the strike committee if it would immediately get the men back to work, but he swore never to sign an agreement with the union.

Local 441 had prepared for a long siege. A broad-based strike committee of twenty-two officers and rank and file strikers was set up and functioned during the whole period. A soup kitchen operated on a daily basis. After a few weeks the majority of the strikers got work wherever they could, and a band of two hundred men and women with picket captains kept the picket line going twenty-four hours a day, seven days a week despite an injunction. No production took place during the strike.

The company used every trick to break our ranks. Wylie Brown again had lunch at the New York Athletic Club, this time with Joe (King) Ryan—"life president" of the International Longshoremen's Association, and enlisted his aid. He sent Anthony Anastasia, then head of a stevedoring company, down with dozens of his goons by boat to land on the dock and give the impression that production was going on. We countered, with the aid of the National Maritime Union, with friendly boats and confronted them, whenever we chose to, on the Kill Van Kull. After a while they couldn't get any more scum to work for them, and Anastasia asked if he could work for us.

But most of all, we organized, on our side, all the friends and natural allies that we had: first a Wives' Committee, then the whole Polish community. Our weekly strikers' meeting was held every Monday morning at the Polish National Hall on Bayway Avenue, several blocks from the plant and Local 441 office. Two successful mass meetings were held at the Elizabeth Armory, where community leaders appeared on our behalf, including Congressman Adam Clayton Powell, from Harlem (the black workers who lived in New York were maintaining a daily picket line in front of the corporate offices of Phelps Dodge at 40 Wall Street).

During the nine months the families of the two hundred pickets received regular food baskets. No family was evicted. Strikers obtained medical attention through friendly physicians and credit at local merchants. All family emergencies were met. Regular collections of food and money were made at factory gates with the aid of the Union County CIO Council.

On special occasions demonstrations were held in front of the Phelps Dodge plant with delegations from the labor movement of the whole New York-New Jersey metropolitan area.

We had faith in our cause, in ourselves, and in the solidarity of the working people who admired the manner in which we fought the good fight and who willingly supported us.

Wylie Brown did not sign the agreement; his chief attorney signed for him. The strikers did not crawl back, but returned as proud union men and women, having won the best contract possible in that period, including $75 for each worker—the "share" of the bribe that the company had offered to our committee at the beginning of the negotiations.

Bert Eckstein was a member of the strike committee in charge of publicity.

Paul Dömény

In 1940 Paul Dömény first became General Secretary of Local 1064, United Catering, Restaurant, Bar and Hotel Workers' Union, and has been returned to office in every election since then. Under his leadership the local gained the first forty-hour week and the first pension plan for restaurant workers in the state of Michigan. Dömény has represented his union on a host of local, national, and even international bodies, including the Metropolitan Detroit AFL-CIO Council Executive Board, the Michigan State AFL-CIO Executive Board, the AFL-CIO Industrial Department conventions, and the congresses of the International Union of Food and Allied Workers Association in Geneva in 1977 and in Munich in 1981.

As a delegate to the first CIO convention, in 1940, Dömény witnessed the dramatic moment when John L. Lewis stepped down as CIO president and Philip Murray took over as the new president. In 1956, Dömény was again present as labor history was being made. He served as a delegate at the merger convention of the AFL and the CIO in New York. More recently he has been one of the founders of the Labor-Community Coalition for Jobs in the Detroit area.

Paul Dömény is Co-Chairman of the Eightieth Anniversary Committee, Magyar Szó.

Paul Dömény.

131

Julius Emspak, Hungarian-American labor leader, founder of the United Electric Workers Union and a friend of our paper.

Julius Emspak:
A Giant of American Labor

J ulius Emspak was only fourteen years old when he went to work at the Schenectady, New York, General Electric plant after his father, a blacksmith at that plant, was killed in an accident.

From office boy he advanced to toolmaker and then tool designer, the highest factory crafts. Taking a leave of absence from the plant, Emspak went back to school, then to college and eventually to graduate studies in philosophy at Brown University, where he earned the highest academic honors.

But his working-class background, and his desire to help working people fight to improve conditions in the factories, brought him back to practice his skills at the GE plant.

There was no union there, since the company had smashed craft unions some years earlier.

Emspak was one of four or five GE workers who, during the 1930s, decided to build an industrial union. With a few hundred members behind them, this group contacted similar organizations at fifteen other GE plants who came together in 1936 to set up what became the United Electrical, Radio and Machine Workers of America, commonly known as UE.

Emspak was elected secretary-treasurer of the new union. UE joined with the steelworkers and the auto workers to make up the "big three" of the Congress of Industrial Organizations.

The UE within a few years organized the big electrical monopolies, something that had never before been accomplished, as well as hundreds of smaller companies. Close to half a million workers were brought into the union.

The union's achievements and Emspak's profound understanding of workers' problems and needs were recognized by President Franklin D. Roosevelt, who named him to the President's National Labor Victory Committee in World War II, along with leaders of the AFL and CIO.

When the war ended, Emspak proposed that the three unions that held contracts with the country's largest corporations in the basic industries—electrical, steel, and auto—form a common front to face these corporate giants.

The three unions together struck in the winter of 1946. It was the first time in U.S. labor history that such a common front had been built and it has not been repeated since.

The gains they made had never been achieved before, and their unity inspired many other unions to present militant stands against their employers.

The UE had, because of its militancy, earned the hatred of the corporations. When the politicians launched the cold war, they sought the backing of the labor movement.

The UE came under severe attack because it refused to let those politicians decide what road members of the union should take, what policies they should follow.

Defending the union's principles of rank and file control, for the right of all in the industry—regardless of age, sex, nationality, or political belief—to hold full union rights, Emspak was called before the House Un-American Activities Committee and sentenced to a year in jail for refusing to bow to that committee's antidemocratic demands.

On appeal, the conviction was overturned by the Supreme Court.

Employers, and government agencies working with those employers, abetted by sections of the labor leadership that saw the democratic nature of the UE as challenging their own bureaucratic policies, combined forces in an attempt to destroy the union. Emspak was among the union's leaders who drew the strongest fire from this combination.

In fighting to preserve the union and its principles, Emspak's health was undermined. He died in April 1962 at the age of fifty-seven.

Julius Emspak served as president of the Council of Hungarian American Trade Unionists during World War II.

"The Diamond Rollers." Cover design of the 50th Anniversary Album of the
Verhovay-William Penn Association, published in 1936.

The "Diamond Rollers"

Hungarians in the Mines—
The Founding of Verhovay

The Miners of Hazelton

Joseph Kovács

Among the Hungarian-American folk songs there are several that deal with the lives of miners. One went something like this:

Könnyeinket szénpor issza,
Kacagásunk füstbe fúl,
Kis falunkba vágyunk vissza
Ahol minden fűszál ért magyarul

(The coal powder absorbs our tears,
Our laughter is drowned in smoke,
We yearn to return to our little village
Where every blade of grass understood Hungarian.)

Others were more defiant:

Ha majd üt az óra,
Akkor virradóra
Felkapsz csodaszárnyon
Repülö hajóra,
Haza mégy és nem türsz
Semmi cudarságot,
Teremtesz magadnak
Uj Magyarországot.

(When the clock strikes
And the dawn breaks
You take to magic wings
On flying boats

Home you return and won't put up
With any base deals.
You will create for yourself
A new Hungary.)

Very few people will remember these miners' songs when the centennial of the William Penn Association is celebrated sometime in the mid-1980s. There will be good reason to celebrate, because this is one of the few ethnic-origin sick-benefit associations that has lasted for one hundred years and has not been buried by the political establishment.

According to legend, the organization was established by 13 miners. By some curious coincidence, when the miners added up their capital, it turned out that they had $13. That's the way it is reported by Geza Kende, the Hungarian-American historian. Why was there a need for a legend? Because the number 13 is, according to Hungarian folklore, the carrier of baleful events, baleful omens. That's why there should not be 13 people sitting at a table. It is obvious, according to this tradition, that our Lord Jesus would not have had such an ignominious end on the cross if he had been aware of this situation and had not sat down among a group of 13 people at the Last Supper. Neither is it advisable to start out on a journey, or to start a new job, on the 13th day of the month, especially if that day is Friday.

The founders of the organization did not believe in the power of superstitious numbers. Had they believed in it, they could have figured out that their association should have been organized a year earlier, in 1885. The number 1885 is divisible by 13. The history of the association would then have started out like this: "Thirteen miners, with $13 in their pockets, decided in the year 13 times 145 to establish this organization of self-help to aid them in case of illness or accident."

But the founders were neither superstitious nor believers in legends. This is proven by the latest historical research, according to which the association was established by 128 workers, most of them miners. Their original capital was also somewhat larger than the legendary $13. It was, to be exact, $17.25. The original name of the organization was the Verhovay Association, the name having been derived from an obscure Hungarian politician of the last century. Let's not regret if we are poorer by a legend. The extent of the founders' efforts and the strength of their determination deserve our respect.

The Verhovay Association in 1955 merged with the Rákoczi Sick Benefit Association (founded in 1888 in Bridgeport); since that time it has been known as the William Penn Association. It was, at the turn of the century, only one of the many Hungarian organizations in the United States. And it wasn't the first one either. A Hungarian society was established at the time of the Kossuth emigration. Another one, long considered the first of its kind, was founded in Newark in 1882. After the turn of the century, there were hardly any Hungarian communities which did not have their own local social or sick-benefit organization. According to another Hungarian-American historian, Geza Hoffman, the number of Hungarian organizations in the first decade of our century was 1,339. Of these, 382 were associated with churches. The rest of them were secular; 191 were socialist-oriented. In the coming years we will find out how many of them reach their centennials.

Hungarians in the Mines

Julia Puskás

In her seminal study, *From Hungary to the United States* (Akadémiai Kiadó, Budapest, 1982), Julianna Puskás, a noted Hungarian sociologist, gives a memorable description of the conditions in the mining area of the United States as they existed in the last quarter of the nineteenth century (pp. 74-80):

The types of job at which the new immigrants could work, especially those from Hungary, were always the most dangerous in every industrial state. It is well known that the mining and the metal industries take the greatest number of victims. The basically dangerous work areas became doubly so for the immigrants. They did not speak the language, so did not understand verbal warnings, while posted notices about danger meant nothing to them. These factors were partly responsible for the shockingly frequent industrial accidents; the other was the system of industrial organization in the United States.

Factories, work places, and labor safety regulations made no provision for the immigrant's ignorance of the dangers of the new environment, and paid no heed to his requiring increased protection and safer working conditions. In fact, employers often did not observe even those labor safety regulations which were prescribed by law. Compensation laws in case of accident were built on the theory of individual responsibility, and common law held only its direct contriver responsible for the accident. Even in states where the provisions of the common law with reference to industrial accidents had been modified, only general compensation was provided for: the worker had the right to sue, that is, to try to get compensation through the courts. But this method of getting redress was rarely used by the immigrants, who did not speak the language and were on unfamiliar ground. At any rate, the courts that heard the evidence on mine explosions that had caused mass accident or death rarely held the mine owners responsible. The accident-compensation law of

Pennsylvania—where the Magyars worked in the largest numbers—did not cover the worker's family, left without its breadwinner, in Hungary.

It is yet to be ascertained what percentage of the Hungarian immigrants lost their lives, or were crippled or maimed simply because they were unorganized Eastern Europeans with whom neither their employers—greedily getting richer—nor the organized American workers felt a sense of community. The accident rate was inordinately high among the immigrants: for example, in the Carnegie South Works of Pittsburgh, 25 per cent of the new immigrants suffered injuries or were killed every year between 1907 and 1910. From 1904 on, the almanac of the Hungarian-American newspaper, *Szabadság*, always had a chapter headed "Fatal accidents" and "Mine disasters." The following summary is based on newspaper reports of some of the catastrophes. "A terrible mine accident took place on the morning of January 25 (1904) in the Harwick coal mine of the Allegheny Coal Company, in Cheswick, 15 miles from Pittsburgh. . . . Shortly after 187 men went down into the mine to work, the pit gas exploded; all of them suffocated." An investigation found that no one was responsible. "It seems that these investigations in America are just like the ones at home," commented the newspaper. Then it continues: "The terrible catastrophe at Cheswick is the darkest page of Hungarian-American history. More than fifty men met their death in the mine, not including their Slovak compatriots, who were, however, much fewer in number. Only a very few of these workers, who died such a dreadful death, had life insurance, so that the widows and orphans, in addition to their irreplaceable loss, are facing a very uncertain future. . . . They buried the dead in a common grave, dug next to the mine. . . ."

In the *Szabadság Naptár* of 1908, we can read: "The past year holds extremely woeful memories for Hungarian-Americans. Great is the number of those valiant Magyars who fell on the battlefield of labor, who were killed by the mine, were crushed by rocks, torn to pieces by machines, and burned to death by molten steel. How often the mailman brought the sad letter with the news that, in one place or another, Hungarians are being destroyed. The mournful list will have no end. Labor is taking its toll by the hundreds, and we stand before the burned and mutilated corpses terrified by the knowledge of our utter helplessness."

The *Népszava* writes: "At the end of the year, just before the season of joy, two indescribably awful mine catastrophes destroyed many fine Hungarian miners. Twenty-four Magyar miners fell victim to the mine explosions in Arnold City, and almost a hundred Slovak miners from Hungary, and a lot of Magyar miners, fell victim to the mine catastrophe at Monongahela." There was an explosion in the Dare shaft of the United Coal Company of Pittsburgh in which supposedly 400 Hungarians (i.e., men from Hungary) lost their lives.

The registers of the Hungarian-American churches also contain shocking data about mass mine accidents, and about the victims of mine explosions and industrial accidents. For example, a Calvinist minister from around Pittsburgh, in Homestead, put down in his church register the ages of those buried and the causes of death. Between 1903 and 1914 the most frequent causes of death were "mine explosion," "deadly contusion," "burns," "hit by train," "typhoid," "dysentery." The majority of victims were young men.

Among the immigrants from Hungary it was especially the mine that became a concept associated with fear and horror. Most of the accidents happened in the mines. "The mine killed him," said the old Hungarian-Americans with the same resignation as if they had been speaking of a bloodthirsty monster, against whom man would struggle in vain. The weight of these experiences in the mines is indicated by their incorporation into songs originating in the old country, and by their becoming the main theme of the evolving American working-class poetry and literature.

It is worth while quoting at length from contemporary reports based on the information collected in 1890 by a United States Department of Labor commission on the life style of Slovaks and Magyars in 16 iron and steel factories of the state of Pennsylvania: "The workers employed here are almost all Hungarians, and the majority of the married ones left their families in Europe. They are unassuming. They generally keep 40 dollars in ready cash on themselves for times of sickness or other unexpected occurrences. They send their savings back to their families regularly. They resolve their lodging collectively: 20-45 men find a suitable house together and elect a *burdos gazda* (usually a man with a wife). His jos is to get provisions, pay the rent, and keep the accounts. At the end of each month all members of the group pay their part of the total expenses, plus 1.5 or 2 dollars for the wife of the *burdos gazda*, who cooks and cleans. Beside this, they pay 50 cents to the *gazda* if he spends all his time taking care of the business of the collective; but if he is a worker who lives on his wages, then he too is a member of the collective and pays his part of the common expenses. The aim is not to exceed 9 dollars a month as the total expense for food and lodging per capita, and if, at the end of the month, they find that they have overstepped this sum, they have a meeting and cut the food, in order to reduce expenses. Everyone provides his own bedding. The furniture is poor, consisting of home-made tables, benches instead of chairs, and beds fabricated out of old boards, and the only well-equipped piece of furnishing in the entire house is the stove they cook on. The houses are chock full: those working the night shift alternate in using the same rooms with those working the day shift; 4-10 men sleep in a room. Once a month, on pay day, they collectively buy a barrel of beer for 3 dollars, if there are 20 of them to do so, and drink it up together. But if there are fewer than 20 men, then they do not buy together, because then the expense for each is too much. They usually have one decent suit besides their work clothes; each spends an average of 18 dollars on clothes annually."

Married women had a harder time getting factory jobs, especially in small mining camps where work opportunities for women were few. Most of them undertook to keep house for the *burdosok* (boarders). The employment of married women in industry in the United States was minimal, 3 per cent according to the 1900 census. There are no statistical data on the employment of the Magyar women, but from numerous contemporary sources it appears that a significant number of the married women at this time worked as a *burdos asszony*. They had no easy time of it. They washed and ironed the clothes and underwear of 10-15 men, which, without a washing machine, was in itself no easy task. They cleaned the rooms and cooked for the men, even filling individual orders on demand. The common meals were called *compánia koszt* (company food) and were paid for collectively by the boarders. The *burdos asszony* prepared the food packages for the men working on the different shifts. They kept the "company books" and handled the money the men left with them rather than put in a bank. The women's job was to carry water, to prepare the baths, and in some places, when the men returned pitch-black from work, even to scrub their backs with the barrels full of hot water that they prepared for them.

That the wife of the *burdos gazda* lived together in the same household with a group of lonely young men, far away from home, loosened the strict norms of matrimonial fidelity that obtained in the old country. At times, jealousy, fights, family dramas, gave rise sometimes even to murder or suicide. As a Magyar immigrant who lived through those times observed, "The roots of all the murders that took place among the Magyars, and there were quite a few, were always in the *burdos* houses."

The boarding-house system had a number of variations and was most wide spread in the state of Pennsylvania. The most uncongenial types were those outside the cities, in factory or mining camps, in settlements generally consisting of only 100 to 200 houses; here, the boarding house was usually company property. In some places, the company compelled the married workers to keep *burdos* houses by way of payment to the company for their own housing. At industrial and mining camps the stores were owned by the company, and the workers had to shop there. They received so-called "company books" for keeping account of the goods purchased; the total cost was deducted from their pay at the end of the month. This system of credit raised prices and was a form of the workers' exploitation, for company stores, having no competition, sold poorer quality products at higher prices.

Such were the economic and social conditions amid which the first Hungarian mutual-aid and sick-benefit organizations were established in the United States almost one hundred years ago.

One of the most important among them, and even today the largest, was the Verhovay Association (today known as the William Penn Association).

Mass burial of Hungarian miners killed in the 1924 mine catastrophe at Benwood, W. Va. 124 miners perished in that tragedy. The person marked with an X on the picture is Janos Lekai-Lassen, editor of our newspaper.

How and Why the Verhovay Association Was Founded

In a touchingly sentimental poem written by the Hungarian journalist Árpád Tarnóczy for the fiftieth anniversary album of the Verhovay Fraternal Insurance Association (now the William Penn Association), the Hungarian miners in America's anthracite coal fields are referred to as "diamond rollers" (Gyémántgörgetök). Maurus Jókai, the great Hungarian writer, titled one of his novels dealing with the life story of a coal baron *Black Diamonds*.

In a sense, Tarnóczy's term is correct. Hungarian coal miners cut and blasted, rolled and pulled up from the bowels of the earth measureless wealth—the equivalent of heaps of diamonds—for the owners of the mines.

"The capitalist, the man of enterprise and the adventurer," says F. P. Dewees in his book *The Molly Maguires*,

rushed pell-mell to a mountain region heretofore offering but small inducement to the emigrants, all hoping to realize sudden fortune from a newly discovered source of wealth. Flourishing towns sprang into existence as if by magic, speculation ran wild, fortunes have been made in a day and all the influences affecting a mining region at fever heat were here in full being.

Those who could not afford to speculate, however, who just worked in the mines, rolled something else for themselves: "The miner," writes Saul Alinsky in his biography of John L. Lewis, "knows that he digs death as well as coal and the death tonnage is appalling. From 1910 to 1945, 68,842 miners were killed and 2,275,000 injured." This represented a carnage greater than the losses of American soldiers suffered in World War I. And this does not include the terrible toll of the black lung disease which affected hundreds of thousands of miners, terminating their lives much too soon.

Among the victims a disproportionately large number were Hungarians.

143

The Founders

Many Hungarians worked in the coal fields around Hazleton, Pennsylvania. A large group of them had boarded in the house of a greedy and brutal woman. The moment one of her boarders became sick or temporarily disabled and could not pay on time, she mercilessly had him evicted.

According to tradition, the following incident took place in February 1886: Mihály Pálinkás, a young Hungarian miner, was coming home from his shift in the mine when, to his deep anguish, he noted an older fellow Hungarian miner out in the yard of the house in a rain-soaked, unkempt bed. The man was coughing heavily. The woman had put him out, together with his bed. It was a dreary cold February day, and it was raining.

Pálinkás was outraged. He took the sick, elderly man into his room and immediately went around the boarding house calling his friends to his room.

"Men, we have to do something," he said to them. "We can't permit such a situation to happen, that when one of us gets sick he should be thrown out, like a dog. Let us establish a sick-benefit fund. Nobody misses very much a few dimes or quarters when we work. Put together, a fund will enable us to help each other when we get sick and can't work." The men agreed and a few days later they held a regular meeting at which some twenty-one Hungarian miners showed up.

It is revealing of the atmosphere of those days that not all of the twenty-one miners dared to participate even in such a purely beneficial activity. Only thirteen of them signed the petition to establish a sick-benefit organization. We offer the names of these thirteen with a great sense of reverence: István Arnóczky, Joseph Debrössy, János Eckbauer, Mátyás Galatha, József Hornyák, Károly Juhász, Ferenc Kriszt, György Mikó, István Mészros, Mihály Pálinkás, András Ráshi, András Spisák and József Ujlár.

Mihály Pálinkás was elected first president of the organization. In 1955 the name of the organization was changed from Verhovay to the William Penn Association. At present it is the largest such organization in the Hungarian community in the United States, with more than sixty thousand members.

The "Subversive"
Sándor Rákosi

"**I** only stopped working, because—and you must understand this—my lungs could not take it any longer. I had to stop every twenty minutes to catch my breath. But even on the last day I spent in the mine, I loaded as much as I did fifteen years ago. But I felt already that my lungs couldn't take it. This is how I went into retirement in my sixty-ninth year." He stuffed his pipe, carefully watching every grain of tobacco. "I brought up decently eleven children. With the work of my two hands. Next year it will be fifty years since I came to America. I worked forty-five years below the ground, in the mines."

Well, you certainly dug a lot of coal in nearly half a century, I said, more to reassure him that I was listening to his words.

"A lot of coal? Well, if you piled it up into a heap, it would, perhaps, match the Empire State Building. True, I have never seen it in its reality, but one of my daughters, who is married in New York, sent me a picture postcard, showing that famous New York building." He drew on his pipe, but did not let the smoke out easily. He turned it around in his mouth, tasted it, and only then let it out. "Yes, I, by myself, with my two hands and a 'shufly' and pickaxe, I too have built an Empire State Building out of coal!"

He was very proud of this comparison, and that he brought up eleven children decently—and that three of his sons had fought against fascism in the war. But he was also very proud that all his life he had been a union man. He was injured three times in the mines. Once he was almost crushed by a rock; another time his left leg was maimed; and the last time some of his ribs were broken. And yet it was not these accidents that had broken him. It was the bad mine air, the pit gas that had destroyed his system.

Why am I writing all this?

It was at one of the meetings of *Testvériség* (brotherhood) that this Hungarian-American miner had pulled me aside: "Tell me, brother, was he thinking of me too, when Secretary Clark of the Justice Department was placing our organization on the list of subversives?" He smiled coyly, and said that upon the urging of his children he had applied for citizenship, after living nearly half a century in America. "If there were enough room on the application form, I would have written there in large letters that I am a union member, and that my insurance company is the IWO. There was not much room, so I wrote it in only small letters. For I am really proud of this organization, and of what they have done for me and my family; I feel I will never be able to thank them enough. Now I am really curious. Will they say in Washington that I do not deserve to be a citizen? I am really curious," he repeated. "I always thought, and told my children, that I worked honestly for my citizenship. I felt myself a citizen already when I loaded my first ton of coal. That was my real first application. And since then, since the first ton of coal, I gave my youth, my power, my health to the building of America. Perhaps I should have written this too in my application," he said, turning his pipe between his teeth.

1950

Sándor Rákosi has been connected with our newspaper as editor and correspondent for more than 50 years.

The Tower Warden
Looks Back

Articles, Letters & Editorials from the pages of our press

The Tower Warden Looks Back

György Bálint

MEPHISTO *(ad spectatores):*
    Here, too, occurs what long occurred:
LYNCEUS THE TOWER WARDEN *(singing on the watch
   tower of the castle):*
        To see I was born,
        To look is my call,
        To the tower sworn,
        I delight in all.

Goethe: Faust

Yesterday I leafed through a German edition of Goethe's *Faust*. I happened to open the book at Act V, Second Part, the act which I believe is the crowning glory not only of *Faust* but of Goethe's entire work:

> Auch hier gescheht,
> was längst geschah. . . .

I read Mephisto's declaration on the top of the page. It reassures us: there is really nothing new under the sun.

Then the scene changes and Lynceus appears, the watchman in his post in the watchtower. He meditates under the starry sky and then begins to sing:

> Zum sehen geboren
> zum schauen bestellt,
> Dem Thurme geschworen,
> Gefällt mir die Welt. . . .

said the watchman in the night, in the Faustian and European night of Goethe's time. He was born to see, he was ordained to observe, he swore fealty to the tower, and at the end he found the world beautiful as he glanced back at the past.

Today, the watchman in Europe's towers can await the night at their posts of differing heights with similar emotions. He who was born to see, he who was ordained to observe and who swore fealty to his post cannot complain. The world, indeed, was beautiful, with all its crises, with all its horrors. It was beautiful in the lofty, watchtower-lofty meaning of the word. For in this sense beautiful is everything that is real, that is living, that is moving and is observable. The rich order and rich disorder of life, the myriad faces of reality, the incredibly manifold possibilities of joy and suffering: all this is beautiful when viewed from the tower. Of course, no one is so fortunate as Lynceus, the watchman, for no one can view the world always from a tower. But even if we are experiencing great turmoil, even if we seemingly get lost in the vortex of life, at the bottom of our soul we must protect our own special tower and occasionally find the great moments, the bird's eye view of life.

This is especially true for those who were "born to see, ordained to observe" and who are tied by their oath to the tower. And if we succeed in remaining faithful to our pledge then, indeed, everything is beautiful.

Whatever we saw, whatever we participated in, was beautiful. The whole world was beautiful: the painting of Giotto in Santa Croce in Florence; the song of the people of Marseilles on July 14; the silent rocks of the Hardanger fjord on light-gray summer nights; the noisy palaver of Spanish working women in the groceries of Barcelona and Valencia; the sterile cleanliness of Hamburg's streets; the swirling filth in Patras. The walk in the mountains of Buda; the cares and worries in the apartments of Pest; the voice of Moissi on the stage, meditating on a sonnet, becoming outraged over injustice. Daydreaming in a London pub with a glass of wine amid dockworkers; walking with Hungarian peasants on a highway and sharing a pail of water with them; observing exotic ducks in the lake of St. James Park, concentrating on political news, sitting with someone on a parkbench, or standing guard, lonesome, in the autumn rain. All these were beautiful, just as the crisis and the turmoil we witnessed were beautiful. And beautiful were the tragedies we viewed on the stage and in the parliaments. The libraries and the factories, the murals in the galleries and the placards on the kiosks were all beautiful. Everything was magnificent, for everything was alive and we saw everything, because we were simultaneously down among the multitudes and up above in the watchtower, and we reported everything. The whole world was beautiful. Let us not regret anything. It is still nice that we can take Goethe and the other classics in our hands. The great texts are still within our reach. Let us not regret anything that happened up till now, and let us not regret what is still to come.

Perhaps we shall no longer have towers, but what we have already seen cannot be torn from our consciousness.

This essay was written by the author, an outstanding Hungarian journalist, in 1939, on the eve of World War II and of the Holocaust. Three years later he perished in the Ukraine as a member of a labor batallion. – Editor

Excerpts from the writings of Rev. L. A. Gross

The overdue second front

The victory is still far off, but the first step toward victory is now only a question of days. The first United Nations soldier who sets foot on the soil of Europe will carry in his knapsack the death verdict of the Hitler crime syndicate. And there will be no appeal from this verdict.

1943

A national organization, uniting all democratic Hungarians, should be formed . . . This organization should seek contact with the underground movement in Hungary, giving them all possible material and moral support. Intense effort should be made to convince the United Nations of the fact that the Hungarian people were not asked for their consent to enter the war on Hitler's side, that they are innocent of the war crimes of their rulers and therefore deserve just treatment at the peace conference.

1943

Today and tomorrow

Some of our leading statesmen still have the illusion that the main objective of the war is the defeat and destruction of fascism. What a mistake! The defeat of fascism is simply the means for the accomplishment of a better international order . . .

When an old, decrepit building ceases to serve the purpose it was built for it wouldn't do to use new material to patch it up. As the Master said:

"No man also seweth a piece of new cloth on an old garment: else the new piece that filled it up taketh away from the old, and the rent is made worse. And no man putteth new wine into old bottles: else the new wine doth burst the bottles, and the wine is spilled, and the bottles will be marred" (Mark II, 21-22). The awakening peoples of the world want to build a new and better house

1945

On the Hungarian Constitution

I was asked by the Secretary General of the World Federation of Hungarians Joseph Balogh to state my view of the new Hungarian Constitution. And they asked me what other churchmen think about it.

I can't say that I specifically know the views of many Hungarian clergymen in the United States. Judging by their statements in some Hungarian newspapers I would say that they have condemned the Constitution without really knowing its substance, because, after all, anything that has been created by "godless, atheistic communism" must be evil. With a few praiseworthy exceptions their thinking is similar to that of Nathanael who, when told by Pplip that they have found the Messiah in the person of Jesus, said, "Can there be any good come out of Nazareth?" Whereupon Philip saith to him: "Come and see" (John 1, 46-47). To the doubter, therefore, I say in the spirit of Philip: Come to Hungary . . . and see!

1949

"He that is not against us . . ."

What attitude should a minister, a disciple of Christ assume in reference to the Soviet Union or the peoples' democracies? It wouldn't take too much effort to find the answer directly from the mouth of Jesus . . . Here is a dialogue in Luke, 49-50: "Master (said John) we saw one casting out devils in thy name; and we forbade him, because he followeth not with us. And Jesus said unto him, Forbid him not: for he that is not against us is for us.'

The "devilcaster" obviously must have done some beneficial act because in those days all evil, all sickness, was ascribed to the work of the devil. But the overenthusiastic John did not consider the fact that man may have performed a useful act. All he thought of was that the man was not one of Jesus' followers, so he was a competitor. But Jesus had a different idea. He made John understand that no one has a monopoly for doing the right thing.

Today the socialist states are also driving out devils: they are driving out poverty, ignorance, superstition and are creating conditions which provide culture, knowledge, health and prosperity for all people. Who has the right today to oppose them just because they followeth not with us?"

1952

About János Kádár

I am quoting from one of my columns that I wrote not long after the catastrophe of 1956 in Hungary:

"It is hard for us to comprehend what almost superhuman task has been given to János Kádár. What tremendous self-sacrifice and courage was needed to undertake the governing of Hungary at that particular moment in history. He had to soothe millions of agitated souls and inspire them to perform the colossal task of again rebuilding a ruined country. He had to provide food for millions amidst a paralyzed economy and agriculture. What strength of character, determination and vigilance was needed to carry out a mission of this magnitude!

"If he would prove to be weak, the tide of history would sweep him away and with him the prospects of a decent future of that much suffering nation. If he appeared to be too forceful he would have been called a brutal tyrant and an executioner. If he would have moved too cautiously he would have been branded a weakling and may not have been able to lead the country.

"Judging by what has already occurred Kádár has proved himself equal to the unprecedented task given to him."

Today, after six agonizing years, as we view the economic, political and ideological panorama of our native land, we can state with profound gratitude that János Kádár fulfilled the confidence advanced to him, that he successfully wrestled with the myriad tasks, acting with cool head but with warm heart. . . . The structure of democracy is so strong now in Hungary that its government decided in a very generous gesture to grant amnesty to those responsible for the tragedy of 1956. This step deserves as much credit as any of the great accomplishments of the past six years.

1963

Thou shalt not go unpunished

"For thus saith the Lord; Behold, they whose judgment was not to drink of the cup have assuredly drunken; and art thou he that shall altogether go unpunished? Thou shalt not go unpunished, but thou shalt surely drink of it . . . For, lo, I will make thee small among the heathen, and despised among men. Thy terribleness hath deceived thee, and the pride of thine heart, O thou that dwellest in the clefts of the rock that holdest the height of the hill: though thou shouldest make thy nest as high as the eagle, I will bring thee down from thence, saith the Lord."

I won't even try to describe that spiritual crisis that moves me—a modest sharer and preacher of Christ's faith and hope—to use the somber lugubrious words of Jeremiah, the prophet of mourning and melancholy, for the text of my Christmas message—instead of using the relevant joyous, uplifting words of the Gospels.

May the Lord forgive me, but instead of the fragrance of the three wise men's incense and myrrh, instead of the fragrance of myriads of Christmas trees, I smell the stench of thousands of corpses lying around in the fields and villages of Vietnam.

Instead of the song of heavenly Choir, I hear the heartrending, pitiful cries of Vietnamese men, women and children agonizing under the exploding bombs rained on them by our air force.

I cannot see the light of the star of Bethlehem for my eyes have been blinded by the flames of napalm bombs pouring upon the innocent people of that distant land.

Forgive me my Lord, I cannot jubilate this Christmas.

1966

Thoughts About Our Paper

If we did not have a newspaper like the *Magyar Szó*, I would wander through the length and width of this great land of ours like a mendicant friar visiting all Hungarian colonies. I would knock at every door asking or begging money to establish a paper like this.

Fortunately, we have a paper. We are not confronted with the terribly difficult task of starting one. We have one, but it will exist only as long as we give it our unstinting support. It is my profound conviction that the progressive Hungarian American community simply could not exist without a paper like the *Magyar Szó*.

1953

When I was an active minister of the Gospel I had many opportunities to witness the generosity of churchgoing people. But I can state with my hand on my heart that I have never, never witnessed the boundless self-sacrifice displayed by the readers of the *Magyar Szó* towards their paper.

In saying this I do not want to belittle the generosity of the faithful; I want to extol that of the rank and file soldiers of our press: our readers.

1962

It is my firm conviction that our paper, this journalistic oil lamp, that has spread light among Hungarian Americans for almost 65 years now, will continue to radiate light and enlightenment for many more years, illuminating the path toward a finer, better society.

Those whose path was lit by this little lamp should consider it their sacred obligation to keep the flame burning so that it can serve the generations of Hungarian Americans that will follow us.

1965

Rev. L.A. Gross, a devoted and dedicated friend of our paper, contributed brilliant columns to it for more than 30 years.

On All Souls' Day, 1915

Ferenc Molnár

Tonight's illumination is not intended for our victoriously advancing troops; this illumination honors the motionless regiments and the silenced trumpets. On this All Souls' Day of the year of the dead, let our eyes, accustomed to watching marching troops and feeling rapture at the sight of galloping cavalry, abandon for a moment the exciting picture of the war: this is the day of the halted quick. This is the evening of the hussar, prostrate on the ground; of the gunner over his cannon; of the stiff footsoldier clutching the clay of his trench. Today is the day of the little wooden crosses and the large crosses, with the markers: "Here rest Hungarian Soldiers." Today is the night of the "Unknown Honvéd [Guardsman]" sleeping lonely in the dark soil of Galicia; today is the day of so many "Hungarian Soldiers" and "Guardsmen" that if a candle were lit on the grave of each one of them, our globe would be more beautiful than the star-studded sky.

* * * *

The true music of Death sounded this year, not the one mankind has declared to be the funeral song. This was his song: the *hurrah* stuck in the throat, the short rattle and the suddenly silenced curse. His true verses were heard, instead of the psalms: the wail broken in half, the echoless cry for help.

* * * *

All Souls' Day—the second already during this war—and how much we have to peel off our brains in order to understand in its real, in its old sense what it means for a young, healthy man to die. We are so dazed by the stupendous first moment that it is true agony to free our minds and to try to contemplate, with that good old sober brain, the grave of only one single soldier. How many official bulletins, how many newspaper strategies, how many false concepts must we cleanse from our brain, how many widespread and approved phrases of complacency, such as: "minor losses," "heavy casualties," "bloody battle," "strong resistance" do we have to dissect and analyze, explain to ourselves, until we return to that state of mind which was still

154

commonplace in the summer of 1914, which perceived clearly the horror of just one person's innocent and too-early death?

On All Souls' Day everyone ought to shake himself, to loosen all the sedimented narcotics in his mind, the many expressions like "forward movement," "action," "landing operations," "countermeasure," "reinforcement," "pincer movement" and all that heavy, mind-boggling muck, to stir and break it up into fine grains, to reveal it in its true form, in the true form that we would have seen it in 1914: in the tortured deaths of innocent men, the men submerging in struggle with the stream, screaming men with sharp bits of steel fragments in their groins. So that, from these military phrases injected into us, a new vision might arise: A Hungarian clerk suddenly recoiling from a sharp steel fragment in his temple (three lines in the obituary column, giving name, regimental number, military rank, the name of the Russian village, everything but the essential itself)—everyone must become free from these burdens, for otherwise he cannot, in his own soul, really light a candle for every fallen Hungarian soldier.

The day must come sometime, even in this world of drunken stupor, if only one day, when one locks the door upon himself, and with eyes shut, he contemplates, at last, his own naked bloody heart, the old one, the real one.

Christmas in the Camp

Sándor Ják

Soft snow blanketed the mountains, the trees, the blocks; a Christmas tree decorated the "Appelplatz" with gleaming colored bulbs on its branches.

The second day of Christmas.

We had macaroni for dinner on the holy evening, plenty of it, and tasty cake too, to round out a little our collapsed bellies. The SS guys and the KAPO's kept a human mask in front of their cruelties, or, perhaps, the Christmas spirit-created illusion exuded from them: for two days we are not working. For breakfast they served us sweetened tea and white bread; for lunch we filled our shrunken tummies with vegetables and a lot of meat. The easily gullible mumbled something like, even among killers there are some with better feelings.

Through the window I beheld the snow, the mountain, and my old life. Gerö, the math teacher, disturbed my meditation: you know, two or three years ago, I am not sure which, my younger son, Pete, wanted to surprise me for Christmas. My wife gave away the secret: he wanted to buy me a silver pencil that writes in three colors. Pete diligently nudged money from me, and I gave. At last my son and his mother . . . yes, my son and his mother . . . you know . . . my son . . . I know, brother, I know, your son Pete—and his mother . . . Yes, that is how it was . . . He did not even have to say it, it was in the eyes of the math teacher: "My son Pete and his mother." After a short silence I said: I traveled to my father-in-law last Christmas, with my Pirkó. The train was jammed, I was taking some wine and cigars for my father-in-law, some stockings for my sister-in-law, for the boys . . . Pain is pressing my chest, it chokes my breath, memories are battering my brain. . . .

This is terrible, this Christmas, the rest, this lugging of bricks, this tunnel digging does not hurt as much. . . . No, I must not think, when I suffer in work, at least I am not thinking.

Remember, Pirkó, my darling. . . .

Dark, black snow.

We are struggling in the pincer of our memories, we cannot free ourselves, and when, unexpectedly, they are calling us for a line-up, we are relieved. We go to stand in line, we will be cold, you cannot think there. But there are some who grumble: they said there wouldn't be any line-ups.

There are optimists who say they will now distribute the Red Cross packets that they have stolen from us till now. Dispute. At last, the majority believes this story of the packet distribution, and we are hurrying to the "line-up yard."

There stood the Christmas tree, the colored lights blinking among the branches, and ten yards beyond stood the gallows. No, this cannot be true.

This will be then the real grand-guignol, says someone near me. You do not really believe they will do hanging today. I am sure there will be some fool speechmaking, that we should make more of an effort, for it depends on us what we choose, peace or gallows, some real Hitlerian work propaganda, says Sándor Farkas in outrage.

We stand up in files. Between the posts the spectacle: the Christmas tree and the gallows.

Cheap gimmickry, I thought, and in very bad taste.

You can hang five persons on the gallows they set up. Until now it stood on the Hoffplatz, where they hanged men in secret. We did hear rumors that the new commander plans to hang people in public. Maybe that is what they want to announce.

We stopped guessing. The loudspeaker announced what numbers had been brought forward. These numbers were men. They called nine numbers, and now nine men stand between the gallows and the huge Christmas tree.

Then the loudspeaker started again. The new commander announces that he just wants verdicts and from now on he will ask us captives whether our "guilty" comrades deserve the gallows or not.

All of a sudden we notice that we are surrounded by guards with machine guns ready for action.

The Blockaltester announces that all we can say is *Jawohl.*

Then the commander asks us whether captive no. 45678 deserves hanging.

Jawohl.

And the grim procedure is repeated nine times. *Jawohl* and *Jawohl.* The "numbers" stand between the gallows and the Christmas tree. These "numbers" are men: fathers and sons, husbands and lovers. And we say *Jawohl.*

The whole thing is like a horror film. We stop thinking, we are not surprised anymore, and we know this is the way it has to be. *Jawohl!* The floor drops from under the feet of the first five. Now they hang from the hook with their tongues sticking out. *Jawohl.* They struggle a few minutes and then the camp doctor announces the death. The next four numbers follow. But no. One hook remains empty. To symbolize that there is always room for one more. If we don't behave.

Jawohl! we shouted, and with this the Christmas celebration has ended. This is what happened in the Don concentration camp near Nordhausen on Christmas Day 1943.

All around us snow has covered everything and up there in the high heavens dwelled God and "that child" for the joy of whose birth there stood that Christmas tree on the Appelplatz.

Jawohl!

Surviving the concentration camp, Sándor Ják was reunited with his wife, Pirkó. Together they returned to Hungary, where Ják joined the staff of the newspaper Budapest, writing occasionally for our paper, too.

John Reed's Farewell

Dr. Béla Pogány

An unusual encounter took place on a sunny fall afternoon in September of 1919 through a whim of chance, or perhaps by the fantastic logic of the forces that move the world. The path of the busy weekday work of the American-Hungarian workers' movement coincided for a moment with the path of one of the most phenomenal figures in America's — or, rather, the world's — labor movement.

The scene of this encounter was the Hungarian Workers' House, where the monthly meeting that night of the executive committee of the Hungarian section of the Socialist Party was in preparation. A Hungarian woman was busy in the room, when, unexpectedly, a man appeared before her: John Reed. He said he wanted to speak with her on a very important matter. We will describe this encounter.

John Reed! This legendary, remarkable man, this matchless figure of the American labor movement, came personally, on an "important matter," to the Hungarian workers. It is as if someone were to recall that Sándor Petőfi once asked him for a favor. It is not without reason that John Reed brings to my mind the figure of Petőfi. They both streaked through the sky like a comet with flaming temperament, so that, after a flashing, feverishly active life, they should offer their youth to their fate, but their names and their deeds shall continue to shine in immortality. Petőfi at twenty-six, Reed at thirty-three — just like Jesus — ended their unforgettable lives.

That ageless book, *Ten Days That Shook the World*, precisely and conscientiously recorded the history of the first days of the Russian Revolution. In a later edition of the work, Lenin himself wrote a foreword, after the Soviet leadership had officially recognized the extraordinary value of the book. Not many writers can lay claim to such recognition. Its author gained worldwide fame in days; the book was translated into many languages; many millions of copies were bought in the Soviet Union, following the wishes of Lenin, who wrote about it thus: "I recommend it without reservation. I would like to see it printed in millions of copies, and translated into all the languages of the world."

John Reed came from a well-to-do family in Portland, Oregon; he finished his studies at Harvard, then traveled widely in Europe. Two wild love affairs stormed through his life; he shaped them himself, not they him. With his awakened conscience he came into sharp conflict with his surroundings, with the world of the prosperous, whose empty and rigid customs he could not stomach. Perhaps even in his stormy youth, when he was thought to be a bon vivant, he was instinctively seeking the life which contains the true fullness of reality, the true freedom of man — at any rate, something other than what the rich call their own, with its false etiquette, barriers, and snobbery. Ignatius Loyola was a carousing officer in his youth, Saint Francis of Assisi was known as a young gallant in his town, and yet they became saints. The feverish youth of John Reed was itself a denial of the gentlemanly lifestyle, and when he got out into life, he did not want to bury himself in a "serious" occupation. His literary inclinations, his thirst for reality, steered him into the field of journalism — the more so because his writings were too advanced for the bourgeois press. His most serious and deeply felt writings appeared in *The Masses*. He fought the same hopeless battles against the bourgeois papers that during his college years he had waged against the conservative, well-off student clubs and the gentlemanly societies.

In 1913, at the age of twenty-three, he gained decisive success with his series of reports on the Paterson strike, and it was then that he discovered his true calling. In the same year the *New York World* sent him to Mexico to write about Pancho Villa's uprising. In the dispatches he sent, he was already on the side of the insurgents, yet the old-fashioned paper was compelled to publish his reports because, if nothing else, of his national fame. Upon his return, he was sent to the Ludlow, Colorado, miners' strike by the *Metropolitan Magazine*, of which he was already a long-time contributor. The Ludlow miners' strike became a turning point in his life. The state militia put the torch to the tent camp of the miners, who were striking for increased wages. The militia massacred two women and nine children. This brutal act brought the strike to the forefront of national attention. John Reed described the shocking picture of the burned camp; he conscientiously interviewed the strikers, the military officials, and the mining company. The facts showed clearly that this was a class war in open battle, caused by nothing else but the company's dirty thirst for profit and its ruthless exploitation of the workers. It became clear to John Reed that he belonged on the side of the workers. And if reality was his interest, he found rich material in the First World War, which erupted in 1914.

His earlier articles and impressions appeared in a book entitled *Insurgent Mexico*. As a war correspondent he went to Europe; he published his experiences in 1916 under the title *The War on the Eastern Front*. By this time he had gained deep insight into the heart of things; he saw that the European war had in it none of the youthful, inspired swing of the Mexican people's revolution, that the European war was but the quarrel of aged criminal interests; and he turned his attention toward the already brewing Russian Revolution. He went to Russia to get acquainted with the leaders of the political parties, and then, returning to America, began to organize progressive-minded workers.

As a representative of this group he attempted to travel to the Soviet Union, but by this time the American authorities looked at him with jaundiced eyes and denied him a passport. This did not deter him from leaving the country, however. He hired himself out as a boiler-stoker on a ship bound for the capital of Norway, Christiania [now Oslo — Ed.], but nobody knew this. It was on the day before the ship's departure that he visited the center of Hungarian workers, the Hungarian House.

The Hungarian woman John Reed spoke to was Emma G. Steiner, who was very much surprised when she was told that two men were looking for her. One of them she knew, the other was John Reed, whom she knew only from fame. She never guessed that the strapping, well-dressed young man with sparkling eyes, whose every movement betrayed the fascinating power of great men, was John Reed, who a year later would be dead, and who a few years later would receive the extraordinary honor of having his ashes buried in the wall of the Kremlin.

John Reed introduced himself and told her what he wanted. Emma Steiner in her memoirs tells the story:

> Reed told me that he had come because they were to have a conference with about twenty-five people, that night, and they could not find a proper room for the meeting. The only place that would be appropriate was the Hungarian House. He asked me, with emphasis, to attend to this immediately, so that they could have a room for this meeting, because he had to leave the country early in the morning; he could not say where to, but I knew. I went promptly to the president of the House, to ask him if there was an empty room. Of course, there wasn't any; every corner was booked. I thought of only one possibility — that is, to cancel tonight's meeting of the Hungarian committee of the Socialist Party, so Reed could have that room. After much scurrying and telephoning, using the excuse that I was sick and could not make a report tonight, I succeeded, and could happily report to the waiting Reed that it was all right, they could have Room No. 4.

Emma Steiner could not be present at the meeting. She does not even mention it. But unwittingly, the question comes into one's mind, what did happen behind the closed doors, of which nothing has ever leaked out to this very day? Who were those twenty-five trusted workers with whom Reed conferred, for the last time in America? Did he have any feeling that he would never again set foot on his native land, but instead, exhausted in mind and body, from overwork and illness, would depart from this earth on Soviet soil? What could he have said to those workers who came to meet with him, John Reed, who helped shape the fate of the American working class and the labor movement, who learned the reality of the class struggle not by reading Marx but by throwing himself body and soul into strikes, peoples' movements, wars? With visionary eyes, could he have glimpsed into the future of the American labor movement? Could he have imagined the tear-stained and blood-soaked road that the American working class would have to travel in its struggle against the world's greatest money oligarchy? Did he offer them his spiritual testament, or did he give them advice and direction in solving the pressing problems of the moment? Those who were there, did they listen to his words? Did it occur to them that this man was not born into a working-class family, but into a rich family, just like Marx, Engels, and Ferdinand Lassalle, who consciously broke with their class? Reed saw that the bourgeoisie would lead the world to a dead end, to morass and destruction, and he recognized that only the working class possessed the ideals of freedom, equality and true humanism—that the working class would be the standard bearer of mankind's development.

They Deported My Mother

Béla Székely

It was about two months ago that they dragged my mother from her apartment, shoved her into a cattle car, and started off toward an unknown Polish railway station—into the death chamber of one of the concentration camps. That is what was in the notice I received from my kid brother. My mother lived in Dés (Transylvania), where she was born, in that little town which got its name from the Latin word for God—"Deus"—and which was forsaken by every God. She was born there—my great-great grandfather's grave is there too—she lived there, she taught there in the middle school. I am trying to figure out how old she could be. Adding the tender years of her girlhood to my 52 years of drudging life, I am guessing she is 74, 75. She could be, if. . . I cannot finish the sentence, something got stuck in me, like a clock that suddenly stopped ticking.

So now they have dragged her away. There was no one to protect her. Dragged her away from her rooms, where every piece of furniture, curtain, carpet, clock, picture was from the time of my father, who passed away thirty years ago. Poor soul, she must have aged terribly during the past few years, but in my mind she lives, like the old picture I have; perhaps I would not have recognized her, she shriveled so much. Those who knew us say I inherited her eyes, and now that I keep thinking of her the last few days, I see with her eye view, as for the last time—yes, the last time—she strokes the old furniture, her old life. I am sure she stopped at the door—I too stumbled once at the threshold—perhaps they crudely shoved her, and thus made easier what is most difficult, to live one's death, the ultimate breaking away from that which, be it ever so difficult, ever so bitter, yet is real, is expectation, hope, freedom.

No, it is impossible to imagine what happened after that. They locked the door upon her lost life, the door of that small, peaceful, once-happy home. I can see her as she tripped across the rough pavement of the courtyard. She stepped out to the street and I lost her from my view, for she was no longer alone. The street that leads to the Synagogue, to the ancient reformed church, already held the sad shipment: old, bearded ancients, wigged women, the sick and the children. For those who had the strength, who could run, ran, escaped to the forest, hid where they were able to hide. They shoved my mother among these.

This is how I wrote it: every old woman in this motley group is my mother. But not only in this one. There were such groups in other streets, other cities, other countries.

Oh, but mine too, and yours too, you who are my brother, for among them is your mother too. And there is no God any more who could distinguish among them, those dragged away, locked in death cells. There is no God any more who could tell which is whose mother, there in Edom, who is whose son here in the land of escape.

There is no feeling of vengeance, nor hatred, that could be just mine alone. Common is our mourning and common is our hatred. Sweet is this hatred, and humane. Blessed and benevolent, for life is rising from it. A new life in which no one any longer makes distinctions between man and man, in which everyone's life is sacred and protected, no matter what color his skin or what the faith in his heart. Their lives, my mother's life, lost for this new world. The life of your beloved ones. Horrible is the sacrifice which they made for us. For this, let their memory be blessed forever.

1946

The Dead Are Warning

William Brandt

Nazism was more than simply mass murder. The Nazis, who, one after the other, are receiving forgiveness and pardon in the Western zones, have developed soul murder into a system. They have, in satanic fashion, already murdered the souls of those who could be forced to perform the task of killing their fellow prisoners, in return for "saving their lives" for awhile. The Nazis have taken away their humanity.

This nightmare cannot be chased away. We are here, we whose mothers, brothers, and children were killed in the death camps. We are here, and even if we know that it was mere chance that they and not us were driven into the gas chambers, we must know why we are here. Otherwise there is no meaning, no purpose, to our own lives. Otherwise we are the living dead. We must act so that by our actions we will help the liberated prevent a repetition of these horrors. The dead are commanding every living being to fulfill this sacred obligation.

1946

Two Soldiers
Florian Paczier

I am idling among the orange trees, when a car stops in front of me in the street. A man steps out, comes to me to inquire how he can buy a few acres of land, here in the vicinity of Elsinore, California. I tell him that I don't know anything about such things, but for him to go to a real estate agent. As we talk, both of us realize immediately that neither of us is a native American. He asks what nationality I am. I tell him that I am Hungarian. Upon hearing this he says he visited Hungary. He asks which region. I say, from Transylvania. He says he was there too. So I ask him what nationality he is. He says Italian. See now, and I traveled in Italy. When? he asks. So I say, in 1918-19. But there was war then, says he. Well, that is just why I was there. You were in that war? Which front? At the Piave, I say. Were you there in the battle in June? he asks. Yes, I said. Then I saw that he became very nervous, his cheeks goose-fleshy and his voice choky. At last he says: I was there too. His tears ran, he came over, hugged and kissed me. I returned this expression of friendliness to this sincere man and we pressed each other's hand for a long time, as if to say, how good that we did not meet at the Piave, with loaded guns in our hands, but here, in a peaceful time, when man's natural instincts rule over us. His name was Marion Penzin. We talked for a long time. He told me that the Italians knew of our plans, and so they emptied their first line of trenches, and we fired away at empty trenches. So I say, it was easy for you to know everything, when our Queen Zita was a cousin of your King Emmanuel. He says, they knew it for other reasons too. He also said that he was born in that region, on the other side of the Montello Mountain, and as a child he used to go to the Piave to bathe and to fish.

When we finished our conversation, we exchanged telephone numbers, and maintained our friendship. Soon after, he called me up to tell me the good news that he had bought a piece of land near Elsinore, and asked me to visit him. When I did, he showed me an album published by the Italian government commemorating the fiftieth anniversary of the battle of Piave. It is a handsome book, and it contains a map which the Italians used in that battle. It is a beautifully made book, full of pictures, among them that of the cavern where our company stayed for two months and where I was taken a prisoner. He said he would give me that book, but first he wanted to show it to a friend who was present.

I visited him once more, but by then he was in a very weakened condition. As I was leaving, he said, let me embrace you once more. And we embraced and kissed each other for the last time. About two weeks later I read in the paper that he had died. I went to his funeral. No one knew me except his wife. After the ceremony, she came over to me and introduced her son, who is a teacher here in Elsinore. We talked at length and he said that his mother wants to give me that album, because it most fittingly belongs to me. The son brought it to me, and inscribed the album thus:

TO FLORIAN PACZIER
a soldier in the battle of the Great War of 1914-18
from Mario Penzin (1893-1976),
also a soldier in this battle.
The politicians called them enemies,
but those who have been made to fight,
know otherwise.
  E. Penzin, son of Mario
  175th U.S Infantry (1944-1945)

Florian Paczier served in the Hungarian army in World War I. For the past 60 years he has been a dedicated builder and supporter of our newspaper.

Storm Clouds of the Revolution
An Editorial

Victor Hugo writes in one of his beautiful novels that when the judge sentenced Marat, the great leader of the French Revolution, and accused him of all the cruelties of a revolution, the dying Conventist replied: "A cloud formed a thousand and five hundred years ago. After fifteen centuries the cloud broke. And you accuse the lightning!"

The storm clouds of revolution gathered over the centuries out of the awful sufferings of the Russian people, until at last the storm broke loose, the lightning of the people's bitterness struck, destroyed and burned the system of class rule of the minority. If the millions of Russian workers, after centuries of knout-rule, extirpated by its roots the conquered ruling class, the tribunal of history would exonerate them, for we cannot accuse the lightning. Responsible for the reaping by the storm are those who sowed the wind.

1919

For Peace
An Editorial

On the traditional holiday of our country, on Memorial Day, the American people render homage to the memory of our nation's heroic dead. This year, the blood shed by America's sons, the indescribable devastation of a country and a people, and the agony of a world drifting toward an atomic war, provide the midnight framework to Memorial Day.

History, in its own good time, will render judgment as to who is responsible for the fact that six years after the greatest bloodletting of all time, mankind is once again drifting toward a new war. But we who are now living cannot wait until Judgment Day. To us is given the task, through our labors for peace, of making sense of the deaths of those millions and tens of millions who gave their lives in order to bring lasting peace to the world.

Only with this struggle can we sanctify their glorious memory; only thus can we fulfill our obligation to our country, to our people, and to mankind.

1951

In Defense of the Workers' Sick-Benefit Society

An Editorial

Why is our organization, the IWO-Hungarian Brotherhood, a thorn in the side of reaction? Ours is one of the soundest of the sick-benefit institutions in the land. The authorities have never found improprieties of any sort in our organization. We never begged for a loan from the Reconstruction Finance Corporation; we did not send mink coats to White House secretaries; we had no connections with Frank Costello, with Joe Adonis, or with any other underworld chieftains. We never bribed the police. We had no associations with the netherworld, nor with the other world, but only with our membership; we had only their interests at heart. And yet the authorities want to smash our organization, in which 160,000 American workers cooperate as brothers and sisters, side by side, regardless of religion, race, or political conviction.

Why? I will give you the answer. Because the members and officers of our organization, in overwhelming majority, raised their voices in favor of peace. Because we have never joined the camp of the warmongers. For this reason the reactionaries entered the swamps of the underworld, pulled from there several well-known plants and informers to use in an attempt to prove that we are subversives.

When Lajos Kossuth set foot in America in 1852, he said, in his first speech, on Staten Island: "There is no better proof of the justness of a cause than when its enemies bring out ridiculous objections to support their filthy interests."

1951

The Crime of Sacco and Vanzetti
An Editorial

Their crime is that they organized the workers against exploitation, for their defense, for strikes.

Their crime is that they sacrificed their lives to serve the interests of the working class.

Their crime is that they were true, and remained true, even shackled in their cells, to their class, the oppressed, the exploited working class, deprived of their rights.

Their crime is the same for which big business strung up on the gallows in Pennsylvania the first organizers of the miners; strung up on the gallows in Chicago the bravest leaders of the workers, after the Haymarket tragedy. In Colorado they kidnapped, in Idaho they jailed the officers of the Western Federation of Miners; they jailed the members of the I.W.W. in Centralia; they condemned and shot Joe Hill, lynched Frank Little; they have kept Tom Mooney in jail now for ten years; they butchered or jailed hundreds of the unnamed heroes of the labor movement.

1927

171

Support the Striking G.M. Workers

An Editorial

T he workers of General Motors are striking for their rights, for the well-being of their families, for greater security in the future: so that their jobs will be secure; so that they cannot be thrown out whenever the bosses at G.M. feel like it; so that their seniority rights will always be assured; so that piecework and speed-up will be abolished; so that G.M. will pay wages in accordance with working conditions and the cost of living, and will pay time-and-a-half for overtime. They are striking to secure a thirty-hour workweek, to enable more workers to be employed. To achieve their goals, to protect the workers, the United Auto Workers Union should be recognized as the sole representative of all G.M. workers.

Hungarian workers, citizens of Detroit! Don't let yourselves be misled by General Motors, nor by a section of the press. The Hungarian community, Hungarian associations, small homeowners, institutions, as well as people of other languages and nationalities, should as one line up behind the auto workers.

Every Hungarian worker in the auto industry should immediately join the union to assure the success of the strike.

Support the strike morally and materially, as individuals, associations, and institutions!

1937

For the Spanish People
An Editorial

With indescribable joy and enthusiasm we received your message, and forwarded it immediately to the entire Hungarian community in America—your message that you are beating fascism and that with your banner you are carrying to victory the cause of freedom and democracy in the whole world. Your report that the followers of progress— among them our Hungarian brothers, from here and all lands of Europe—are fighting shoulder to shoulder with you fills us with unlimited confidence in the invincible power of international solidarity, expressed in a great thought: "To win the war, to chase out the intruders, and to fight for a government of the Spanish people based on the ideal of freedom!"

Your struggle is our struggle too. Your struggle is also the struggle of our enchained brothers in Hungary, against oppression, fascism, and war; for peace, for the freedom of all other peoples.

1937

Israel and the New Golden Calf
Dr. Béla Pogány

The pages of the history of this freedom-loving people contain impressive chapters filled with the groans of the people, the curses of the peoples' prophets, the frightening picture of corruption from above, never-ending wars, limitless bloodletting, misery, regicides and strife, and especially the democratic demands of a restless and excitable people. The repeatedly trampled-upon Jewish masses were perhaps the first people in world history to have democratic strivings, and from their ardent aspirations was born that Christ whose moral concept had such dynamic effect upon the shaping of the world. Does the history of this people, with its great past, teach us the lesson that the tragedy so characteristic of its history will repeat itself — that is, that its leaders, once again, will betray them, as they have in the bloody storms of the past, and defraud their democratic strivings? Will the Israeli democracy, born at the critical period of imperialism, experience the same fate that was so often the lot of its ancestors? Will the people be corrupted by the new golden calf — imperialism?

1952

Ordeal of the Bier
András Bódog

In 1950, on the night of March 7-8, in a little New Mexico village with a tongue-twistingly long name that lies sixty miles from the famous Los Alamos atom plant, a tragedy occurred: a fire broke out in the jailhouse of the military experimental station, and fourteen imprisoned soldiers burned to death behind bars.

Let us examine closely what happened that night in the vicinity of Albuquerque, in the jail of the secret military experimental station of Sandia, sixty miles from the world's largest and most expensive industrial wonder, the Los Alamos atom-smashing plant. The jail was a barracks-like wooden structure along whose lengths rows of cells with heavy iron rails stood one after the other. In the cells were imprisoned soldiers. The nights are cruelly cold in that desert, and at both ends of the building an old-fashioned petroleum stove burned and spread its fumes. The generators of the Los Alamos atom plant consumed and produced millions of watts of electric power. The heat from the famous atom heap could warm a city of half a million, but that energy went to waste. That energy could have been used for a thousand and one things, but it remained wasted, for no one had the time to bother with such petty things. A whole new world could be created out of nothing in this place, but all its energies were concentrated on producing a bomb so perfect that an explosion could completely destroy half the world, while the other half would not be even slightly affected.

In light of all this, understandably, the barracks prison was heated not with atomic power but with old-fashioned oil stoves. "The building is safe," said the experts only a month before, and this was confirmed by the leadership in Washington. The leadership consisted of generals, and generals always know what they are talking about, even when they arrogantly assured us that according to God and the laws of physics, the atomic bomb can explode only in Moscow or Tobolsk but never in New York. And so the director of the jail either hid the keys or took them with him — we do not know — but when one

175

of the oil stoves exploded and the building started to burn, the unfortunate ones in the cells could not get out and they perished — they were roasted alive.

Who was at fault in this horrible disaster? If there was a mistake, who committed the error, and when, and where? Was it because we spend millions for destruction so fervently that we would not even consider putting the waste products to good use? So it is that in the shadow of the miracle of atomic energy they build wooden barracks, and the soldiers, who are learning how to handle weapons of destruction costing hundreds of millions, are kept warm by hundred-year-old stoves. Did the fault lie in the belief that we should change only death, but not life? Was it this kind of thinking that allowed the leadership to approve the wooden barracks and the oil stoves? And the director of the jail could not very well be blamed, because, after all, the experts and the leadership considered the building safe. If only the oil stove had also respected the rules of the military and the laws of physics, there would have been no trouble and no need to open the cells at night in an emergency. Hence, the fact that the director took the keys with him, maybe even slept with them, would not have mattered. It is clear as daylight.

Nevertheless, the oil stove did explode, the "fireproof" building did burn down, and fourteen unfortunate young soldiers met their deaths. Who was at fault? The military expert, who only failed to figure out how oil explodes and how wood burns, or the leadership, who only failed to figure out how many mistakes an expert can make? Are the fourteen unfortunate dead at fault, for being born human, for breaching discipline and winding up in jail, or is the oil stove at fault for daring to contradict the experts of the highest military rank? We do not know.

And who can say that they know the answer? Still, in the name of the fourteen human beings who suffocated and were burned alive, in my own name, in the name of my fellow human beings, in the name of the living and of the dead, in the name of 1,500 million humans, I speak to those concerned. Listen, you — experts, soldiers, big boys, powerful ones, lords of life and death, omniscients!

You are as sure of yourselves as the experts of that small military jail in Sandia, who could not predict the explosion of a measly little oil stove and its consequences. Sixty miles from the exploded stove, you are huddling and swirling around a somewhat larger stove. What you are concocting there and in other places is many millions of times larger and more vicious: atomic bombs, and what is even more vicious than bombs, the poison of arrogant thinking. You think that everything has been figured out. That is why you are playing with fire, with world catastrophe, wars, hydrogen bombs, and are shouting that all the results depend on you. Experts of the world! You forgot to take into account the explosion of a few drops of oil and you want to light the flame of world conflagration and keep it within bounds.

Powerful ones, soldiers, experts, diplomats — you are lying! The corpses of fourteen unfortunate ones burned to charcoal are testifying against you. Don't believe what these "experts" say — 1,500 million fellow human beings — don't believe them. If we become blind and believe what they say, we too can just as irrevocably and horribly burn and perish on the Earth, like those fourteen unfortunate young imprisoned soldiers, shut away in that "safe" prison in Sandia, while the experts and the director — the latter with the keys of the cells under his pillow — slept and dreamed the sweet dreams of the righteous.

András Bódog, attorney, friend and co-worker of the great Hungarian poet Attila József, was a devoted reader of and contributor to our newspaper.

People who love our paper. Members of the Los Angeles Hungarian Workers Club. Similar groups are existing in many other cities, such as New York, Miami, Fla., Detroit, Mich., Cleveland, Ohio.

Watergate

In its editorial of November 4th, demanding the resignation of the President, the *New York Times,* conveying the message of America's real rulers, the monopolists, the oil trusts, the armament makers, the great Wall Street banks, the steel and copper barons, told Nixon: "You have miserably failed in the task given to you, for the implementation of which we invested more than 150 million dollars in your election campaign. Your fumbling destroyed the people's trust in you and it is beginning to destroy the very basis of the capitalist system, so get out, resign!"

In this demand the entire nation concurs. As convincing and proper as the demand of the *Times* is, however, it is not complete. It fails to demand the impeachment and indictment of those who originated and developed Nixon's policies, his illegal plans for the subversion of the Constitution and the democratic system based on it, for the trampling of all legitimate interests of the people under foot.

Nixon did not operate in a vacuum. His policies evolved with the cooperation—the connivance—of the most influential circles of the Establishment. Much as he managed to line his own pockets through various transactions in connection with his San Clemente and Key Biscayne residences, tax evasions, and the like, the overwhelming beneficiaries of his policies of mischanneling the revenues of the government were the leading monopolies, the giant banks, the milk trust, the oil trust, the grain trust, firms like I.T.T., Lockheed, Boeing, etc.

This is the time to begin the long overdue investigation into the wholesale squandering of the national wealth of the American people and its relationship to the economic, social, and moral crisis affecting the entire nation.

All the tools for such an investigation are available to the people and to their elected representatives in Congress in the form of existing legislation (Sherman Antitrust Act), congressional committees (committee to investigate trusts and the multinational corporations), and executive apparatus (the antitrust division of the Justice Department).

Unless such an investigation is ordered immediately, unless the monopolists responsible for the corrupt, antidemocratic policies and practices of the Nixon Administration are called to reckoning, the grave problems of the nation cannot and will not be solved. They will, indeed, become infinitely more serious. For even if Nixon resigns, the moving forces behind him, the monopolists, will remain intact, and while the immediate threat to the constitutional system and to the freedom and safety of the nation may be temporarily averted, the relief will prove to be but transitory.

Can anyone imagine that the monopolists who financed Nixon's rise to power for the avowed purpose of emasculating the democratic system have undergone a change of heart? These powerful interests are too deeply mired in the crisis of their system, both domestically and internationally, to permit the full and effective functioning of the democratic process any longer. They will devise—perhaps they already have done so—new schemes to destroy democracy.

To accomplish the tasks outlined above, by compelling their representatives to launch such an investigation and to implement its results, the American people will have to go through the deepest soul-searching in our history. As the all-pervasive corruption, deceit, and treachery of the Nixon Administration emerge into full view, Americans must become aware of the process by which they were manipulated into voting for the perpetrators of this crime against the people. They will inevitably see the connection between the sacrificing of thousands of American lives in the Vietnam War, which was part and parcel of this deception, between the cold war ideology, the anti-Soviet propaganda, and their domestic counterparts—racism, suppression of dissent, the attempts to subvert their democracy and rob them of their freedom.

With a clear understanding of the nature of the crisis and of the forces responsible for it, with a relentless resolution to fundamentally cleanse not merely the temple of our government but the entire edifice of our democracy, the people of the United States will overcome the present crisis and will lay the foundation of a better future for themselves and for posterity.

1973

Prometheus of the Moneybags
Joseph Budish

In the *N.Y. Times* of June 12 economist Leonard Silk said that George Gilder's book, "Wealth and Poverty," has been "hailed by the President as a vital expression of his own philosophy" and by David Stockman, the budget director, as "Promethean in its intellectual power and insight." The intellectual level of this latter-day Prometheus is epitomized in the following quotation from Gilder's book: "A successful economy depends on the proliferation of the rich, on creating a large class of risk-taking men who are willing to shun the easy channels of a comfortable life in order to create new enterprise, win huge profits, and invest them again." Silk's own comment is: "The President's tax program would make these words into flesh."

There is no doubt that the Reagan crew will break its collective back for the "risk-taking men" of big capital, but winning "huge profits" is not exactly a new experience for the great interlocking blocks of financial-industrial monopoly. If we can raise our heads above the flood of verbiage coming out of Washington, we can take a quick look at the record.

In the five years from 1976 through 1980 all corporate profits, net after taxes, totalled just over 800 billion dollars, officially. This does not include $623.8 billion in "Capital Consumption Allowances." The 500 largest industrial corporations (not including banks or utilities like ATT or Con Edison, etc.) were about 23% of the roughly 220,000 corporations but made over 40% of the net profit for the five years, or $323 billion. This profit slice of the top 500 increased from 31% in 1976 to a hair under 50% of total corporate profits in 1980.

Rockefeller's Exxon deserves special mention. Exxon's net after taxes more than doubled, from $2,422,494,000 in 1977 to $5,650,000,000 in 1980, for an unbelievable total of $15,131,207,000 for the four years, a real hardship case that moved the soft-hearted Mr. Reagan to lift all controls on oil prices as soon as he took office.

As for the banks, they are not exactly in need of welfare. Net income after taxes of insured commercial banks in the U.S. went from $7,843,277,000 for 1976 to $12,838,487,000 for 1979 (the latest FDIC figure available), or a profit increase of 83% even before Reagan took office. Here also the biggest take the cream. In 1979 there were thirty-three banks, 0.233% of the 14,159 insured commercial banks, that had assets of over $5 billion. These thirty-three made $3,971,396,000, or 31% of the total net banking profit.

What good did all this flood of "huge profits" do you and me, the average citizen who works for a living? How much of these billions "trickled down" to us? Zilch. In fact, less than zero. The "trickle" went up, not down, and it was not such a "trickle."

Department of Labor "Spendable Average Weekly Earnings" for all private nonagricultural workers, in constant 1967 dollars (that is, adjusted for inflation) are (1) married worker with 3 dependents, $91.42 in 1976 and $83.56 in 1980, a drop of 8.5%, and (2) single worker with no dependents, $84.05 in 1976 and $76.45 in 1980, a drop of 9%.

Under Reagan policies, the contrast between rising profits and declining standard of living will certainly become sharper. No wonder that as Silk says, "On the whole, business is content. . . . They are happy to see a return of the biblical principle that rural America once expressed as 'Them what has, gits.' "

1981

Condemning the World's Children

The chief beneficiaries of UNICEF, Mr. George Rubin asserts in a letter to the *New York Times* (6/21/78), are the Palestinian Arabs, Vietnam and Cuba. UNICEF funds, he claims, helped many children grow up to be "Arab terrorists and Cuban soldiers." Implicit in Mr. Rubin's observation is the proposal to diminish or altogether abolish UNICEF. Let hundreds of millions of children continue to starve throughout the world and if, as a result of the proposed cutting off of UNICEF aid, additional hundreds of thousands of children will die, so be it.

The mentality that Mr. Rubin displays in his inhuman utterance is not altogether unknown in history. As recorded in Matthew 2:16, King Herod, fearing that one of the children of Bethlehem would grow up to be a contender for his throne, had all the children in and around Bethlehem under the age of two massacred. Mr. Rubin seems ready to doom children of all nations and all ages.

The story describes how the mothers of Bethlehem cried, fulfilling a prophecy that "In Rama was there a voice heard, lamentation and great mourning, Rachel weeping for her children."

Given present-day world conditions, the fate of our children, of all children, is in jeopardy. Millions of Rachels are crying throughout the world over their starving children. Do not help increase their grief, Mr. Rubin, by your heartless proposal.

1978

Letters to the Editor

The following letters are typical of the thousands we have received. These letters are unsolicited testimonials expressing the sentiments of the readers toward our newspaper.

Greetings to our beloved newspaper, which has sustained through all these years our faith in the real Hungarian Resurrection, in the coming victory of the people.

Glory to the people of the land of my birth, who are today realizing all the dreams which our ancestors dreamed amid immeasurable suffering. They are building today a nation in which all the power and all the wealth will belong to those who with their two strong arms and hands have created it.

Adam Hadnagy
Linden, New Jersey, 1951

Beloved Teacher:

I have been reading you, my beloved teacher, my newspaper *Magyar Szó*, since 1914, the year we first arrived in Bethlehem, Pennsylvania. Since that time it has been my lot to wander all over the United States, but you, my beloved teacher, have always been with me. Never give up, dear teacher! Keep teaching the people! With all the warmth of our hearts we wish you many, many years of success, our deepest gratitude to the board of editors, and greetings to all its readers.

Mr. and Mrs. Frank Tittelbach,
Bell, California, 1948

To the Editor:

I hope that this outstanding, truthful paper, every line of which I read with utmost appreciation, will live to the milestone of its ninetieth anniversary, for the joy of all of us, and especially for the generation coming after us.

Dr. L. B.
Denver, Colorado, 1982

Raised as a second generation American, imbued with a special pride of nation (both my father and brother served in the U.S. Army) another value was added when I married a native-born Hungarian. Until then I had not fully appreciated the richness of another heritage and its contribution to the best in American life.

Encounters with many people publishing this paper brought insight and helped focus it properly. Along with providing a true connection between the old and new world and its role in the building of America, came a better understanding of the ideas and people involved as anti-fascists in Horthy Hungary of World War II.

What bearing does this have today? American society is still grappling with its own concepts of democracy and needs all available reinforcement. In its outreach for standard-bearers who are still contributing to human freedom, this group of American-Hungarians, proud of their democratic heritage, must be included.

Lee Heimlich
New York, 1980

I am asking God's help so that we can enjoy for many more years this precious newspaper. May the blessings of God be upon you for many years.
Your sincere reader,

Freda H.
Florida, 1982

To the Editor:

I am sending my own and my neighbor's renewal subscription. I would like to do more for the paper but the trouble with my eyes keeps me from doing more. I have just passed my ninety-second birthday, have been a reader of the paper for sixty-eight years, and will stop reading it only when they nail the top of my coffin over me.

John Szabo
Trenton, New Jersey, 1982

To the Editor:

Like most of us I have to read the English newspapers for the latest news. But, when after reading them I take our paper in my hands, I feel like a weary traveler who finds cool spring water in an oasis. I am past sixty but I hope to live long enough to celebrate with you the hundredth anniversary of our newspaper.

E. R.
Los Angeles, 1982

A Greeting from Porcupine Plains

I wish a peaceful, happy new year for all those who read the Magyar Szó, Hungarian Word. Together with the editors, they carry the banner which many previous generations held aloft trying to make this world a better place for our children.

I myself fought for them in Spain. On August 24, 1937 I was wounded there; I told my comrade-at-arms, Joe Cserni: "Carry on Joe, for the death of one soldier the struggle cannot stop." I thought I was going to die. I didn't, but he did; two weeks later he received three gunshot wounds and died.

We live in an era of historical change and there is nothing nobler than to fight for the generations that are coming after us. Life belongs to those who live and the dead cannot help. Except through their example.

Forward, friends, for the defense of peace, for building a better future and . . . building our paper.

Dennis Kozma, Spanish Civil War veteran
1978

As Long as I Live . . .

My husband and I have been faithful readers of the Magyar Szó for sixty-four years. Following its teachings, he always did what he could for organizing his fellow workers. He lost his job many times when he was caught distributing leaflets. But all this has been forgotten. The young people are earning enough but for the old ones life is difficult.

I am sending my renewal for our paper, although I can't read it anymore. I can't see. But as long as I live I want to have it coming to my house.

Mrs. Jolan Blasko,
Palm City, Florida, 1980

Emma Kinces died at Frenchtown, N.J. on Jan. 30, 1981. She was 84 years old. Came to the United States around 1910, or 1912 to Bridgeport, Conn. Survivors are 3 daughters, 4 sons, 12 grandchildren, 14 great-grandchildren.

Mom Kinces was a very kind woman, many people ate in her home, there was always room to pay a friendly visit.

I first got to know my stepmom in Windber, Pa. in 1922 at the time of the coalminers' strike. Mom Kinces' was one of those families that were evicted during the strike. The family's furniture was ruined from living in a tent that the union supplied. The 1922 strike was a long one. Mom was a working-class woman until her last days. Always on the side of the union where workers were struggling.

Speaking for myself I am glad to tell people how many of these things rubbed off on me. One is what I learned from all the Hungarian coalminers, union miners that is. They would get together at our home, talk about struggle of the miners. One of the prize moments was to hear them say: you know how we never scabbed!

Much more could be written about Mom Kinces but this was the life of all workingclass miners' women.

A lot rubbed off from the "Uj Elöre" and now the Hungarian Word. Your paper is doing a fine job.

Thank you good people,

Frank Kinces,
Philadelphia, 1981

Elegy

Alas, fate compelled me to flee my native land. How I would have loved to stay home and live there. I always wanted to return but somehow things never worked out so that I could go back and live in a decent, humane society.

The better times for which I fought for thirty years are now unfolding in Hungary, and, alas   I still can't enjoy it. I have become old in America; I became a citizen, I brought up my children here, and now the poet's command is meant for me: ["You have to live and die here" part of the Hungarian National Anthem: "*Manifesto (Szózat)* by Vörösmarty—Ed.]

Imre Boron, Magyar Jövö, *March 15, 1945*

Our dear reader Imre Borona passed away on June 6, 1970.

The Tisza, most beloved river of the Hungarian people.

Hungary,
Oh Beloved Land!

Endre Ady, the greatest Hungarian poet of the 20th century.

A Message to Our American Brethren

My countrymen, you whom our common curse
has taken from us and dispersed afar
perhaps—too often in your thoughts we are.

But, oh, our Magyar life is overwhelmed,
and from the deluge they alone emerge
whom distant shores from present peril urge.

You far-off Magyars, how I envy you,
for from the very first here all was lost;
you, happy race, are far from ruin tossed.

Translated by Anton N. Nyerges

Endre Ady (1871-1919) was Hungary's greatest poet of the twentieth century.

Hungary Is Songs

Mrs. Zoltán Kodály

More than half a century ago, when the waves of emigration drove so many Hungarians to foreign shores, Zoltán Kodály also set out upon the path of the wanderer on a road of discovery, in search of Hungary.

The land he was searching for had no boundaries. It had no present; it had only a past and a future. It was a land truer than reality, a country ripened by history, one that can materialize only during the time that a song can be sung or a ballad can be recited.

The Hungarian people found its very soul in the Hungarian song, which is as old as the people itself. It found that reality which throbs in the rhythm of the shepherd's dance, in the mystic illuminations of ballads, or, transformed into lines and circles, emerges in the ornament of a peasant blouse.

The songs and ballads that have lifted their audiences for centuries into the ethereal regions of poetry have for a long time now been existing only in the strictly delineated and rapidly dissolving peasant life. Yet we sense the picture they transmit to us about the world to be as complete and as self-sufficient as the messages of modern poetry. We accept their human messages as valid for all of us.

At their birth, the comprehensive and expansive thrust of tradition was at work. The strict and mainly unwritten technical commands that unerringly defined the area of native creative genius removed from the folk songs everything that was casual, disposable, or valueless.

The fire of this living, traditional foundry is diminishing with the passing of peasant life. We must realize that once this fire goes out it will mean the cessation of the communal form of creativity which brought about the master-pieces of folk poetry. The fate of the treasures of Hungarian folk songs and folk ballads entrusted to us is our common responsibility.

The pearl taken out of its shell no longer develops. But it receives life, luminous rose-hued coloring from the wearer's body. The song and the ballad

190

similarly become alive when we read them, when we recite them, or, better yet, when we sing them. They become part of our daily lives.

That singing Hungary which Zoltán Kodály dreamed of more than half a century ago is now materializing.

We want all of these to whom, even in a strange land, the Hungarian song is the message of the mother tongue, to sing with us.

A 1946 photograph of Zoltan Kodaly with the great composer's dedication to the photographer, Gabor Hackett.

Once I Rang the Church Bells
Tibor Bálint

When I close my eyes and think of the place of my birth, the suburbs and the downtown streets, of the Házsongárd and of the Hostat quarters, of the Irisz settlement and Csillaghegy, of Calvary Church and the Garden of the Prisoners, tender scenes flow before my eyes, as in a spring twilight dream, and at such times I realize how many things I remember. I feel that my breath smells of milk, that my ribs almost crackle from the fresh air, and that each grain of sand separately tickles my soles, hardly accustomed yet to walking, while I descend into the bed of some semidark brook, among the leaves of the huge, green burdocks, from which the cool smell of mud oozes up and a purple-colored pot is hiding behind the mysterious elder bush on the shore.

My native land is a tub, floating on the water of the mill brook, shaded by the elders; it is also the happy intuition that after many unknown turns and passings under many bridges, along the tomato- and mint-fragranced vegetable gardens, I will eventually reach the endless blue sea.

My native land is three yellow plums on a black gravestone and that childish conviction, that while I am munching the plums, warmed by the gravestone in the Házsongárd cemetery, I am feeding on the flesh of my great-grandfather, to whom the roots of the plumtree reach down.

My native land is a vigil, smelling of the linden tree, a picture which reminds me that I am crouching among the branches of the old tree of Farkas Street, carefully picking the flowers, lest people trudging by on the sidewalk should notice it and call me to the attention of the policeman, and I spy into a nicely furnished room where a young couple are embracing.

My native land is a tiny fish, caught with my mother's silk stocking from the stagnant water of the closed-up mill brook, for me to put into a tin can and gallop with across town as if the belly of the little fish contained diamonds.

My native land is a supplication, emerging from a candle-lit hut, the whisper of a woman who pledged nine Tuesday's fasts if only her yellow-spotted tabby cat will return.

My native land is a sweet, metallic sound of churchbells, which rocks the noodles in Sunday's chicken soup.

My native land is the puffy-faced trombonist of the army band, pacing along with rocking steps, while the pony, carrying the great drum, breathes on his back.

My native land is a giant mushroom, from the top of which one can see the lovely city enveloped in a blue mist.

My native land is the blond Szamos River, which in an insane moment rushed down from the snowcapped heights of Gyalu to the city at such speed that the oil lamp was still timidly blinking in the hut carried away by it. . . .

My native land is the ancient reformed collegium, and in its window János Apáczai Csere is resting on his elbows, with pale but perspiring face.

My native land is the boots of King Mátyás, and I glanced into them with as much curiosity as if they were the crater of a volcano.

My native land is the sparkling of wet belfries, sunshine after the rain, the fragrance of dill and the soft chords of Samuel Brassai's piano.

My native land is the city where I too once rang the church bells in the belfry of Saint Michael's Church, entwined in the heavy rope, while I felt like shouting in glory and wailing in fright, because sometimes I felt that the bell would swing me up and I would fly through the narrow window where the pigeons come and go; but the tower warden just stood there mutely and severely beside me as if to egg me on: pull on, sonny, pull, you are ringing the evening bells for your city and it would behoove every resident to ring the church bells once in his lifetime in this belfry!

And since that time my native land is a soft continuous ringing of church bells, which gently rocks the sunshine and the golden noodles in Sunday's chicken soup and the pigeons in the heights and the dust around King Mátyás's boots and engraves the wrinkles on the face of Apáczai, but also evokes a smile on him and sways the blond foam of the Szamos and the bows of the linden trees and the memories and the strawberry-colored photographs on the wall, the faces of my grandfather and grandmother. It rocks my heart, to strengthen in it the conviction that it was good to live here, in this city, even if fearful times surrounded it.

I cast down my eyes and looked at the ground so as not to see the town's embarrassment. But I did not long to be away in Paris, in London, or in Rome. After all, one cannot choose his parents. As for the rest: I knew that even on the gravestones I could find two or three plums or red-meaty pears, because the whimsical inhabitants of Kolozsvár, even in the cemetery of Házsongárd, planted fruit trees.

1980

Tibor Bálint was born in Kolozsvár (Cluj), in Transylvania.

"Farewell, Aelia Sabina!"
Dr. Alfred Henley

"**W**e were once citizens of the same empire," my English friend remarked. He was speaking to the curator of the Roman museum at Aquincum, on the edge of present-day Budapest.

The curator gave us a startled look but then he smiled broadly. He pointed to the large map of the Roman Empire, which took up an entire wall of the lobby. There the enormous span from Britannia to Pannonia, the Roman name for Hungary, stretched more than a thousand miles, less than half the Empire's length.

That morning the two of us and an interpreter had set out for Aquincum, the ruins of an entire Roman city, once the capital of Inferior Pannonia (actually eastern Transdanubia), dating back to A.D. 19.

We were intensely engrossed in whatever we saw, particularly in the Greek and Latin inscriptions on the tombstones and on jewelry. The curator showed me a golden pendant inscribed in Greek. I wrote out the translation:

Let them talk as much as they like,
I do not care
Do love me: it will serve you well.

Clearly the lady was the mistress of a Roman officer. In ancient times the Roman military was not permitted to marry and each encampment was surrounded by their "wives" and children. The curator thanked me and said that the woman's tomb was found intact with all her jewels but her name was missing from the stone.

What does this pile of ruins say to us almost two thousand years later? Greek and Roman civilization has a deeper fascination for us than any other ancient society. Why? Karl Marx, who was a profound student of Greek culture points out:

A man cannot become a child again unless he becomes childish. But does he not enjoy the artless ways of the child and must he not strive to reproduce its truth on a higher plane? Is not the character of evey epoch revived perfectly true to nature in child nature? Why should the social childhood of mankind, where it had its most beautiful development, not exert an eternal charm as an age that will never return? There are ill-bred children and precocious children. Many of the ancient nations belonged to the latter class. The Greeks were normal children. The charm their art has for us does not conflict with the primitive character of the social order from which it had sprung. It is rather the product of the latter, and is rather due to the fact that the unripe social conditions under which the art arose and under which alone it could appear can never return.

Apart from Italy no country in Europe has as many ruins and remembrances of its Roman past as Hungary. The reasons are evident: from the days of Augustus at the beginning of the first century A.D., when Pannonia was conquered by the Roman legions, it was a frontier against incursions by the Celts and Huns. Made secure by encampments and the Danube, it quickly became a vacation spot for wealthy Roman families, a crossroad for all of eastern Europe and a departure point for further conquests in Dacia (now Romania), in Thrace (now Bulgaria), and into the territory of what is now Armenia.

In Hungary itself there are many reminders of the widespread Roman occupation. In western Hungary (Superior Pannonia) the two great Roman towns of Scarabantia (Sopron) and Sabaria (Szombathely) were the junctions of the European north-south trade route and the east-west trade route used by Byzantine merchants. It is interesting that Sabaria was founded in A.D. 43 by the great Roman emperor and administrator Claudius. In our own day Claudius was maligned by a television series based on the gossip of the Roman historians Seneca, Suetonius, and Tacitus. Yet it was in Claudius' reign that Britain and Pannonia were added to the Empire. Claudius was the first emperor to admit Gauls to the Roman Senate, to make freed slaves his advisors, to write his own speeches, to reject the worship of emperors as gods, and to enforce tolerance toward the religious practices and traditions of the Jews in Asia Minor and Northern Africa. . . .

From the tombstone he erected to his wife we learn that the name of the town organist was Titus Aelius Justus. The inscription also tells us that his wife Sabina had a lovely voice, played the harp well, was liked by the people, and made him a very good wife. "Happiness to you, whoever may read these lines," is the message of the bereaved husband of nearly two thousand years ago. "May the gods guard you, and may you cry piously,' 'Farewell, Aelia Sabina!'"

Where does the evocative power of such ruins lie? Why does the story of the grieving organist Aelius and his wife move us? It is just here that one's own life comes out of the past, not just the personal history of any single individual. And it is clear that Marx in the words quoted above does not refer only to the childhood of mankind. He tells us that every period, which is a moment in a peculiar and never-recurring past, can actually be experienced by us today.

1978

Dr. Henley, noted Marxist scholar, engineer, and educator, frequently contributed articles to our newspaper.

Attila Jozsef, greatest poet of the Hungarian working class.

Elegy
József Attila

Smoke, under a low leaden sky, swirls hooded
in thick banks over the sad land:
and so my soul, back and forward,
sways like the smoke.
Sways, yet stays.

Iron soul you are—yet tender in images!
Going behind the heavy tread of the real,
look deep into yourself, see
where you were born!
—Here, under a sky once supple and flowing,
across the loneliness of thin dividing
walls, where the menacing, impassively imploring silence

of misery slowly loosens the melancholy
so solidly
packed in the thinker's heart
and mingles it with the heart
of millions.

The whole dominion of men
begins here. Here everything is a ruin.
A tough euphoria has spread
its umbrella over the abandoned factory yard.
Into a damp darkness
the days go down by stained steps
from shatter of paltry windows.
Tell me:
is it here you are from?
Here, where you are tied to your gloomy wish
to be like other wretched souls
in whom this age, the great age, is

straitjacketed: the others whose faces
are marked by every line that's made?

Here you rest, here where the rickety creak
of a fence guards the greed
of the moral order,
and watches it all.

Can you recognize yourself? Here the souls
wait in a void for the towering beauty-filled
future, as the dark and desolate shacks
have dreams of houses, lifting high
a nimble web of murmurs. Set
in the dried mud, fragments of glass
stare with fixed eyes, cut off from light,
over the tortured meadow-grass.

From the low hills a thimble
of sand rolls down at random . . . and there's a flash,
a buzz of some fly–black, green or blue–
attracted here from richer neighbourhoods
by the rags,
by the leavings of man.
Good is mother earth, tormented in her care,
also in her own way
preparing a table
A yellow weed springs in a saucepan there!
What have you to say
to this dry heart's-leap of recognition which draws me–
to a landscape that is bone of my bone?
What of my rich torment–coming back, back here?

So a mother's son,
after the cudgels of strangers, will return.
Here, only here, you may smile and cry, and
here, here only can your sinew endure,
my soul! This is my native land.

(1933)
Translated by Edwin Morgan

József Attila was one of the most outstanding poets of Hungary in the twentieth century (1905-1937).

I Don't Know
Miklós Radnóti

I don't know what this land means to other, this little country
circled by fire, place of my birth,
world of my childhood, rocking in the distance.
I grew out of her like the fragile branch of a tree,
and I hope my body will sink down in her.
Here, I'm at home. When one by one, bushes kneel at my feet,
I know their names and the names of their flowers.
I know people who walk down the roads and where they're going,
and on a summer evening, I know the meaning of the pain
that turns red and trickles down the walls of houses.
This land is only a map for the pilot who flies over.
He doesn't know where the poet Vörösmarty lived.
For him factories and angry barracks hide on this map.
For me there are grasshoppers, oxen, church steeples, gentle farms.
Through binoculars, he sees factories and plowed fields,
I see the worker, shaking, afraid for his work.
I see forests, orchards filled with song, vineyards, graveyards,
and a little old woman who weeps and weeps quietly among the
     graves.
The industrial plant and the railway must be destroyed.
But it's only a watchman's box and the man stands outside
sending messages with a red flag. There are children around him,
in the factory yard a sheep dog plays, rolling on the ground.
And there's the park and the footprints of lovers from the past.
Sometimes kisses tasted like honey, sometimes like blackberries.
I didn't want to take a test one day, so on my way to school
I tripped on a stone at the edge of the sidewalk.
Here is the stone, but from up there it can't be seen.
There's no instrument to show at all.
We are sinners, just like people everywhere
and we know what we did wrong, when and how and where

but innocent workers and poets live here, too.
Knowledge grows inside, nursing babies,
and it shines in there. Hiding in dark cellars they guard it
Waiting for the day when the finger of peace will mark our land
And their new words will answer our muffled ones.

1944

Miklós Radnóti, one of the great Hungarian poets of the century, was murdered by the Nazis in 1944.

G.D. Hackett

Hugo Gellert with Julius Zilzer at their joint exhibit in 1960.

For a Happy, Free Hungary

Dr. János Gyetvay

We are a part of the Hungarian people's body. We left the cradles of our families there, our families who still live there. We never forgot, never denied our beloved native land. While struggling desperately to earn a living here, we ceaselessly think of our brethren there, and were and are ready to support with all our strength, all our might, our beloved, long-suffering homeland and its people.

We did not come willingly. We were driven out, torn away from our native soil. We had no land alongside the ten-thousand-acre estates. Tortured, downtrodden servants have we been of counts, barons, and their myriad henchmen, the target of their gendarmes. In the cities we had no work, and no wages; we had no roofs over our heads. We had no right to organize, to associate freely with each other. We walked in tattered clothing on the streets of the cities alongside gentlemen and ladies dressed in velvet and velour. We were homeless in our homeland, displaced in the land of our ancestors.

We wanted bread, land, freedom, and happiness. We had been deprived of them for centuries. And at last when we saw no other way out, we grabbed our only heritage, the wanderer's stick, and set out for the wide world. We were drawn here by hopes, dreams, illusions. Thus have one and a half million of the finest of the Hungarian people stumbled out of their native land, most of them to the United States.

We believed we would find everything we sought. Yes, indeed, we found perhaps a bigger piece of bread, more humane shelter and somewhat more freedom. But only through toiling for others, for the manufacturers, for the barons of mine and mill. We couldn't escape the capitalist system here either. We remained an oppressed class here too.

Torn from the body of the Hungarian people we became flesh and blood of the American working people. Now we are struggling among their ranks for liberation—for untrammeled political freedom, for democracy, and against the fascism that is threatening catastrophe for all mankind. We are giving our total support to our Spanish brothers and sisters in their mortal struggle against the vanguard of fascism, the forerunner of World War II.

Did we become alienated from our brothers and sisters in Hungary? Never, not for a moment. Haven't we been and are we not now ready to support our brethren in the old country?

We love the land of Hungary. It is of that land that we demand more for our people in Hungary. We support the Hungarian people but not the government that invited alien forces, Rumanian and Czech armies, into our land.

We support our Hungarian brothers against the thousand-year-old oppressors. For land, for bread, for freedom, for happiness, for liberation. Against war, for peace, against fascism. For a happy, free Hungary in the Danube Basin.

This is the battle cry of Hungarian-Americans for the Hungarian people, for Hungary.

March 15, 1937

Dr. Gyetvay was editor-in-chief of our paper from 1932-1946.

Hungarian Good Friday
Reverend L. A. Gross

The scale of emotions experienced by the people these days, especially those who are concerned with the fate of their native land, approaches the feeling of that little band of disciples at the time they left the scene of the Crucifixion, where they all thought that "it has been finished." They were so much under the influence of the terrible tragedy they had just witnessed that they forgot the comforting message the Master had given them only a few hours earlier in the Garden of Gethsemane:

> Verily, verily I say unto you, That ye shall weep and lament, but the world shall rejoice: and ye shall be sorrowful, but your sorrow shall turn into joy.

> A woman when she is in travail hath sorrow, because her hour is come: but as soon as she is delivered of the child, she remembereth no longer the anguish, for the joy that a man is born into the world.

and then,

> Your heart shall rejoice and your joy no man taketh from you (John 16:21-22).

But this joy has a great price. It seems that only that has value and meaning whose acquisition involves sacrifices. We know from history that great popular movements which resulted in the awakening, in resurrection, were always preceded by a period of crucifixion. Do not believe, therefore, that "it has been finished." On the contrary! It is only the beginning. The unearthly darkness of Good Friday must precede the ecstatic joy of Easter. The night is darkest just before dawn. And believe me, my brother, dawn is approaching. Have faith, fight, and render sacrifice. Easter is coming!

And when you and your children celebrate the joys and blessings of Easter will you take a piece of paper and pencil in your hand and make a reckoning: What was the price of Easter? I doubt it. You will say what I am saying now: I will joyously suffer the pains of hundreds of Good Fridays if that be the price of eternal Easter for myself and for my fellow men.

Resurrection is necessarily preceded by the Calvary of Good Friday. Jesus had to die on the cross before he could offer his followers the gift of the belief in Resurrection. We can really say, without Golgotha there is no Resurrection. Without Good Friday there is no Easter.

Many countries are passing now through the horrible experience of Good Friday. They are being crucified by the gendarmes of their own people who have allied themselves with their own Judases. They, too, could cry out: "Eli, Eli, Lomo Shabaktani?" "My God, my God, why hast thou forsaken me?" And God does not answer now, just as He did not answer on that other Good Friday. But the elements have answered:

And behold the veil of the temple was rent in twain from the top to the bottom: and the earth did quake, and the rocks rent. And the graves were opened; and the many bodies of the saints which slept arose, and came out of the graves after his Resurrection, and went into the holy city, and appeared unto many (Matthew 27:51).

Soon there will be earthquakes in many lands. The people will rise irresistibly and will smash the rocks of tyranny with their bare fists, will smash to smithereens the fortresses of feudalism hitherto believed unconquerable, will rend the veil of false traditions, false doctrines, the veils which only serve to cover up the blood-curdling reality. And the people will see to it that the same fate should befall their own Judases as befell the original Judas.

1944

Reverend Gross was a devoted friend of and regular contributor to our newspaper.

Hungary, A Special Country

Paul Elouard

I am now going to talk about a country which is the very flame of laughter and life. About a country and a people which knows that the present carries within itself the seed of the future. About a country which knows that there are tomorrows and that one can think of tomorrow without fear. About a country which is the embodiment of optimism and gaiety. About a people that lifts its head and knows what light, hope, and happiness mean.

The Hungarians paid with their blood for their conviction that men and women are the master of their fate. This Asiatic people settled in the Danube Basin a thousand years ago. In the eleventh century it adopted Christianity and established a powerful kingdom.

But the rich and enticing Hungarian plains that stand wide open to the winds, to marauders, to the greed of strangers, always attracted conquerors—Turks and Germans alike. In order to free themselves from the one, they surrendered themselves to the other. Ultimately they had to fight for their independence and in the struggle against Germanic influence the Hungarian people hammered out its own patriotic tradition. The history of this country had for centuries been the history of resistance to conquerors. And, as usually happens, the people had to struggle simultaneously against the external and the internal enemy, against those who collaborated with the external enemy—to speak frankly, against the landlords, against the aristocrats.

This struggle for independence and freedom climaxed in 1848. Under the influence of the ideas of freedom emanating originally from France, the Hungarian people had to fight on two fronts, or apparently on two fronts. We know now that the fronts were actually one and the same. In fighting against the rule of the Hapsburgs, the Hungarian people wanted to shake off the yoke of the large landowners, who didn't object to foreign oppression because its burden weighed exclusively on the masses of the people. For them it was a highly profitable arrangement.

That is when the great historical idea dawned upon the Hungarian scene: that in a national struggle, it is basically only the people who fight for the country. This is what Jaures tried to express once, in a little-known statement, when he said that "the poor people have nothing but their fatherland." This is the lesson of the Paris commune, which took place because the privileged classes left France. This is the lesson of the French resistance, of which François Mauriac had to admit that "essentially it was the working class which in its great masses remained faithful to France."

The Hungarian people were aware of the symbiosis between the people and the land. They learned it by experience, with the sword in their hand, much sooner than other peoples. The poets of Hungary sang of this noble struggle. In the recent past, the Horthy fascists drove Hungary into World War II. After they went through the agony of German occupation, after they were liberated with the help of the Red Army and their own partisans, it was this spirit which permeated them. It infused life into the moribund body of the nation, opening the way for renewal, for freedom, for love. And it showed the world what a people can accomplish when it can carry out its own will.

Having been rebuilt on the ruins of World War II, Hungary today emerges as a marvelously rich country, utilizing the immensely rich cultural and material heritage of the past.

And Budapest, this dual city is like the embodiment of a dream, spreading like a dream, the most human embodiment of beauty on both banks of the majestic River Danube. It is one of the most beautiful of Europe's capitals, where joy is flowing in unison with the waves of the river.

It is a city to which one can apply Rimbaud's words: "It knows the joy of new work." An eternal city dedicated to the happiness of its entire population.

1949

Paul Elouard, the great French poet, was a true friend of Hungary.

An Address by Paul Robeson

Speech by Paul Robeson at Our Celebration
of the Anniversary of the Hungarian Revolution, 1952.

A century can be momentous in the history of any land. In 1848 my beloved father was a boy of five and a slave, one of millions descended from those torn from their native soil to labor and toil, that wealth and ease might accrue to a few powerful landowners and their vassels.

But beneath the surface, torrents were rushing, and a few years later the deluge came. It represented an historic leap in the history of my land and the world. My people, allied with the John Browns and the Garrisons and the Lovejoys and the Harriet Beecher Stowes, led by their heroic Frederick Douglass, Harriet Tubman, and countless heroes unnamed, moved swiftly toward emancipation and an America realizing, in some part, its dedication to the proposition that all men are created equal and stating anew that this America must be the land of government of the people, by the people, and for the people.

No country lives unto itself, and the world-shaking events of 1848, the stirrings toward liberty of Europe's millions, were closely bound to the winning of the Negro people's right to full freedom and participation in the human family.

No more glorious page was written than in the beautiful Hungary of your forebears and of that great and heroic figure Lajos Kossuth. As your and my people were joined in deep and common sympathy and struggle, so today— this very occasion—marks the ever-abiding unity and friendship of our two folks.

These bonds have been and are forged in toil and in the knowledge that we and ours, together with generations of others (as the ballad says), have built this great America. Yes, we are true Americans—Irish, Negro, Jewish, Italian, French and English, Spanish, Russian, Chinese, Polish, Scottish, Hungarian, Lithuanian, Swedish, Finnish, Canadian, Greek, Turkish, Czech and double Czech.

Yes, we and ours, workers in the fields of cotton, rice, and tobacco, workers in the dark satanic mills and mines . . .

Yes, this America belongs to us. Today the whole country is rising against the fascist tactics of McCarthy. Progressive America was the first to sense the danger, the first to sound the alarm. Millions of other Americans are now becoming alerted and moved into action.

Remember the Mundt-Nixon bill, leading to the Smith Act and the McCarran legislation!

But we can, as part of the vanguard, work ceaselessly, fearlessly, to do much to save the land which must be passed on as one of peace and plenty, to our children and our children's children.

My most heartfelt greetings to the great people of the land of Lajos Kossuth, to the Hungarian People's Republic, one of the mighty lands of socialism. May they ever rest assured that there stands on guard an honest America, an honest America stretching out the hand of friendship and peace to all the peoples of the earth.

The danger spots remain, especially here in our own beleaguered land, but today this is an all-embracing, worldwide struggle. The powerful camp of peace, led by the great people of the Soviet Socialist Republics, together with the peoples' democracies, will deter war, will be joined by millions of peace-loving fighters in every corner of the earth, will impose peace.

Peace will conquer war: "A béke legyözi a haborut!"

Again, my love to the people of Hungary, to the parents and children who have written me so many kind letters.

Hail to you at this historic moment! As the words of your famous song go: "Éljen a magyar szabadság, éljen a haza!" ("Long live Hungarian freedom, Long live the fatherland!").

Paul Robeson was a friend of our paper who frequently honored us by his appearance and participation at our commemorative meetings.

The Destruction of the Hungarian Jews

Peregrinus

The destruction of Hungarian Jews was called by Churchill, "the greatest and most horrible crime in the whole history of the world." The overwhelming part of the losses occurred in the provinces where very few Jews escaped deportation; those who survived came back from the death camps. That shows that incredibly few attempts were made for the rescue of half a million people. There are no recollections of clerics who tried to help them or protested against the deportations as had been done by priests in other countries.

But on a higher level there were attempts to prevent or to stop the deportation on the part of prelates and foreign heads of state and statesmen. It has to be admitted that in 1944 the Hungarian hierarchy rose above its earlier attitude of sympathy with rightist ideas and systems and of antipathy toward the Jews. But it was not easy to change their attitude as quickly as the speed of events required. They were accustomed to excommunicate leftist, but not rightist political leaders; to preach against Socialists and Jews but not against Fascists; to protest against the murder of Spanish priests but not against the massacre of Spanish workers; against the murder of the Tsar but not against pogroms in the Ukraine.

Thus, not they, but Angelo Rotta, then the Apostolic Nuncio initiated the rescue action in Hungary. Two days after the occupation of Hungary by the Germans, on March 23, 1944, he conveyed to the new Prime Minister the message of the Pope warning the government not to commit cruelties against the Jews. On May 15 he declared in the name of the Pope: "the whole world knows what the deportation really means." He castigated *all* persecutions while Cardinal Serédi intervened only in the interest of the baptized Jews, a minute part of the 500,000. Finally, on June 8, the Nuncio demanded a more energetic intervention of the gremio of the bishops, to defend not only the converts but *all Jews*. Unhappily, through no fault of the Nuncio, it was too late, because the deportations had begun a month earlier; more than half of the Jews had been deported already from the provinces and most of the deported probably were already dead. Also, Bishop Baron Vilmos Apor reproached the Prince-Primate for not protesting loudly against the persecutions, but Serédi procrastinated and answered: "the time is not yet ripe for the intervention of the Church." He allowed the sermons to deal only in general terms with injustice and cruelty. He rejected the demand of Calvinist Bishop Ravasz that they issue a common declaration, although this also would have been too late by that time. Finally, the Pope demanded an unambiguous declaration from the bishops, "in the defense of Christian principles and of the bishops' Hungarian compatriots, *especially the Christians* (emphasis mine) unjustly hit by racial dispositions."

Even had the primate obeyed the Pope, it would have been useless, because at that date, June 27, the great deportations ended. But the circular letter of the bishops was not promulgated at all. The government told Serédi that the deportation of the Budapest Jews would be left pending, baptized Jews would not be deported any more, and relatives of priests would not be required to wear the yellow star. At that the Cardinal retreated and ordered his priests only to inform the congregations that his negotiations with the government were continuing. They continued although 500,000 Jews had been deported to Auschwitz under the most horrendous circumstances.

The Protestant bishops tried to act more resolutely, though equally belatedly; the protest they sent to the Prime Minister could not have had any effect because it was dated June 23. Finally, they too were content to read in their churches, two weeks after the deportations, a short declaration which promised the continuation of their talks with the government. That was less than nothing.

There were isolated bishops who condemned from the pulpit the cruelties; some dared to utter the word "Jew." One bishop succeeded in exempting a few baptized Jews from deportation. That was all that was done for the salvation of 500,000 people.

The developments in Budapest were different. When in July, 1944, Eichmann tried to deport the 250,000 Jews there the situation of the Germans was so desperate that they could not spare the troops necessary for it. Regent Horthy, encouraged by foreign interventions, suspended all further deportations and on October 15 he attempted to quit the war, but he was overthrown by the Germans who put an Arrowcross government in power.

This regime committed innumerable murders of Jews and leftists, caused the death of thousands by marching them afoot to the west, put a great part of the Jews under inhuman conditions in a ghetto and sacrificed many thousands of Hungarian lives for the continuation of a hopeless war. But the majority of the Budapest Jews survived, partly because the breakdown of administration made it impossible for the government to catch all those who had gone underground and partly at this time the foreign missions and the churches of the capital did all they could to defend the Jews by giving them hiding places and furnishing them either false personal papers or letters of safe conduct. The population of the city, surrounded and besieged by Soviet armies, was uneasy and did not participate much in the uncovering of fugitives and in denouncing them to the authorities. One part of the city, Pest, fell to the Soviet armies in January, 1945, the other part in February—and for the Jews the nightmare was over.

Peregrinus is the pseudonym of a noted Hungarian jurist and essayist who has been writing for our paper for the past twenty years.

Béla Lugosi, president of the Hungarian-American Council for Democracy.

Questions on Hungarian Society

György Aczél

Our critics in the West often allege that the countries of Eastern Europe have failed to bring genuine liberation to their people; moreover, not even materially have they been able to offer them any more than economies wrestling with permanent shortages, economies of scarcity. This—in addition to being contrary to the facts, that is, it is not even objectively true—is utterly unfair because it judges these countries in the context of the most developed Western capitalist ones without taking into account their economic history. . . .

Any one of a number of standards may be used to measure the economic development of a country. Let me mention only three. First: what it has achieved in comparison to its earlier self. Second, and this is objectively the most important: how many of the socio-economic objectives it had set itself have been realized. Third, and this receives considerable attention today: the country's position in the world economic hierarchy. I think the most decisive change in that development in Hungary is shown to be sound, not only by the first two standards, but also by the third.

According to economic historians the socialist construction of the past twenty years—although development was not free of contradictions—has meant the fastest and most balanced rate of economic growth in Hungarian history. . . . People do not have to worry about the morrow; they do not have to fear unemployment; they are not plagued by the spectre of bankruptcy and by the prohibitive costs of hospitalization and medical treatment. I mention in the second place, but not as a secondary factor, the widening and ever increasing opportunity of participating in decision-making. In keeping with their interests and inclination, everyone can have a say in the affairs of their immediate or broader community. In keeping with their abilities, and the force of their arguments, they may shape the course of public affairs, and can freely express their opinions. True, they may find themselves facing conflicts due to the vanity or jealousy of a boss or bosses, but they are not defenceless, and not endangered in their being as breadwinners. Then there is the chance to satisfy cultural needs. I think that if a competition were run on how many books on an average are in the possession of one citizen of a given country, or how many cultural functions he attends—we Hungarians would finish somewhere up front. I might also mention the increasingly available options open to individual talents. How many children of workers and peasants study at universities and colleges in capitalist countries, and how many do in this country? Last but not least, let me mention a good and clear conscience. Man is a moral being, injustice offends his very being. Poverty and exploitation and human suffering may become, for a man of sound moral sense, the source of constant mental disequilibrium and conflicts of conscience. What is instrumental in the sound state of morale in Hungarian society is also the awareness that Hungary takes the side of progress in international life, that we support those who fight for a just cause: for independent nationhood, for progress and a life worthy of man.

On the "red bourgeoisie"

Another lot accuse us of not having abolished classes, but, on the contrary, of having produced a new class, the "red bourgeoisie." Those who lend an ear to propaganda against us may consider this to be a problem of considerable weight. No use denying, there are men, some in positions of authority, who abandon their earlier selves in the image they project, their way of life and thinking, and this can, in turn, become manifest by distorting their behaviour, working style and methods. But they are individuals, not a whole section of society. A whole series of safeguards operates against unhealthy isolation. The way leading officials are selected, judged and rated is one such safeguard, the point of view of mass organizations being considered as well. The basis of this is a three-fold requirement those in charge at all levels have to meet: political suitability, professional skills, qualities of leadership. Of course, it is necessary to size up every individual as a person, all the essential features of his character and behaviour. Another safeguard is the particularly critical attention to which public opinion subjects all office holders.

Our relationship to the Soviet Union was, has remained, and will be of outstanding importance to us. Our opponents look with favour on any kind of hostility to the Soviet Union, whether it originates from Pinochet or Pol Pot. . . .

Of course, there is no lack of manifestations disparaging our country today either. Our being a "satellite" is deplored, the old phrases are repeated: if it rains in Moscow, umbrellas must be opened in Budapest; Hungary is a vassal state of the Soviet Union; in Hungaro-Soviet economic relations only Soviet interests count, and so forth. To those who says things like that it would be useless to explain, for example, that our relationship with the Soviet Union, Hungaro-Soviet friendship, is the most decisive external factor which has ·ensured that the past three decades have been a period of the most dynamic development in the history of the Hungarian people. There are some who cannot understand this, and others are not willing to do so.

Hungary supports and advocates extensive and ever intensifying international contacts. Openness to the entire world is imposed on us, just as on Austria, not only by the country's resource endowments—the scarcity of many raw materials and fuels—not only by the country's specific economic situation.

What is even more important: peace is our vital interest. Again and again we insist with all our might that the historic confrontation between capitalism and socialism be decided under the conditions of peaceful coexistence. . . .

In the spirit of confidence in the strength of our ideas and in the people, the country has taken up a slogan formulated by János Kádár that "he who is not against us is with us." The soundness of this basic posture has been proved several times over by the facts and results of almost a quarter of a century. This is why we look on religious people as our allies, with whom we have fundamental ideological differences, but apart from that we are united in a common front not only by the fight against armaments, bloodshed and war, but also by the construction of our socialist country. History has taught us that our cause is rendered a good service by a policy that is looking for what we have in common, not for what divides us, and by the tolerance which this entails.

This need not in the least be at variance with the consistent maintenance of our principled steadfastness. Internationally, we consider as our ally everybody who is capable of objectivity, everybody who is not an addicted or fanatic anti-Communist, spoiling for a fight and always ready to hate, everybody who is a supporter of peaceful coexistence. . . .

These days we are often praised for our results and ambitions; what is more, we are called "an example" and not always with sincere motives. But we judge ourselves and our place, our role in the world, in an objective manner. Our results cannot make us overconfident, if for no other reason than because we are not protected against errors today either. . . .

Far be it from me to prettify the real situation. Much remains to be done to get socialist democracy off the ground. But we have already laid the groundwork, and what I mean here is shop-floor democracy in the first place. I am convinced that in this field we are a long way ahead of the capitalist countries. We are progressing towards a point where a working man on the job gets more of a chance to shape his working conditions, to express his opinion on the problems, tasks and plans concerning the team, and to find remedies for possible grievances. It is our intention to learn from experience, to do away with mere formalities, to lend a lively substance to the already established and still developing institutions, and to prune the shoots of bureaucracy. This is today a key issue of shopfloor democracy. . . .

János Kádár is doubtless an historical personality. Not only because he became a leading figure in Hungary at the time of an historical turn of events, but mainly because he is, and has turned out to be, exceptionally suited for his post. If I may express myself in this way: our people have the historic luck to have found the right leader whose principal ability, in addition to his own good qualities, is that he can learn from history, recognize what the facts demand and is able to see the perspectives, that he can make people accept the tasks ahead, that he can unify a diverse society.

János Kádár's fate has always been one with that of the people. He has lived through, and knows from experience, the past half-century of Hungarian history: all the misery and suffering during the Horthy era, the brute force and prisons of fascism, the suffering of the Second World War, the joys of Liberation, the distortions of the personality cult. His life—one could say—coincides in many respects with the history of the Hungarian working class, of the people. His personality has been formed by this high amount of experience and knowledge, and at the same time he has preserved the virtues of a working man. The fundamental principle of János Kádár's life is that without the people there is no way of engaging in politics; a good leader does not take decisions on his own, he must ensure that as many as possible take part in making and implementing decisions. He regards the party not as a ruling authority but as an organization in the service of the people. His every ambition is that the largest number possible should make the policy of the Hungarian Socialist Workers' Party their own, representing and pursuing it ably and actively.

Nationalism is a deadly peril which has shrunk and expanded at the same time. We think of honest national feeling and patriotism to be an inalienable, fundamental human right, for socialism also grows within a national framework; moreover, the criteria of national existence find better expression in it than in other kinds of societies. We look on national pride based on genuine values of the past and present as justified. But we regard as manifestations of nationalism, and condemn as such, any intention, ambition and sentiment which openly or covertly incites to, and builds upon, the despising of other peoples, in its extreme forms racial hatred, occasionally the falsification of the history of the nation, and the embracing of sham values and chauvinistic passions.

Nationalism is dangerous everywhere and is looming in Hungary, too. It is enough to recall that after the Great War the imperialists of the Allied and Associated Powers reduced the territory of Hungary—not least as a punishment for the Republic of Councils—to one-third of its former size. For this reason, as well as others, one-third of Hungarians live beyond the country's frontiers.

Nationalism was given a boost by the Horthy regime responding to the serious socio-economic problems of the country in a chauvinistic way. It poisoned our people by stirring up nationalistic-chauvinistic passions for a quarter of a century.

We have broken radically with this evil and mendacious tradition. We rely on our Marxist principles, on the genuine interests of the nation, in building and shaping relations with neighbours as well as with the national minorities in Hungary. Owing to the well-known political distortions, it was not easy to take the first steps in the years following Liberation: excesses weighed heavily on the Suebians (Germans who settled in Hungary during the 18th century are known there as Suebians, whatever their tribal origin) and later the South Slav minority was subjected to serious abuses. Today all this is only an instructive memory.

In spite of all this we have not yet succeeded in grubbing out the roots of nationalism. We do not deny that there are frictions and some unfinished business in this respect. We take issue with all those who hold wrong views of the national minorities question; and with those who deal with this problem as if it were the only vital question of the nation. We have to argue with those who are mistaken, but there is no common ground with narrowminded chauvinists. We take it that our task is to set an attractive example, and not to excite hatred. Our aims include rational and sensible management, raising living standards all round, and creating an attractive life fit for human beings. All this, taken together, means a really socialist policy that suits the interests of the nation, and it calls for a sound national minorities policy.

215

Because of the complexity of the national problem things can be set right only by internationalism making vigorous progress everywhere. Where the principles of internationalism are violated, harm is done not only to the national minorities but also to the nation concerned. At the same time we know full well—no matter how stubbornly a feeling of solidarity with the Hungarians living in many places abroad persists in us—that the destiny of the nation depends on what we construct here at home, and on whether we are able to construct a socialist Hungary which we can look to with pride.

György Aczél is a member of the Political Committee of the Hungarian Socialist Workers' Party, and Deputy Chairman of the Council of Ministers.

BY GYULA ZILZER

FASCISM MEANS WAR!
FASCHISMUS IST KRIEG!
LE FASCISME - C'EST LA GUERRE!
EL FASCISMO - ESTA LA GUERRA!

Julius Zilzer's antifascist cartoons created a sensation in France in the early 1930's. They were praised by Albert Einstein, Louis Aragon, Romain Roland and other outstanding personalities.

Transylvanian Feast

Excerpts from the Foreword

Paul Kövi

The rich traditions of one's native land can truly be appreciated only by those who left it a long time ago. The elusive, haunting memories of events, along with food flavors and aromas—the overpowering emotions surrounding our childhood and early youth—unexpectedly burst forth like a long dormant volcano especially when we are traversing *mezzo giorno*, the middle years of our lives.

It was not Transylvania where my Mother sang her lullaby while rocking my cradle; it was not the land from which I departed to cross the Atlantic Ocean. But my old Alma Mater, the University of Kolozsvár, has given me such princely spiritual provisions for my long, long journey that as years passed a gnawing feeling of indebtedness has begun to develop within my psyche. I was pursued by an internal warning perpetually reminding me of an unsettled human obligation; somehow I felt I had to reciprocate my adopted home for the marvelous experience it had given me, and that I must express my gratitude in some way for making me the man I am today. Because it was there, in the land of Transylvania, that I had acquired not only the desire for knowledge, but also a deep respect for other people, their traditions and religious convictions, as well as the infinite variety of other experiences pertaining to the flavors of different cuisines popular in this beautiful region.

While living in Kolozsvár as a college student, I also absorbed the spiritual inheritance of that historical place. During the centuries, this lovely capital city of Transylvania bore several names: Kolozsvár in Hungarian, Klausenburg in the Saxon tongue, Cluj in Rumanian, and, finally, Napoca, so named by the Roman legions.

Kolozsvár and the entire region known as Transylvania had been a unique place in South-Eastern Europe. During the centuries of persecutions in the wake of devastating religious wars, it was here that, for the first time, religious freedom was declared and had flourished. It was here, in this miniature melting pot, where five ethnic groups, Hungarians, Rumanians, Saxon Germans, Armenians, and Jews, had lived for many a decade in peace and mutual respect. This is the country that had often been called "an East Europe Switzerland." Transylvania as a historical reality is gradually disappearing and becoming a "Fata Morgana," no more than a fading dream, unfortunately beset by ideological and nationalist fanaticism. This was one more reason for embarking upon this adventure.

But the most important motive still remains my deep love for Transylvania. I felt compelled to find a way of reciprocating at least some of the intellectual and emotional riches I had received there. My work in the restaurant field—more than work, a real vocation—has inspired me to study and collect Transylvanian gastronomic treasures and family traditions hidden in old books and manuscripts in different parts of the world. I have been engaged in this activity for more than two decades. Finally, five years ago I decided to publish a book about the exciting and varied cuisine of this region, before its colorful tradition became caught up in the onslaught of grey uniformity we are experiencing throughout the world. This volume thus is my humble gift of gratitude for my real education in Kolozsvár, my beloved second home.

Some years ago in Italy, I visited St. Lazzaro Island near Venice, the site of an old Armenian Mechitarist Monastery. There, to my utter surprise, I found a unique collection of books dating back to the 17th and 18th centuries, describing customs and foods of the Transylvanian Armenians. These incunabula, written both in Hungarian and Armenian, also contain a large number of recipes (many of which are included in this book).

While reading through books, manuscripts and various menus for festive dinners, I began to feel the presence of the "Chinese Connection," and recognized definite similarities between the Transylvanian and Chinese gastronomical expressions. For example, ginger, one of the most important Chinese spices, was equally popular in China and Transylvania for a long period of time. To my knowledge, it is only in these two cuisines that the combinations of cabbage, pork, and river lobster are in existence. In both places this combination was served in egg-pastry rolls. Similarly, the almost identical serving of river crab, pan-fried with vegetables and spicy sausages, must be more than a coincidence.

Subsequently I came across Baron Radvánsky's recipe collection compiled in the 16th century. The Baron discusses the use of Oriental spices, condiments and herbs commonly used in the Transylvanian kitchen at that time. The question automatically arises: how did these spices find their way to the remote Transylvania? In my opinion, the short, very hot paprika-pepper, popular both in China and in Transylvania, is of Chinese and not of Mexican origin, as most other pepper of Europe. My theory is based on the assumption that during the Medieval times and well into the 16th century, the continental trade route from China to Europe must have had in Transylvania its end station. Other information supported my hypothesis. Having read the stories about the art of serving food in Andreas Milos's writings, I found another unmistakable Chinese influence. In Transylvania the festive hunter's dinners had always been served in groups of three—a custom common even in today's China.

Yet another interesting discovery was learning that in the 17th century black coffee had already been popular in Transylvania, long before it became widespread in Vienna, Austria. Coffee was used not only as an after-dinner drink, but also to thicken sauces. I found several statements regarding the sale of coffee to Transylvanian noblemen's households from Greek merchants in the early 17th century. Conversely, I was able to find exotic sauce recipes prepared with coffee.

The more I studied the culinary habits of the various ethnic groups—Hungarian, Saxon, Armenian and Jewish—in Transylvania the more I realized their intrinsic interrelationships: each represented a special flavor in Transylvanian cuisine and each enriched the other.

Transylvanian Sunday Soup
Tibor Bálint

I once wrote that the sweet and clanging ring of the noontime bell of my homeland which rocks the golden dumplings in the Sunday soup and still floats to my desk from the fading limits of my memories is the fragrance of that meat-soup of old which arouses so much joy and hope in me about the future of the world. Because this soup wasn't just a food, it was a symbol too, a solemn ceremony, an appeasing sacrifice, in the mist of steaming frankincense, myrrh and other scented spices which seeped out to the courtyard and from there to the garden and from the garden even further into the *world*, proclaiming that a large but modest family had sanctified the seventh day as its deserved day of rest according to the law, having acquired the necessary meats and bones for it . . .

Sundays seemed more dazzling in those days, maybe because we could sleep longer, and by the time we opened our eyes the room was full of light. This light was given a rainbow look by the balmy aroma of the simmering consommé which, like a quiet psalm, praised existence and human initiative. I must confess that I still feel the weekday cooking of this soup to be profane. It can be featured on menus of restauranteurs every day—which makes them suspect—but for me it needs the fitting occasion, a holiday.

Because only in tranquillity, peace and some sort of expectant devotion and reverence can it smell so heavenly: only in authentic surroundings, among people who are convinced that tastes and smells lead us to a higher knowledge and appreciation of our existence, and nurture humanity and good intentions. After all, it's unthinkable that someone joyfully spooning up Transylvanian meat-soup, for instance, should not wish similar gourmet delights for the table of the whole world.

Even the meat brought home from the butcher has a special effect on us: beautiful pieces of rump steak, (spare)ribs, topside and shin with the porous bones, and the hen plucked to a fresh yellow. While we are looking at this still-life the primeval instinct to search for edibles even in things of beauty is roused in us simultaneously with the artist's excitement, who keeping his greed at bay, only notices the shape of the meat, its color and alluring texture, and luxuriates in the cross-bone with gristle which glistens like a pearl.

For a while only the serious and promising fragrance of the various meats issues forth from the kitchen, a kind of ancient puritan savour which as yet is unaware of the cunning collusion from the addition of spices and vegetables which preserve the tasty salts, secret minerals, and flavors of the earth.

After the vegetables have been added, however, when the meat is almost soft and the steaming vapour permeates all ingredients, an uplifting process begins: the symphony of aromas. I could never resist the temptation of stealing a peek into the kettle of secrets: of marveling at the cuts of meat bathing in shimmering melted gold, red carrots and the sticks of parsley-root which the liquid gold embraces as giant jewels. I watched as the peppercorns—like tiny heads of little Black children swimming—popped up and bobbed down again: the lovely meat flowing like a veil from the topside, a delicacy of gourmets. In the pink bay of mushrooms new flavors dissolved and set out on the sea of savours: the pepper glimmered green beside a piece of savoy cabbage and a blood-red tomato: the hen had scattered glittering eighteen-carat coins around itself, like its fairytale counterpart . . . . As the vapours escaped from under the raised lid it felt as if a fleeting spring shower had crossed some exotic forest and I, waking from my gentle reverie, would smile at this enchantment.

Oh, Sunday soup, let the sweet and clanging ring of the semolina dumplings—the never-silenced voice of my homeland—lull you forever and ever!

Translated by Imre Szász

The Secret of Strudel Making

Paul Kövi

I have always loved poppy seed strudel. During the tender years of my youth I was wont to say that if there was a maiden anywhere in the world, even in Egypt, who could make the most delicious poppy seed strudel, I would make the pilgrimage there on foot, to taste it for myself. And if the rumor proved true, I would marry her at once. For me reaching my destination on foot meant crossing chains of snowy mountains, hills and countries, even the stormy seas, walking on the billows like a new Jesus Christ. Thus I would go, never failing, until I arrived, and then, show me a lassie—if there has even been one—who could resist me.

Time passed and I became a university student at Kolozsvár. There my purse grew flat quickly following the frolicky revelings that marked the initiation of Freshmen into college life. All year round I had money only at the beginning of each month: my allowance usually lasted for a few days at best. During the ensuing meager weeks only my Mother's tenderly prepared food parcels assured my sustenance. (In my soul the postal receipts are still preserved and stored with affection as eternal proof of motherly love translated into tangible evidence.) And every one of these weekly parcels contained several feet of poppy seed strudel, the sole request on my part.

The demanded monotony of the contents made my poor Mother feel ashamed after a while: she kept saying that my colleagues might think that she was incapable of baking anything else. But as far as I was concerned, her poppy seed strudel guaranteed the perfect continuity of my ties to home and showed the only imaginable sign of motherly love toward a starving child.

Even years after that, whenever I returned home to spend my vacations or to celebrate some holiday, my arrival automatically granted the logical excuse for Mother to prepare the inevitable poppy seed strudel. This tradition did not seem to disturb any of my friends who happened to accompany me; they devoured the delicious pastry with similar enthusiasm. Thus my joy was doubled by the knowledge that I could share this pleasure with others.

In 1947 I left home for good and started globe trotting which eventually ended with my settling in America. Only in 1968 was I able to return home again; at that time in the company of my fourteen-year-old son. Up until that period I had never been able to explain the primordial, somewhat unique relationship that existed between grandparents and grandchildren. What was the secret of that unfathomable, harmonious love-chain that tied them together with such perfection? To solve this puzzle, I decided to take advantage of our visit and observe how such a relationship between the twice removed generations developed.

My son spoke Hungarian fairly well and subconsciously he was searching for his past, his heritage, his roots. At first Mother only looked at him, silently examining his features, his eyes, his gestures. Then, serenely and with no little pride in her voice, she declared: "our kind!" With this utterance their forever lasting blood-pact had been concluded and sealed. After this there was only one more test left. "Well, my child," she asked, "what would you like to eat? What should I make for you?" My son's curt but all-encompassing reply poured forth immediately: "Strudel!" Next morning, when the lanky lad woke up at seven, the freshly made strudel awaited him. But not just one kind like in my childhood, but three! (Despite this incident, I am still unable to comprerhend the deep mystery of the bond between grandparents and grandchildren.)

Let us talk about those strudels that awaited him. Oh, they were masterpieces! Mother has been famous in the region for her strudels. Even now—she is approaching 82—there is never a wedding in the county to which Mother is not invited. Every ardent bride is eager to have her demonstrate her legendary art.

I can think of nothing that would equal in magnificence the all-enveloping taste-and-aroma harmony of the freshly baked strudel. Let us admire first the enthralling, mouth-whetting, glorious poppy seed strudel which combines all the secrets of the mysterious East. Next to penetrate into our gastronomical psyche came the dizzying aroma of the walnut strudel. As Mother made it, with a touch of cinnamon and scented rum, it connoted the ambiance of luscious tropical fables. Its heavy, intoxicating smell intermingled with the cherry strudel's refreshing delicacy: a juxtaposition of an epic and a lyric poem. And finally the cottage cheese strudel studded with raisins and spiced with vanilla . . . I still remember how I used to gaze at this supreme creation while it baked. The sugar caramel, oozing through the dough's pores, slowly formed a fancy glaze, a golden crown, on top of this royal masterpiece.

All my life I have been watching strudel making, trying to memorize the process step by step, stealing the inner-most secret of this global art through its minute components. Because verily I say onto thee: strudel making IS a mysterious procedure comprising scores of well concealed secrets. As a matter of fact, it is impossible either to describe or learn this ritual; one must pilfer the formula, breathe it in through the pores of the skin; then, one has to shape it, mold it, develop it as a fine sculptor manipulates his clay in unending devotion.

I often noticed Mother examining the quality of the two different kinds of flours she used, caressing the substance while sifting it through her fingers. When she was making strudel she closed every window and door; no one could enter or leave the kitchen in those sacred moments because as she was wont to say: "the draught makes holes in the dough." Gradually I have become convinced that preparing strudel is like eating it: replete with complicated, intrinsic mysteries.

At those lucky occasions when I was privy to the entire process, I observed her jigging the mixed flour through a fine sieve onto a board. In the center of the heap she formed a well for a special mixture. The elixir had been prepared earlier from a cup of water, one egg, a touch of salt and a dash of vinegar. This concoction was poured into the hole and working from the middle outward, she stirred and kneaded it forcefully, meticulously, for about fifteen minutes, until the dough was smooth and easily removable from the bowl.

Having shaped it into small loaves, she placed them on a generously floured board and spread melted butter or fat on their top with a tiny brush made out of goose feathers. The dough was covered and rested undisturbed for 25 minutes.

The next step was the delicate "stretching." To get ready for this maneuver, she covered our big, rectangular kitchen table with a clean, white, oversized table cloth which she again floured in abandon. Then she began rolling and pulling the dough carefully, stretching the flexible texture until it was hanging off the four corners. Circling the table innumerable times, with her hand under the thinning dough, endlessly manipulating, she never made a hole in the process. I stood there mesmerized by the incredible dexterity of her magic hand, admiring the technique as her wrist rapidly continued its spiral movements in stretching the dough layer further and yet thinner. Her arms moved like a rotating machine. In the end the dough was so light and translucent that one could blow it off the table or even read a newspaper under it. When the desired thinness had been achieved, she tore off the uneven ends and put them aside. Later she would knead these into another loaf again.

After the paper-thin dough was sprinkled with melted butter or fat, she placed the already mixed stuffing on one third of the sheet or spread it on the whole surface. Holding the two corners of the table cloth in both hands, she slowly lifted then rolled up the filled dough, cut it into varying lengths to fit the different baking pans. The top was once more anointed with the remaining butter, then it went into the pre-heated oven to bake until it was ready.

In my youth I was quite surprised by her use of vinegar; it seemed such an unlikely ingredient. But I know now that vinegar helps start the bonding process, whereas the touch of salt provides "life" to the precious dough.

Small wonder my friends from Transylvania are often called "crafty highlanders." In one of the Szekely counties, in Haromszek, people must be extremely cautious of every move made, every word uttered. Short of that one may lose one's shirt. Each gesture has its own meaning, every sentence hides a secret double entendre and every word a playful pun. There, even the poppy seed strudel consumption has its own trick; one must eat very fast and a lot of it, because this pastry is such a heavenly feed that if one looks in another direction even for a second, after turning back there will not be as much as a morsel left.

Translated by Clara Györgyey

My Mother's Starter-Dough
Paul Kövi

Bread—the staff of life—played a crucial, almost sacred role not only in our lives, but also in that of our neighbors in the small town where I grew up. The very idea of bread was expressed symbolically in our daily language, embellished in poetry, or used in prayers. No other food deserved to be extolled as "life giving, God given, or blessed." Bread literally was and remains the gift of life.

The assigned chores on bread baking days played an especially important part in my childhood memories. The dough for our bread was home-made. The baking was entrusted to a master baker in the part of town where we lived. For over half a century this marvelous old artisan with his charcoal heated brick oven produced the perfect loaves for all of us in the neighborhood. On baking days I could hardly wait for the sound of the midday bells and immediately would dash to the little bakery on the corner to pick up our freshly baked breads. Running home with my precious load, I would indulge in its beautiful mouth-watering, tempting aroma. How I longed to break off and taste a hunk of the crunchy, still hot bread, but this would mean betraying a sacred trust.

My Mother was the only person in our house privileged to cut our bread first. In my home, bread was never simply broken—it was a family ritual. Before we could eat, Mother made the sign of the cross over the bread and blessed it. Symbolically touched by the sign of eternal life and hope, the bread was declared ready to be tasted. We would vie for the crusty end pieces. No bread ever tasted better than those still warm, crunchy, brown morsels.

Even now, when I recall the process of bread making, I am overcome with awe. Bread making was a century old tradition, repeated ceremoniously generation after generation in our family. There was much of the miraculous in this ritual. Since my family is of strict, old Lutheran stock, the word "holy" was not trifled with; it was applied to God alone. The process of bread making, however, was held in the greatest reverence, a small step short of holiness. Everything that constituted part of the bread making process belonged to this beautified, privileged category.

How well I remember the special baskets, a large oval and a smaller round one, in which I carried the dough to our baker. They were always kept separately on the shelf, never used for any other purpose—it was indeed sacrosanct. The smaller one I have taken with me on my peregrination as a constant reminder of home. Four fine white linen napkins lined these baskets. These linens were also used only on bread making days and only felt the soft touch of my Mother's hands. They were permeated with the wonderful aroma of good fresh flour.

But the single most important thing in this miraculous ritual was the starter yeast-dough. Every family had its own little yeast reserve, and somehow it was even shameful to borrow one. That woman was not much thought of who did not respect and keep clean the starter-dough, or who—"Heaven help her"—would squander it.

Because surely the starter-dough was received by my Mother from her Mother when she got married and began her own household. My Grandmother meanwhile got it from her Mother, and this way, in its order, back through generations into centuries. The little starter-dough represented not only our family's past and history, but its present also, thus, its desire for living, therefore its future. And principally, it meant—for all of us—the connection with our native land. For we lived off the fat of the land, and so did my Grandparents. Whatever we had produced and grown gave the substance to our daily life.

On the occasion of each breadmaking, my Mother pinched off about a one pound piece from the bread-dough, flattened it and put it aside in a dry place to "dry and crack." The two baskets and the four little cloths were folded nicely and took their places next to it. Then our little starter-dough waited its time there patiently, till the next baking. But it was there and at this particular moment that the little, raw yeast-bread's eternally important role really began. Inside it the yeast fungi slowly but surely multiplied, and the little starter-dough continuously breathed its atomic bread particles into the house's air, which we sniffed in and made our own, and they in turn became our bodies' life participants and ingredients. This process was reciprocal, as our house was filled with the very essence of ourselves.

We also filled the air with our own human bacteria, with our basic chemical make-up's little particles, with the tiny atoms of our hopeful dreams, tired sweat, our love-making's scent. The little yeast-dough absorbed all these bacteria from the air, formed and multiplied it longer in its own selfishly decided way, creating, in this manner, our little house's bacteriological balance and chemical set-up—a unique micro-cosmos. Our starter-dough was unlike others, it was a composite of us.

And thus, every house in that little town had its own specific chemical-bacteriological make-up, a historical and spiritual micro-cosmos which differed from its neighbors'. Our home was a self-defined unit in the immense universe and in this specified unit, my Mother's little starter-dough represented the dominating center. The little yeast-bread was the depository of our family's and our individual, human character; the key to tradition, continuity, beauty and love.

How I pity today's people who don't have a tiny little starter-dough of their own, as a statement of their own individuality which they could pass down to their daughters and sons. Oh, how I pity all those who simply go to the supermarket, and take home some sort of bread; although it might even be nice, and good, and varied in taste . . . since the little machine-made loaf tries to accomplish the duties assigned to it, but this poor bread . . . has no soul of its own.

Demonstration in support of the persecuted Jewry of Hungary organized by Rev. Geza Takaro in New York in 1944.

Members of our business office in the early 1950's. From left to right: Alex Rosner manager, Clara Reich circulation manager, Clare Vago editorial assistant and correspondent, Kato Gyarmaty, Editor of the Nok Vilaga the only women's magazine in the ethnic field in America. Steve Horvath foreman of our printshop.

John Albok

"How beautiful the feet
of him . . . that
publisheth peace."

–Isiah LII• 7

"Caput Mundi"

Gabor Goda

The dual existence of unspeakable evil and transcendental good is one of the basic characteristics of all history.

Every high school student is aware, of course, that the inquisition which for centuries paraded as the defender of the faith of love formed one of the bloodiest chapters of world history. Yet the same centuries that are disfigured by its horrors gave literally numberless geniuses to the world.

He who ascends the hills of Fiesole may recall the march of great geniuses as they passed over those roads of history. Should you on the other hand happen to step into the church of Santa Croce in Florence, you will involuntarily bow not before the altar but the tomb of Michelangelo. Who can, furthermore, describe the emotion when you stand before the casket of Galileo? Who can resist the overwhelming emotion when viewing the mausoleum of Machiavelli? Who can say that he or she is not viewing with the eyes of a child the ashes of Dante? Who does not shudder upon hearing the name of Columbus or even Amerigo Vespucci? But then almost every city and town in Italy has given birth to geniuses who changed the world.

It is through such experiences and emotions that one begins to realize that man is indeed a giant And I do not mean to minimize the contributions of other nations or the giants of ancient civilizations.

These colossi of beauty, of science, of progress are the milestones that reassure me that the trend of history is toward higher, nobler grounds.

Why do I then soliloquize on the glories of Italy? I have recently visited the Capitol of Rome. It was my sixth or seventh visit. The residents of today's Rome call it Piazza del Campidoglio. At the time of the Roman Empire it was called "Caput Mundi," the "Head of the World."

The whole square, with the Museum of the Capitol, with the Palazzo del Conservatori and the Palazzo Senatori, is built on that marble carpet that was designed by Michelangelo, who furthermore designed every window, every column, every stairway and that magnificent gate that seems to beckon to the whole world.

This is where students and masters alike can learn what space means both as an architectural and a symbolic element. This is where one, even the greatest, can learn what proportion means.

This square was witness to Caesar and to all the little caesars. It saw the fall of a united Italy and its resurgence. The blood of Rienzi flowed on its cold slabs, and it was covered by the flag of Garibaldi. The whole world served as inspiration to Michelangelo because he couldn't be bothered by anything less than majestic, anything local, anything irrelevant.

The entire square is like a peak from where you can view the whole world. It is not merely an architectural triumph but the testament of a mental superpower, about the endless possibilities of art.

Yet there was a man, an unspeakable monster, a murderous fascist who raised his hand against this inspired beauty and who attempted to destroy or gravely injure it. He placed a bomb in the portal of the City Hall so that it broke into smithereens. Every bit of stone has since been recovered but it is just too horrible to think that there existed on this earth a monster in human form who dared touch this priceless diamond, this common treasure of all mankind.

How many people died in world wars? How many perished in local wars? How many were killed in the name of an idea? How many cities were destroyed, how many homes, how many hospitals, how many schools were ruined? I stood in France before Gothic cathedrals of breathtaking beauty whose horrendous wounds are still visible. Still I believe that there is a basic humanism binding us together.

I still want to participate in the laying of the foundation of a better, more human future, even if I know that I personally will not see it emerge in my lifetime. I still believe in every possibility that is beautiful, that is human. I believe in all this.

But one thing I do not believe. I do not believe that the worst enemies of mankind against whom we fought World War II have given up their efforts to fight and subdue humanity. It is their vanguard that are besieging in their anger the masterpieces of civilization in so many countries.

And I do not refer only to that madman who almost destroyed Michelangelo's Pietà or slashed the canvas of Rembrandt's *Night Watch*. I tremble when I think of the fact that in Rome, in the San Pietro in Vincoli, the statue of Moses is only at arm's length from the Pietà! Moses who is not a leader and a legislator, but THE leader and THE legislator.

We have reached a point when we have to tremble for the continued safety of the greatest treasures of our civilization. We have already defeated fascism. I fear that their wounded vanity, coupled with their insane ideas, will make them try once more to exterminate everything that is human in man. That is the reason why whenever I see or hear the word *Peace* written or uttered I feel that I see or hear an ally, one who even if by different ways and means is trying to defend everything that I consider precious.

That which has happened in the Capitol of Rome or is happening beneath the headlines of terrorism in Italy or in other countries should make all decent people join in the defense of common human values.

The attack against the Caput Mundi is a symbol of a newly forming attack against not merely the head but the heart and life of all mankind.

Let us join forces to halt and defeat it.

1978

Christmas 1981
Zoltán Deák

The heavenly host, who has been ordained to praise God with the Angel, has descended, unbeknownst to most of us, from the pages of the Gospel and is now marching with the peace demonstrators on all continents, in all the great cities, yea even in the smallest hamlets, crying, "Peace on Earth and good will toward men."

Huge as the number of the heavenly host is, it is outnumbered by an even mightier contingent that accompanies it and the peace marchers wherever they appear.

The silent victims of all previous wars, of all previous acts of inhumanity, are now participating in the demonstrations. The victims of two world wars and all other massacres have emerged from their graves and are following the host. The victims of the Holocaust have reappeared in great columns of smoke, the shape of gigantic exclamation points, to stand alongside the marchers.

Who can resist this united front of the heavenly host, of the living and the dead and of the not-yet-born?

May the hellish gates of the warmakers' citadels be shaken to their poisonous foundations! May the monstrous clouds of war disperse forever! Let the glorious, life-giving sun of hope and peace shine from now on forever over us on earth!

1981

Zoltán Deák is editor-in-chief of the Magyar Szó.

Mankind at the Crossroads—Nuclear Destruction or an Abundant Life

Bishop Dr. Károly Tóth

It is . . . neither an exaggeration nor a mark of false political pathos to say that mankind must choose between two alternatives: either the utter destruction of the human race or work for a new era of peace. There is no third possibility!

In the given critical situation, the testimony to peace of the Christian faith and the encouraging force of the hope of life relying on God's promises have become of decisive significance. Indeed, there is no church—and even less any international Christian organization regardless of denominational differences—which would not say some word or other for peace in this critical situation.

In this situation it is understandable that people are beginning to realize the untenability of peace based on deterrence and the failure of the balance of terror. It is certain that the new nuclear weapons which reduce the threshold between traditional and atomic arms to a minimum do not serve the cause of deterrence; rather, they produce an illusion of invincibility. We have seen that a nuclear war entails the threat of utter annihilation for both parties because of the possible retaliation of the other. The reduction, and then elimination, of this risk is what is being aimed at in the new phase of the arms race. What this means theologically, ethically and in the context of a "just war" needs special investigation. In any case, it is true that the armament race, i.e. mutual deterrence, has "ensured" the peace of Europe for 36 years. But there is no guarantee that this can be continued "ad infinitum," because the policy of mutual deterrence has proved a fiasco on account of the very armament race itself. For the world has not availed itself of the period of peace forced by the atomic stalemate to take effective steps in disarmament, much less stop any further armament. In our search for an alternative to the balance of terror, the question is raised: whose interests are served by the escalating armaments? Who is making use of the slogan of "liberty" to justify imperialism and exploitation? . . .

In our search for an alternative to the balance of terror, we are immediately faced with the problems of security. As the concepts of national security and national interests are alternately used, this gives rise to a lot of confusion. In this respect, too, a certain change in the way of viewing things can be seen in the policy of the new American Administration which speaks sometimes about "national security," sometimes about "national interests" or "vital interests." But "vital interest" means two things on the other side of the Atlantic Ocean: first, free admission to the raw materials on which American economic life depends; then the maintenance of the existing order of the world which means the maintenance of the social status quo, even in the case of the most oppressive regimes.

If we want to advance along the path of peacemaking, we must inevitably reconsider more profoundly the concept of security. We must elaborate the theory that security is possible not only by power but in other ways also, and that the very existence of nuclear weapons makes any further step in global dimensions impossible. We must strongly emphasize that security is not only a military question—it is basically a political issue, because "it is inacceptable that the security of human society should be based on a security system which, in the final analysis, reckons with the termination of human history."

The arms race is based on a threat. The psychosis of fear can reach a point at which it automatically maintains and increases fear, apart from the original cause of that fear, and the situation therefore changes as a consequence of the new circumstances, while the image of the enemy remains unchanged. To be concrete: there are many in Western Europe in whose eyes Communism is the threatening enemy, the incarnation of evil. This invention of nationalist-socialist propaganda "has become since 1945 a dogma dangerous to the general public in the so-called 'Christian West.' ". . . This is the cause of the rise of the misleading alternatives: atomic bomb or Communism, as if any other choice were out of the question. The anti-Communist approach and the suspicion of a political alliance with the East have made Christian peace activity difficult in Western Europe and even in the Third World. Conscious or subconscious anti-Communism and anti-Soviet feelings are always present everywhere and constitute, on the pretext of standing up against an atheist Marxist ideology, an immensely great temptation for Christians.

The question of whether cooperation for peace and against atomic death is possible or not, in spite of ideological differences and even conflicts, has already been answered by life not only through the service of the Christian churches in the socialist countries, but also in the work of anti-war movements having the broadest bases. In these spheres, Christian personalities and groups are playing a very important role. . . .

The world situation—the situation of humanity—is grave indeed and is even close to a catastrophe. "Adequate words are lacking to express the full seriousness of our present situation." The armament race is "of such grotesque dimensions as to defy rational understanding.". . . In order that the world may get out of this vicious circle, the priorities must be seen correctly. First, we should attempt in the most diverse ways to see to it that the relativism of the existing political and ideological differences is recognized and our common humanity, behind the opponent's views, is discovered. As Albert Einstein wrote in one of his last letters: "We appeal as human beings to human beings: Remember your humanity, and forget the rest." . . . To put common interest into the foreground in every way—that is the most urgent task of the peace movements and of the most differently inspired peace organizations. Anyone who stirs up or intensifies strife today commits a sin against humanity.

1981

Bishop Károly Tóth, of Hungary, is president of the Christian Peace Conference (CPC). The Conference is a non-governmental organization registered at the United Nations. Its continental branches are active in 90 countries in Europe, Asia, Africa and Latin-America.

Better Days Coming
Endre Ady

Better days are coming
And once
(How happy is he who will live to see it)
Fed up with horrors
And remembering
We will stop
The evil misleaders:
The times of yesteryear.

And will ask quietly:
"What death will you choose,
You stupid, worn
Ancient, senseless swords?"
Once
Filled up with remembrance
We will dare to ask
Overdue questions.

Better days are coming.

1918

PARTIAL LIST

of artists, editors, editorial staff members, poets and reporters who have contributed to our press—1902-1982.

*Ádám Abet
*John Albók
Emil György Austin
Imre Bálint
*Oscar Bán
*Imre Bárd
Sándor Barta
Lajos Basky
*Lajos Bebrits
Dr. Elek Bolgár
*András Bódog
Dr. Vilmos Brandt
Joseph Budish
Dr. László Bükkhegyi
Victor Candell
Gyula Czinczar
*Peter Csont
Louis Dattler
Fay Deák
Zoltán Deák
Géza Dénes
Dr. István Domán
*Lajos Egri
*Béla Eörsi
*Mihaly Erdei
*József Fehér
*Lajos Fehér
Árpád Fodor Nagy
Erna Fodor
Dr. Éva Gábor
*György Gábor
*Dr. Zoltán Galambos
Ilonka Gaál
Emil Gardos
Hugó Gellért
*József Geréb
*Margit Gencsi
Tibor Gócze
*Kató Gyarmaty
*Rev. L. A. Gross
*Dr. János Gyetvay
*Dr. Alfred Henley
Lee Heimlich
*Dr. Jenó Holló
*Dr. József Hollós
Klára Hollós

Gabriel D. Hackett
Ágota Illés
*Sándor Ják
Susan Joseph
István Kántor
Ferenc Kálnay
Frigyes Karikás
Viktor Kelemen
József Kovács
Erzsi Kovács
Duci Kovács
Lajos Köves
Zoltán Koós
László Kubinyi
Dr. László Kun
Dezsó Landó
*Aurél Leitner
*János Lékai
James Lustig
*István Lutherán
János Mácza
György Miklós
Dr. Oscar Miklós
Péter Moór
*Jenó Nagy
Emery Nánásy
*Jenó (E.H.) Neuwald
Endre Olexó
Florián Paczier
Peregrinus
*Pál Petrás
*Dr. Béla Pogány
*Eugene Práger
Clara Reich
*László Rácz
Sándor Rosner
János Román
Sándor Rákosi
József Sislay
*Dr. Mózes Simon
*Pál Somogyi
Károly Spáring
Barbara Striker
Dr. George Striker
*Emil Schaefer
*Vilma Schaefer

*Zádor Szabados
*József K. Szabó
József Szebenyei
Lajos Takács
Ferenc Talyigás
Ákos Tasnady
A. Ternay
*János Uhrin
József Varga
Claire Vágó
Oscar Vágó
Anna Saitta Vrbovska
György Vidor
Antonia Wechsler
*William Weinberg
Lajos Weinstock
Rózsi Weinstock
Gyula Zilzer
Péter Zvara

*Deceased

234

We are proud to list here the names of our readers and contributors in Canada, the United States, and Hungary whose aid has helped to produce our annual Year Book, and this anthology. We are deeply indebted to them for their staunch support and their confidence in the success of our common goals of world peace, social progress and friendship between the United States and Hungary.

CALIFORNIA
Julius Kiss
József Kosogovits
Alex Ungár
Margit Faragó
Mr. & Mrs. Louis Curtis
Ethel Soós
Flórián & Rózsi Paczier
Helen Piotrowski
Bözsi Magyari
Mr. & Mrs. J. Schubert
Sándor Szilágyi
Ethel Koncsek
Helen Alsó
Elizabeth Misánsky
Louis Hayes
Erzsébet Gecse
Mr. & Mrs. Kálmán Tengolich
Lajos & Julia Ruby
István & Ilus Kardos
Margit Szabó
Samuel & Annus Bartha
János & Erzsébet Varga
Ferenc & Flóra Jéhn
Lajos Blahm
Mihály Váralyai
Ilonka Gaál
Lajos & Rózsi Weinstock
Geza & Teréz Komjádi
Matild Zala
Gizi Berkowitz
Aranka Schlesinger
József & Ilonka Weisz
Dezsö Nánásy
Sándor Ackerman
József Kálmán
József & Gizi Bischof
Clara Friedman
Rose Ruhig
Alex Goldman
Helen Jánossy
Jolán Belmont
Irén Weiss

Paula Yanow
Erzsébet Neorcsics
János Illés

CANADA
F. Hegedüs
Steve & Helen Kovács
Mr. & Mrs. Antal Nádasdi
Anna & Frank Csetneky
J. Bangha
J. Stephen Hills
Frank Knaus
Emre Libor
Fred Váno
Mr. & Mrs. István Farner
Andy Pocik
Márton Kovács
Steve Papp
Louis Nagy
Mr. & Mrs. Dezsö Nádasdi
József & Betty Tóth
Rose Biczók
Anna Komlósi
Rose Szabó
Leslie Gyene
John Berekáli
András Tirpák
Lórinc Kovács
John Schmidt
James Tózsér
József Németh
Joe & Elizabeth Visnyei
Julia Vass
Helen Czukár
Andy Nyerges
Steve Pintér
Joseph Forray
Alex Kopi
Elizabeth Tücsök
Bertalan Billik
John & Katalin Sipos
Mary Répas
Mary Erdödy

Sándor Eged
Jenö Irinyi
Elizabeth Ossó
József Gál
György Palotás
Andor Gózs
András Krajnák
Mária Gabura
Béla Vágó
John Bartók
Johanna Gencsi
Annie Jutai

CONNECTICUT
James Kázmér

FLORIDA
Gáspár Vizinger
Endre Szigeti
Theresa Medve
Gábor Farkas
Mary & Michael Földi
Freda Haig
Zsigmond Szabó
István Kántor
Paula & Gabi Lustig
Theresa Bikó
Betty & John Tóth
Ernö & Lili Róth
Erzsébet Buja
Jessie Brieger
Margit Práger
Gábor & Lili Farkas
Lola Austin
Péter Jánossy
Mary Abjanich
Frank & Lujza Kash
Aranka Klein
Klári Komlós
Pauline Kiss
Susie Szomy
Károly Ujváry
Peggy Zoltán
Mihály Mátyus
Péter Kiss
Daniel & Anna Sauser
István Scheible
Anna Kocsis
Mr. & Mrs. Joseph Knerly

Rose Károly
Olga Kruchay
Margaret Zámbory
Elizabeth Velecky
Anikó Kotler

ILLINOIS
Mrs. József Kozma
György & Barbara Jámbor
József Sauser
Anna Malitsch
Joe Pilát
Alex Smied
Victor Steiner
Helen Paule
Géza & Julia Stein

INDIANA
Vera Gyurkó
Elizabeth Füleki
György Lukács
Susan Nagy
Mr. & Mrs. Louis Cifra
Mr. Paul Tóth Sr.

MARYLAND
Magda Bernád
Joseph Deák

MICHIGAN
Mr. & Mrs. Pál Dömény
Mária Oltman
Gabriel Kerekes
Charles Udvarnoky
Juliska Yoó
Alex Herczeg
Lajos Kiss
Szabó family
Anna Dobos
M. András Heck
György Gombásy
Ferenc Csikós
Joe & Helen Valentine
Anna Márkus
Katalin Almándy
Bill Kocsis
Anna Leny
István & Mariska Józsa
György Miklós

Rose Spáring
Mr. & Mrs. Ludwig Gebnár
Pál & Mary Szöke
Rose Pavloff
Mr. & Mrs. J. Czulák
Amália Papp
Mr. & Mrs. Ferenc Takács

NEW JERSEY
Pál Miszlay
Mary Tomory
Sándor Rosner
András Szimcsák
Rose Krause
Rózsika Németh
John Horváth
Joe Barna
John Szabó
Louis Odor
Lajos & Marika Iván

NEW YORK
Mary Csorba
*Mr. & Mrs. János Albók
Adéla Stern
Gusztáv & Terus Gamauf
Margaret Friedman
Paula Gross
Anna Mesics
Viktoria Reisz
Jusztina Imre
Gitta & Jack Delman
Mihály & Annus Schill
Mihály & Elza Dengelegi
Feri & Ilus Markovits
Sam & Duci Fishman
Brigitta Weinberg
Clara Reich
Dezsö & Rózsi Lusztig
*Juliska Lutherán
Eddy & Sarah Weiss
István Kócs
Árpád N. Fodor
Steve & Annus Flecker
László & Marika Heldák
Béla & Teréz Schwartz
András Mészáros
Dezsö & Elsie Mihályi
Mr. & Mrs. Alex Bennett

Pál & Helen Sweet
Fay & Zoltán Deák
András Jackó
Rózsi Gartner
Imre Lusztig
Oszkár & Klári Vágó
Muriel Nerenberg
Margit Schenker
Lajos & Bözsi Dattler
Margaret & Robert Rosov
Hugó Gellért
István Sallai
Mr. & Mrs. József Haluska
Mária Fábián
Ida & Gyula Csernovicz
Mr. & Mrs. Alex Heller
Anna Saitta Vrbovska

OHIO
Paul & Bözsi Takács
Gáspár & Mary Szabó
Kálmán Berke
Mike & Mary Kintz
Éva Németh
Imre & Julia Füves
Veronika Nagy
Julia Staudt
Mary Hegedüs
Helen Kaincz
Béla & Erzsébet Novák
Alex Muzik
Imre Farkas
György Kisman
Magda Kálótzy
Irene Kóbor
John Incefy
Lajos Takács
Erzsébet Molnár
László Boross
Zsigmond Krauthammer
Berta Papp
Mihály Keresztesi

PENNSYLVANIA
János Szarka
Teréz Halász
Ferenc & Julia Takács
Mr. & Mrs. Gyula Pável
István Doncsecs

János Babirák
Gyula Nemes
Frank Kincses
József Pika
András Rum

TEXAS
Anna Tatár

WISCONSIN
Mary Böde
Magda Schaff

HUNGARY
György Austin
Erna Fodor

Emil Gárdos
Mr. & Mrs. Feri Hirsch
Mrs. Ignác Grünfeld
Eta Kádár
Mrs. Sándor Mezó
Mr. & Mrs. Béla Gadanecz
Sándor Nichta
Tibor Lieberman
János Rozgonyi
József & Anna Péter
György & Barbara Striker
Béla Zenkó
Anna Mester
Mrs. József Washling
Mrs. Gyula Lusztig

*Deceased

Our first press committee in 1902.

Our Family Album

Happiness
Carl Sandburg

I asked professors who teach the meaning of life to
tell me what is happiness.
And I went to famous executives who boss the work of
thousands of men.
They all shook their heads and gave me a smile as though
I was trying to fool with them.
And then one Sunday afternoon I wandered out along the
Desplaines river
And I saw a crowd of Hungarians under the trees with
Their women and children and a keg of beer and an
Accordion.

Readers of our newspaper, the Előre, picnicking along the Desplaines River, near Chicago, about 1908.

Janós Lekai-Lassen, a hero of the international youth movement, brilliant editor of our paper in the 1920's.

Lajos Kövess, brilliant member of our editorial board in the 1920's.

Lajos Bebrits, one of the most outstanding editors of our newspaper. Returning to Hungary via the Soviet Union in 1945 he became transportation minister and later Ambassador to Sweden.

Editor James Lustig speaking at a Hungarian Liberation Day banquet. Seated next to him is Hugo Gellert.

Dr. John Gyetvay, editor of our paper from 1932 to 1946. Returning to Hungary he eventually became Hungary's ambassador to Turkey.

The lovely young bride of Oct. 1911, Mrs. Stephen Jánossy is today, at the age of 92, still a devoted and dedicated friend and supporter of our paper. Her beloved husband passed away in 1967.

A group of lovely Hungarian beauties added charm and glamour to our 50th Anniversary celebration in 1952.

Delegates to the convention of the Hungarian brotherhood Fraternal Association in 1947. The organization was destroyed by the Judicial branch of our government in the early 1950's.

John Albok

*The Etus Serly dancers perform
at our vintage festival in 1937.*

Zoltan Kodály being interviewed by our reporter, George Vidor upon his arrival in the United States on Oct. 30, 1946.

Béla Bartók with his wife Ditta and son Peter in his Riverdale, N.Y. home in 1940.

Eugene Prager, popular Hungarian-American radio program director, a dedicated friend and former manager of our paper.

László Moholy Nagy, world famous designer, leading member of the Hungarian-American Council for Democracy.

Alexander Farkas, outstanding Hungarian-American pianist and music teacher.

László Kubinyi, brilliant Hungarian-American artist.

Members of Hungarian-American Brotherhood demonstrate against German occupation of Hungary in 1944.

György Miklós, one of the early organizers of the sit-down strikes in Detroit. A devoted friend of our paper.

President Roosevelt's letter to a group organized by our paper which collected 110,000 signatures in support of the Social-Security legislation.

THE WHITE HOUSE
WASHINGTON

April 20, 1939

My dear Mr. Kiss:

My attention has been called to the Resolution of the North American Democratic Hungarian Federation bearing one hundred and ten thousand signatures and which expresses approval of the program of my administration.

I wish to thank the delegation which presented this Resolution and through them the members of your Federation for the confidence which they have seen fit to express in me.

Very sincerely yours,

Franklin D. Roosevelt

Arpád Fodor-Nagy, President of the Hungarian Social Club of New York, secretary of our paper's National Press Committee.

Zoltán Deák, Editor in chief of our newspaper and Rev. L. A. Gross, outstanding columnist, at a wreath laying ceremony at the New York Kossuth statue in the early 1950's.

Paul Robeson, a true friend of our paper, speaking at our 50th anniversary.

John Albok

Rep. Vito Marcantonio speaking at one of our picnics.

The renowned operatic composer Gabrial von Wayditch with his son, staunch friends of our paper.

Noted Hungarian-American composers Mr. and Mrs. Leslie Kondorossy, friends of our newspaper.

Prof. George Striker, of Budapest, member, presidium of World Federation of Hungarian-Americans, a devoted and dedicated friend of our newspaper.

In our editorial office in 1951: Hugo Gellert, Eugene Holló, Zoltán Deák and Dr. Béla Pogány.

A recent portrait of our national Press
Committee.